DIGITAL
CAMERA
SOLUTIONS

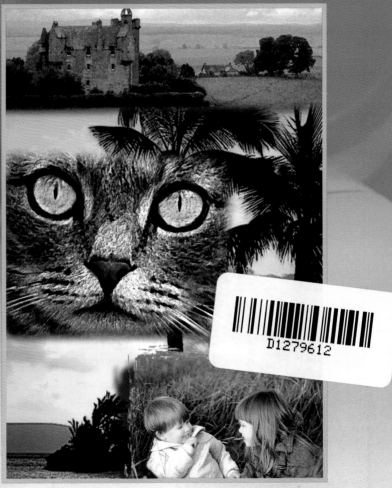

D1279612

Gregory Georges

Digital Camera Solutions

Library of Congress Catalog Number: 99-068481
ISBN: 0-9662889-6-3

5   4   3   2   1

Educational facilities, companies, and organizations interested in multiple copies or licensing of this book should contact the publisher for quantity discount information. Training manuals, CD-ROMs, and portions of this book are also available individually or can be tailored for specific needs.

MUSKA LIPMAN

Muska & Lipman Publishing
2645 Erie Avenue, Suite 41
Cincinnati, Ohio 45208
www.muskalipman.com
publisher@muskalipman.com

This book is composed in Melior, Columbia, Helvetica, and Courier typefaces using QuarkXpress 4.1, Adobe PhotoShop 5.0.2, and Adobe Illustrator 8.0. Created in Cincinnati, Ohio, in the United States of America

Credits

Publisher
Andy Shafran

Editorial Services Manager
Elizabeth A. Agostinelli

Managing Editor
Hope Stephan

Development Editor
Al Valvano

Copy Editor
Bill McManus

Technical Editor
J. Eric Slone

Proofreader
Julie MacLean

Editorial Assistants
Audrey Grant
Jasper Hawke

Cover Designers
Dave Abney
Michael Williams

Production Manager
Cathie Tibbetts

Production Team
DOV Graphics
  Stephanie Archbold
  Michelle Frey
  Tammy Norton
  Kevin Vollrath
  John Windhorst

Indexer
Kevin Broccoli

Printer
C.J. Krehbiel

About the Author

Gregory Georges
ggeorges@reallyusefulpage.com
www.reallyusefulpage.com

Using medium-format, 35mm, and digital cameras, Gregory has amassed a personal collection of more than 12,000 pictures—all taken purely for the fun it. He has, in one way or another, used computers extensively for work and at home since taking his first computer class in 1969. As an experienced photographer and avid user of computer technologies, Gregory has the perfect background and passion to write about digital cameras and how to get the most from digital images.

Nearly every weekend and often during the week, Gregory can be seen pacing up and down the sidelines of soccer and lacrosse fields, taking pictures of his son, daughter, and their teammates or watching his son play ice hockey in hockey rinks. When time allows, he plays ice hockey in adult leagues and works on a growing portfolio of digital fine-art images.

Dedication

To my wife, Linda—for *everything*.

Acknowledgments

Without Carole McClendon of Waterside Productions (the best computer book agent I could have), this book would not exist. Thanks, Carole, for believing in my ideas, for focusing and refining them, and for finding an excellent publisher.

Without Andy Shafran of Muska & Lipman, this book would not exist, or at least not in the form that it does. Thank you, Andy, for making it a full-color book, for allowing me the freedom to write it the way I wanted to see it written, and for giving me the time to do it well—a most unusual combination in the computer book publishing industry.

Without Elizabeth A. Agostinelli and Al Valvano, I would not have enjoyed writing this book as much as I did. Your much-needed support, encouragement, and a kick or two when needed has been very much appreciated. Thanks very much to both of you.

"Thanks" also to all of the other members of the editing and production team, especially Hope Stephan, who truly on occasion was a source of hope; Bill McManus, a word-craftsman with skills that make me envious; and to J. Eric Slone for technical editing.

Without this book, my son, Graham, and my daughter, Lauren, would have seen much more of me during the several months that it took to write it. Thanks for understanding why I missed so many ice hockey, lacrosse, and soccer games and practices and other important events. Thank you also for pictures of both of you, which you allowed me to use.

Without digital camera and computer hardware vendors, imaging software companies, Internet companies, and many photography-related service companies, none of us would have the opportunities to enjoy and share images in as many ways as we do today. Thanks to those companies for the useful, innovative, and increasingly easy-to-use products and services that are now available.

The biggest "thanks" of all goes to those of you who have purchased this book. After all, the book was written for you, and it is important to me to know that it is useful to you. Thanks…

Contents

Introduction

Welcome to *Digital Camera Solutions*—a practical, solutions-oriented book intended to help you learn about digital cameras and how you can use digital images. The goal of this book is to "paint a picture of the possibilities" that are now available to you when you combine the capabilities of digital camera technology, the Internet, and a PC. After reading it, you will have a thorough understanding of the many, many ways you can edit, use, and share your digital images.

This introduction briefly outlines what you will find in the various chapters and describes conventions that will be used throughout the book.

What you'll find (and not find) in this book

Besides lots of valuable content to help you learn about digital cameras and how to get the most from your digital images, this book also offers the following features:

▶ **Hands-on projects** that will enable you to experience first-hand how you will complete specific tasks or projects.

▶ **Extensive overviews** of software applications, Internet services, photo-processing services, and photography-related Web pages that will help you get the most from your digital camera and digital images.

▶ **Hundreds of digital images** showing screen-shots of various software applications and Web sites, plus the results of using specific software tools or services.

▶ **Tips** for selecting and buying a digital camera, safely storing your images, getting better at digitally enhancing your images, choosing the best application for your needs, and more.

▶ **Techniques** for taking better pictures, creating digital images, applying digital filters, sharing digital images, and more.

▶ **Application notes** that provide specific examples of how particular products and services have been used for a particular purpose.

▶ **Money- and time-saving tips** to help you save money and time while enjoying and sharing your digital images.

▶ **Recommendations** for additional sources of accurate and up-to-date information on products and services, as well as books to help you learn more about specific topics.

▶ **Companion Web site** for online examples, book updates, galleries, and other resources.

In this book, you won't find product or service evaluations, nor will you find recommendations of one product offering over another. Instead, you will be presented with a wide range of products and services to show you what is available.

You also won't find complete lists of all the products or services in a particular category. While most of the products and services in this book are considered to be the best in their respective categories, the inclusion or exclusion of any specific product or service should not be construed to mean anything other than the fact that it was or wasn't included!

Who this book is for

This book is for anyone wanting to learn about digital cameras and how digital images can be used, enjoyed, and shared with others. It is for both consumer-level photographers and more advanced or professional photographers. It is for those wanting to use digital images for business or for personal use. If you want to learn about creating slide shows, sending images on electronic postcards, digitally editing images, posting images to a Web page, making an image-based product catalog, electronically stitching images together to create panoramas, using the Internet to share images with hundreds of people, and much more—then this book is for you.

How this book is organized

Digital Camera Solutions is divided into the following four parts, which are further divided into fourteen chapters.

Part I: Starting with a Few Good Digital Images

▶ Chapter 1, "Introducing Digital Cameras." Find out about digital cameras, what you can do with them, and why you ought to have one. You'll also learn how to locate and buy a digital camera to meet your needs.

▶ Chapter 2, "Learning to Take Better Pictures." Get practical advice and twenty-five techniques to help you take better pictures.

▶ Chapter 3, "Turning Photographs into Digital Images." Find out about the five different approaches that you can take to turn your photographs into digital images.

▶ Chapter 4, "Managing and Storing Images." An introduction to software applications and image storage media that can be used to make managing and safely storing your digital image files easy.

Part II: Transforming Ordinary Images into Extraordinary Ones

▶ Chapter 5, "Getting Images into Shape." Gain first-hand experience in digitally editing images and learn about digital image files.

▶ Chapter 6, "Performing Digital Imaging Magic." Learn all about digital image editors and what they can do. Digitally enhance three images on a step-by-step basis.

▶ Chapter 7, "Filtering for Special Effects." Investigate the use of digital image filters and how they can be applied to transform your images into outstanding images.

Part III: Useful and Cool Ways to Use Your Images

▶ Chapter 8, "Displaying Digital Images Electronically." See how you can use digital photo albums, slide shows, and screen savers to enjoy and share your pictures electronically.

▶ Chapter 9, "Other Useful and Fun Things to Do with Images." Find out about many image projects that you can complete for home, business, or just for fun.

▶ Chapter 10, "Doing Extraordinary Things with Images." Explore some of the more extraordinary ways that you can display your images. Find out about tools that can stitch images together, create 360-degree panoramas, morph images, animate images, and more.

Part IV: Sharing and Enjoying Your Images

▶ Chapter 11, "Sharing Images Electronically." Examine ways that you can share your images electronically with e-mail, e-postcards, e-greeting cards, chat, and instant messaging applications.

▶ Chapter 12, "Using the Internet to Share Images." Learn about the services offered by photo-finishing labs that enable you to share your images on the Internet. Investigate how you can share your images in Internet photo-sharing communities and on your own Web pages.

▶ Chapter 13, "Turning Digital Images into Prints." Learn where to go to get prints made from your digital images and find out about desktop printers and a wide range of print media.

▶ Chapter 14, "Using AOL and You've Got Pictures." Investigate the many resources on AOL to help you more fully enjoy photography, your digital camera, and digital imaging. Learn how you can use AOL to share your images with others.

Conventions used in this book

The following conventions are used in this book:

All Web page URLs mentioned in the book appear in **boldface**, as in **www.reallyusefulpage.com**.

The book also features the following special displays for different types of important text:

TIP

Text formatted like this offers a money- or time-saving tip that is relevant to the topic being discussed in the main text.

NOTE

Text formatted like this highlights a specific application of one or more of the products or services discussed in the main text.

Keeping the book's content current

For chapter examples, book updates and corrections, a digital image gallery, and other information related to the content of this book, please visit **http://www.reallyusefulpage.com/dcs**.

The images used in this book

The author has taken all the pictures and has created all the images in this book. The majority of them were taken either with a Kowa Super66 medium-format camera, a Canon EOS A2E, or a Nikon CoolPix 950 digital camera. Prints were scanned either on an HP ScanJet 4c or by a photo-finishing lab offering Kodak digitization.

Part I
Starting with a Few Good Digital Images

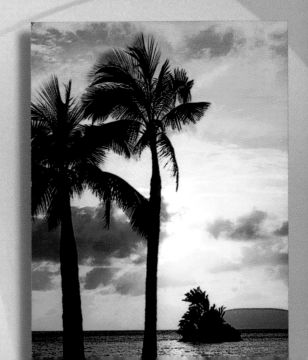

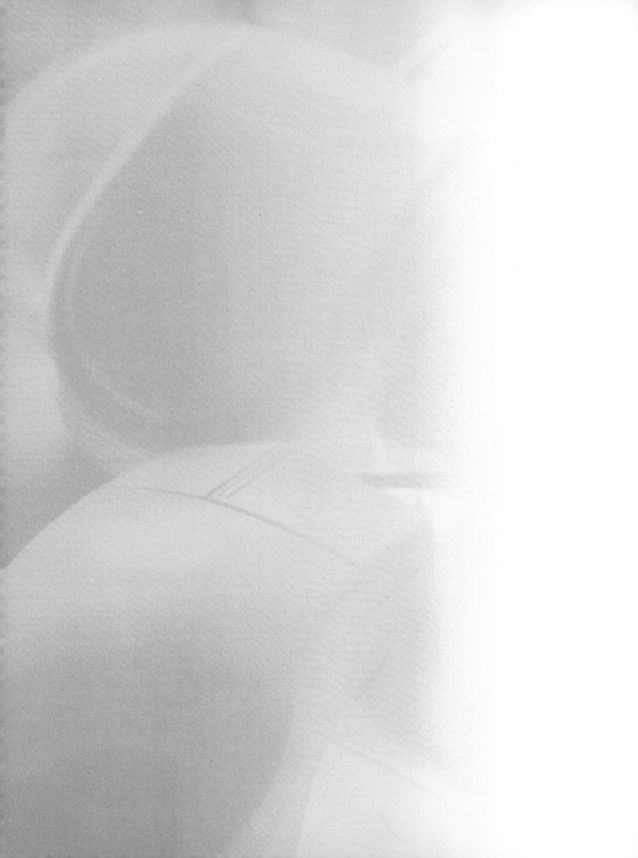

1

Introducing Digital Cameras

Do you have a digital camera? If not, you need to get one! Digital cameras are the newest "must-have" technology gadgets around. They are fun to use, they are useful, and they enable you to do so many things so quickly that you'll wonder why you waited so long to get one. When I took my first sixteen digital pictures and viewed them on the computer screen, I was astounded! I was amazed! The images looked so much better than I thought they would. With the excitement of a child with a new toy, I headed back outside and took another sixteen pictures and then another sixteen. Before I knew it, I had ten excellent images from the forty-eight that I had taken, and I hadn't even read the user's manual yet—nor had I used any film or paid any film processing or printing fees!

Pleased with my results, I wanted to share those ten best images. Using a simple software application, I was able to create a slide show and put it on a free Web site in less than ten minutes. I then sent an e-mail, with a hot-link pointing to the slide show, to my wife at her office. With a double-click of the mouse and a few seconds' wait, she was able to see the slide show and hear my recorded voice say, "I got the camera an hour ago. Look at these pictures!" Yes, the digital camera is going mainstream. It is instantaneous. It is digital. It is fun to use. The images look great, and they are exceedingly easy and inexpensive to share.

In 1998, about 2.7 million digital cameras were sold. Conservative estimates predict that more than nine million digital cameras will be sold in 2000. Fast-changing user requirements, fantastic product innovation, and the lowering of costs by digital camera vendors are creating this tremendous growth. Couple these trends with the fact that more than 50 percent of American homes have one or more computers—many of which can connect to the Internet—and you begin to fully understand the reason for the sudden growth in the sales of digital cameras.

The most exciting thing about digital cameras

The most exciting thing about digital cameras is *what you can do* with them. Let me explain. A few years ago, one of my college marketing professors made the point that when you buy a drill bit, you are really buying a hole! He went on to say that he knew of no one that actually wanted the drill bit—the drill bit itself held no real value. The value was in the many holes that it could drill. There was even more value in the thing that contained the holes that the drill-bit made possible.

Like the drill bit, the digital camera itself is just a tool. In fact, it is just one tool out of many tools and services that are needed to get what you really value the most—*images* that can be enjoyed and shared with family, friends, and business contacts. Based on the fact that you bought this book, I'll bet that you are excited either about already owning a digital camera or about buying one soon. I'll wager that you are *even more* excited about the things that you can do with the images that you will produce with your digital camera!

Not surprisingly, then, most of this book's content concerns *what you can do* with the images once you have them—not the digital camera itself. If you are interested in learning more about digital cameras, I highly recommend a book by two of my favorite computer and photography book authors—Deke McClelland and Katrin Eismann. Their book, *Real World Digital Photography—Industrial-Strength Techniques* (PeachPit Press 1999, ISBN 0-201-35402-0), covers the different types of digital cameras, how digital cameras work, the mechanics of digital imagery, and much more for the technically inclined. I owe a hearty "Thanks" to Deke and Katrin, because I can now skip that part and focus on how to use your digital images! Incidentally, you don't need to know all the technical stuff in their book to be able to successfully use and enjoy a digital camera.

Before we begin looking at what you can do with your images, let's correct some misconceptions about the digital camera and learn about its benefits relative to the film camera. Toward the end of this chapter, you will find practical advice for selecting and buying a digital camera to meet your needs. After this chapter, we'll concentrate on the things that you can do with your images.

Correcting misconceptions about the digital camera

Have you looked at a photograph or a digital image made with a digital camera lately? If not, you really ought to look—don't just take my opinion. For years, digital cameras produced low-quality images and were expensive, bulky, and fragile. Consequently, the older technologies have created a misconception about newer digital cameras that has caused many people to avoid even looking at new digital cameras. However, this isn't the only misconception that keeps many people from investigating digital cameras—in fact, there are many misconceptions about digital cameras that need to be corrected. Look at the digital camera again, I say.

Digital pictures are better than you think

Setting aside all the features, capabilities, and cost issues of a digital camera, picture quality is an important—if not the most important—reason to use, or not to use, a digital camera. As camera vendors are now beginning to introduce 2-megapixel (more than 2 million pixels, or about a 1600×1200 pixel image) digital cameras in the consumer price range, it is safe to say that picture quality is getting to be quite good. Undoubtedly, "good" is a relative word. What is "good" to me might not be "good" to you. If you haven't looked at one lately, however, you are likely to find that pictures taken with a digital camera are better than you expect.

So, how good is a print that has been produced from a digital image that was taken with a digital camera? The answer to that question is difficult to demonstrate, but I'll try. First, consider some of the variables that determine picture quality:

- ▶ Picture-taker's photography skills
- ▶ Optical quality of lenses
- ▶ Camera's features used to enhance (or degrade) overall picture quality, such as digital zooming versus optical zooming, adjusting white balance, or using metering
- ▶ Quality of the digital camera's image sensors
- ▶ Pixel resolution (e.g., 1600×1200 versus 640×400)
- ▶ Type of file format (e.g., TIFF, JPEG, or proprietary format)
- ▶ Level and quality of image file compression used
- ▶ Image editing software used
- ▶ Print size
- ▶ Printer type and quality
- ▶ Paper quality

As you can see, many variables affect the ultimate quality of a print. A series of similar variables works for, or against, getting a high-quality print at a photo-finishing lab as well. If you use a one-hour photo-finishing lab, you are probably aware that you sometimes get great pictures and sometimes get not-so-great pictures. My experience is that many of the better, new digital cameras in the $800 range and up produce digital images that enable you to produce a quality print that is equal to or even better than the prints that you get from a one-hour photo-finishing lab.

For comparison purposes, let's look at two pictures of a log cabin. One was taken with a $1,000 Canon EOS A2E and a Canon Ultrasonic 28-105mm f/3.5-4.5 lens, using Fuji 400 ASA film. This picture was developed at a one-hour lab, and it was scanned with an HP ScanJet 4c, so our comparison is not perfect—but it should give you a good idea of how good the digital camera is.

The other picture was taken with a $1,000 Nikon 950 at 1600×1200 resolution, using the "fine" setting for JPEG-image compression. By the way, the Nikon 950 will also store an image as a TIFF file, which would have produced a higher-quality image, but it would consume about 5.5MBs of storage instead of 700KBs—so I used the lower-quality setting, as it is the setting most digital camera owners are likely to use. Well, which picture was taken with the digital camera—the one shown in Figure 1.1 or Figure 1.2?

Figure 1.1
Was this picture taken with a digital camera?

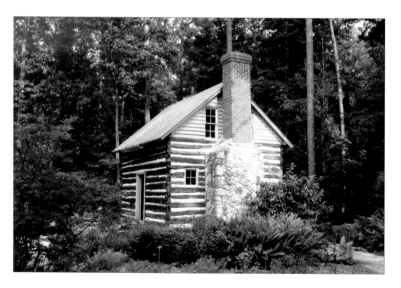

Figure 1.2
Was this picture taken
with a film camera?

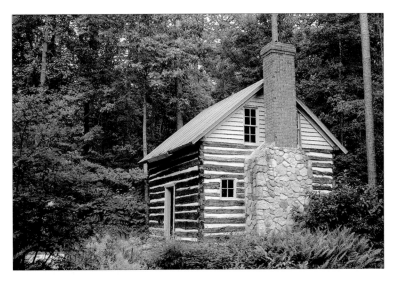

Admittedly, they do look different—but is one necessarily better than the other? What do you think? With a little work in a good image editing application, the picture taken with the digital camera, shown in Figure 1.2, could be made to look even better.

Once you learn that Figure 1.2 was taken with a digital camera, you might say that I did not take a very good picture with the film camera. Or for that matter, as the picture-taker, I might claim that the one-hour lab did not do a very good job printing the photo—or maybe it was a combination. Still, the fact remains—there are many variables to control, and the digital camera can often take as good a picture as one taken with a good film camera.

Finally, as one last proof of the digital camera's capability to take a good picture, look at Figure 1.3. This picture, taken in a used bookstore with a digital camera, is almost clear enough to enable you to read the titles on the books! The camera was set for fluorescent lighting and automatic flash, and the image was saved as a 5.5MB TIFF image. If you are not yet convinced that a digital camera is worth using, try one out at a local camera store. For the cost of a $10 print, you can shoot a picture in or near the store and have them print out an 8×10-inch print on one of their digital printers. If you buy the camera, they might not even charge you for the print!

Figure 1.3
Picture taken with a
Nikon 950, using the
TIFF file format.

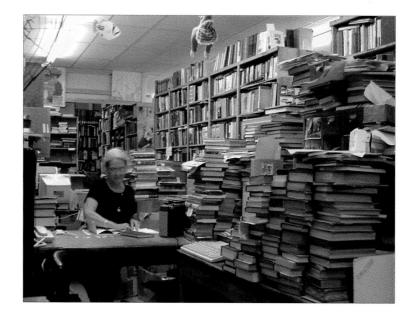

The digital camera is not like a film camera

A traditional camera uses film that needs to be chemically processed at a
photo lab. A digital camera, on the other hand, almost instantaneously
produces a digital file that is stored on small magnetic storage media that
is similar to that used by computers. Digital cameras enable you to store,
erase, and reuse digital image storage media.

Although the digital camera does not constantly require new rolls of film,
as does a traditional camera, storing the images after they have been
downloaded from the camera does require storage space on a hard drive or
on removable storage media, such as a floppy disk, Zip disk, or CD-ROM.

To compose the picture that you want to take, digital cameras typically
offer a 1.5- to 2-inch-wide LCD screen, which is similar to a miniature
television screen (see Figure 1.4). The LCD not only can be used to
compose images, but it also can be used in a textual function mode to
change camera settings, or it can be used as a playback screen.

Figure 1.4
Kodak digital camera
with LCD screen.

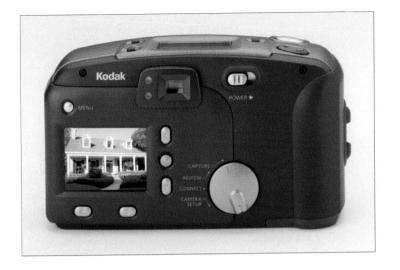

Depending on the camera model, a digital camera can have more than 100 features! These features enable you to do things that are not possible with a film camera, such as adjust white balance (set for sunny, incandescent, fluorescent, or cloudy conditions), increase brightness (for dark conditions), or even auto-white balance lock for shooting panoramas.

Camera features, size, shape, and cost vary dramatically between vendors and within each vendor's product line. Like many of the leading digital camera vendors, Kodak offers a wide range of cameras for entry-level consumers to professionals. You can purchase Kodak consumer-level cameras from $250 to $1,000 and at just about every $100 increment in between. Figure 1.5, 1.6, and 1.7 are just three of about ten models that Kodak offers in the under-$1,000 price range.

Figure 1.5
Kodak DC215 Zoom
digital camera.

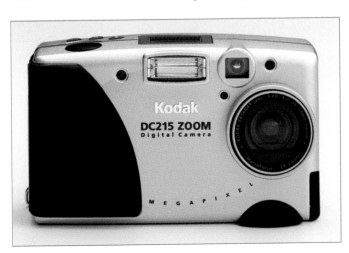

Figure 1.6
Kodak DC280 Zoom
digital camera.

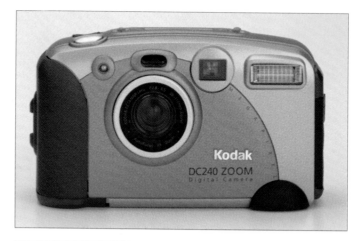

Figure 1.7
Kodak DC290 Zoom
digital camera.

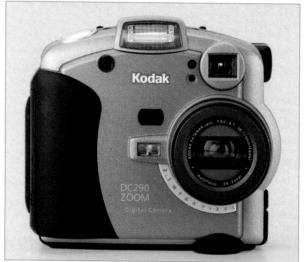

You won't use a digital camera like a film camera

For years, I took pictures only with a medium-format camera that
exposed a 2.25×2.25-inch negative (and generally required a tripod). Then
I bought a 35mm camera. It was a different camera entirely in comparison
to the medium-format camera. I used it differently and shot pictures of
things that I never would have taken (or couldn't have taken) with the
medium-format camera. However, I continued to use the medium-format
camera, because it was far superior for landscapes and stationary objects
when I planned on getting a print larger than 8×10. In contrast, the 35mm
camera was superb for action shots, for catching "life moments" that
vanish quickly, and for all-around general use. Now I happily use them
both—each where it is best suited.

My camera collection now also includes a digital camera, which I use to take all kinds of pictures—especially when I need to have a digital image for use with a PC. However, purchasing a digital camera doesn't mean that you can't continue shooting film-based pictures. If you use each type of camera where it is best suited, you'll get the best results.

Odds are that you, too, won't use your digital camera the same way that you have traditionally used your film camera. The real advantage to the digital camera, of course, is that it creates digital images. We now live in a "digital world" and, thus, need digital images. As an increasing number of people create electronic documents and use the Internet, they will want an easy way to share their digital images without going through the scanning process. In many cases, they won't be concerned about whether they have a printed version of the image. If they do want a printed version, there are many ways that they can get one. My advice is to not look at a digital camera as a replacement for a film camera—they just aren't the same!

It might (or might not) be cheaper to shoot digital

Is it cheaper to shoot pictures with a digital camera or with a film camera? It all depends on how you use your images and how you compare costs. There are so many variables to consider:

- ▶ What pixel resolution will you need?
- ▶ What level of compression will you use to store images?
- ▶ Will you store all the images you shoot or only a few from each series?
- ▶ What storage devices do you intend to use: CD-ROM, Zip disk, hard drive, tape drive, or another kind of storage device?
- ▶ Do you need to purchase a PC?
- ▶ How many software applications will you need to purchase and at what cost?
- ▶ How many batteries will you use?
- ▶ Do you already have an appropriate printer, or will you have to purchase one?
- ▶ How many pictures will you print?
- ▶ How large will the prints be, and how much ink might they use?
- ▶ What kind of printer will you use, and how much do the ink refills cost?
- ▶ What kind of paper do you intend to print on, and how expensive is it?
- ▶ Will you use an outside service to print your images, and how much will they cost to be printed?

Part I Good Digital Images

There are more variables than these, but you get the idea, I'm sure.

My guess is that, for most of us, shooting digital images is not likely to be any cheaper than shooting with a film-based camera. However, if you intend to save only the best few pictures from each series and use them only on Web pages and in digital slide shows, you'll find the digital camera to be a real bargain. Conversely, if you are a snapshot photographer and shoot ten rolls of film while on vacation, and you want to have double prints made of each of them, then digital photography is going to be much more expensive for you.

Excluding computer hardware, software, and a color printer, the three major PC photography costs are image storage media, paper, and ink. Assuming that you take advantage of the new 1600×1200-pixel cameras and use "normal" compression (which slightly reduces image quality, while greatly decreasing file size to about 650KB), the equivalent of a 24-exposure roll of film will take about 15.6MBs. Considering 100MB Zip disks cost about $13.50 per disk and have the capacity to store about 6 rolls of film, that equates to about $2.25 per roll or about a dime per image to store them. If you decide to store only your best images, you can vastly reduce the number of images that you need to store and the cost (unless, of course, you are Ansel Adams and nearly all of your shots are worth keeping).

A CD drive is more expensive than a 100MB Zip drive, but CDs hold many more images and they cost less than $1. A CD-R with a capacity of 640MB can store the equivalent of 41 rolls of 24-exposure film for a cost of less than a $.01 *a roll,* compared to a dime *an image* with a Zip disk.

Chapter 13, "Turning Digital Images into Prints," covers the topic of paper types and printing high-quality photographic prints. However, for the present purposes, we can make a quick estimate of printing costs. Premium Kodak Photo Paper costs about $.60 for an 8×10-inch page. Determining exactly how much printer ink will cost is much more difficult. Print cartridges cost between $23 and $37. As an educated guess, a full 8×10-inch print might cost between $.30 and $.50, depending on the type of printer and the cost of the cartridge. Considering photofinishers charge $6 or more for an 8×10 enlargement, the $1 cost of photographic quality inkjet paper and ink is relatively cheap! If you were to print two 4×6 images on a single piece of 8.5×11-inch paper, the cost might be about the same as ordering two reprints at $.40 each.

In conclusion, storage costs for high-quality images range from less than a penny to as much as a dime per image. An 8×10-inch photo print on photo-quality paper costs another $.60 for paper and $.30 to $.50 for ink, for a total of more than $1 per 8×10-inch print. Printing four photographs per page, you can get four prints that are slightly smaller than 4×6 inches for about $.25 each. Obviously, you can substantially reduce these costs by using paper that is less expensive than "premium quality" photo paper, but you will also reduce the quality of the image.

While this might sound like a bargain, you have not factored in any of the costs of the PC hardware and software, which can total well over $3,000, if you are serious about PC photography and image quality. Allocating $3,000 of hardware and software costs over the number of pictures you take over a three- or four-year period can make each image quite expensive. In most cases, though, the PC is used for many things besides imaging.

You can't shoot "everything" with a digital camera

The limits of what you can and cannot successfully shoot with your digital camera are very dependent on the cost of the camera. The more expensive the camera, the more you will be able to do with it. At this time, even the $1,000 digital camera won't work well for action photographs, such as soccer games, bicycle races, or a BMX bike jump, as shown in Figure 1.8, for two reasons:

► A considerable delay occurs between when you actually push the shutter-release button and when the image is taken, which makes it hard for you to get the picture that you want to take.

► Consumer-level digital cameras are not yet able to capture fast-moving objects, because their processor simply isn't able to process all the necessary pixels fast enough to focus and to store that many pixels—but I'm guessing they will soon.

My recommendation is to plan on taking pictures of fairly slow-moving subjects—and then you will not be disappointed with your purchase. Also, if you enjoy taking time exposures at night, as I do, use a film camera instead of a digital camera. Most digital cameras do not allow time exposures of more than a few seconds.

Figure 1.8
Blurry action photo taken with a digital camera.

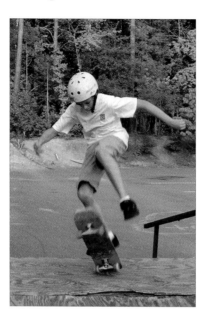

If a digital camera meets your needs now, don't wait for new technology

When buying electronic devices, the natural reaction is to avoid buying until the next new model is out. Such a view will put off a purchase for a long time. Unfortunately, most of us have experienced the severe drop in the price/performance curve in a way that can be sorely felt in our wallets. A rather common experience is to buy a new electronic gadget and then see the price significantly drop within a few weeks, as a new model is introduced that not only does more but also costs less than what you just purchased. That is the inevitable result of an innovative industry working hard to meet the increasingly educated needs of prospective buyers who always want more for less. The good news is that if you buy a digital camera that meets your needs today, it should continue to meet those needs for a reasonable period of time, even if there is a newer, better, faster, and cheaper model on the market. Unless you have an unlimited supply of cash, don't plan to always have the most technologically superior digital camera—they simply change too fast. This is my advice, that is, unless you are exceptionally good at buying and selling at online auctions, such as eBay.

My advice is to buy when you can afford to buy and when the technology enables you to do the things that you want to do. Be thankful that we live in a world full of innovative companies that are constantly introducing new products and services. Don't worry about all the new stuff that arrives right after you make a purchase. Shoot your pictures and share and enjoy them—your enjoyment will more than make up the difference in price and feature disparity.

Reasons why you'll love your digital camera

Digital cameras are fun and useful. There is no question about it. Here are just a few of the many reasons that you will love your digital camera:

▶ **Digital images are instantly available and usable.** As soon as a picture is taken, the image is ready to be used. This is true even if you decide to take only a single picture—there is no need to wait until you shoot the rest of the roll of film, as you do with a film-based camera—just shoot and use it!

▶ **You get instant feedback.** Using the LCD, you can see the picture that was just taken. You'll know right away whether you got the shot you wanted. If you didn't, you can reshoot until you get the perfect picture. The real benefit is that you will get better pictures.

▶ **Digital images are Internet-ready.** You don't have to scan or convert the file into another file format. Most digital cameras allow images to be saved as a JPEG image. You shoot it, and it's ready to for Internet.

▶ **Your subjects can see how they look.** Sometimes, *thinking* that you took a good picture isn't good enough. Using the LCD, you can immediately show those in the picture how they look. If they aren't happy with the result, take it again. Guaranteed "picture perfect!"

▶ **No cost for "bad pictures."** If you don't like an image, just delete it. It won't cost a penny to store or print!

▶ **Digital images are so easy to use.** You'll find many ways to use digital images once you find out how easy it is to shoot and download files to your PC. E-mail attachments, newsletters, Christmas letters, greeting cards, and short notes to friends and family are just a few of the many ways that you can use your images.

▶ **Digital images are easy to store and manage.** Unlike film-based photographs, digital images are easy to store on high-capacity digital media, such as CD-ROMs and Zip disks. You won't need shoeboxes, and you won't have the problem of finding a negative for a picture that you want to print—just find the digital image and print it.

This list could continue, but the message is already clear: The more you use your digital camera, the more you are likely to love it!

What can you do with a digital camera?

Finally, we get to the proverbial million-dollar question: What can you do with a digital camera? That is exactly the question that this book was written to answer. There are so many topics to cover that it will take 13 more chapters to examine the possibilities. For now, though, look at Figure 1.9, which shows many of the ways in which you can use a digital camera.

Figure 1.9
Things that you can do with a digital camera.

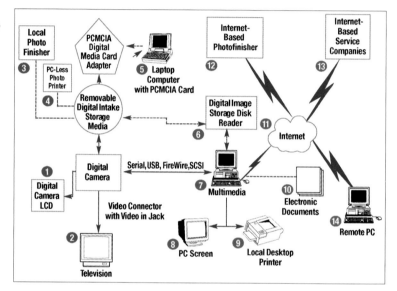

1. View images as a full-screen image, as a sheet of thumbnails, or as an automatic or manual slide show in the digital camera's LCD.

2. View images on a television screen as a full-screen image, as a sheet of thumbnails, or as an automatic or manual slide show, by connecting the digital camera to a television or VCR through the VIDEO IN jack.

3. Get photo-quality prints "on the spot" at sizes up to 8×10 inches by taking your removable digital image storage card (digital film) to a local photofinisher with an onsite digital file printing service.

4. Use a "PC-less environment" photo-printer to select, edit, and print images directly from a digital image storage card. It also can be used to save images to storage media such as a Zip drive.

5. Use a notebook computer to access images directly from a digital image storage card by using a PCMCIA digital image storage card adapter.

6. Directly access digital images from any PC, with an inexpensive digital image storage card reader that connects to your computer. The card reader is viewed by the operating system as an additional drive, enabling images to be transferred bilaterally between the PC and the digital image storage card.

7. Use a PC to view or transfer digital images directly with a digital camera by connecting the PC to a digital camera via a cable (serial, SCSI, USB, or FireWire) and using software supplied by the camera vendor.

Once your digital images are accessible by your PC, you can do the following:

8. Use the PC screen to view the images in slide shows, screen-savers, photo albums, and more.

9. Print your images with a photo-quality printer on photo-quality paper or on other types of papers, including labels, business cards, fabric transfer papers, folded greeting cards, fine-art papers, and so forth.

10. Use images in electronic documents created with desktop publishing programs, word-processors, spreadsheets, calendars, and more.

11. Make images available to everyone on the Internet by posting them to a Web site.

12. Upload images to online Internet photofinishers and order photo-quality prints, photo calendars, T-shirts, barbecue aprons, hats, and more.

13. Send images via the Internet to service companies to get professionally printed business cards, wedding invitations, letterhead, brochures, and more.

14. Share your images with others via the Internet, with chat applications or instant messengers, or share images in online communities or forums.

Selecting and buying the "best" digital camera

My commitment to you, as the author of this book, is to provide you with accurate, practical, and up-to-date information about digital cameras. However, as much as I would like to be able to include an entire chapter comparing and contrasting digital cameras, the time it takes to write a book, print it, and make it available for purchase is vastly more time than it takes for camera vendors to introduce new products and drop prices on older models. Consequently, I cannot make such recommendations. But don't worry, because some fabulous resources are available on the Internet for comparing up-to-date camera specifications and prices. I'll make sure that you leave this chapter either knowing what you need to know or knowing where to go to get all the latest information and advice to make an excellent choice on a digital camera. First, here are a few tips on selecting a digital camera.

Deciding how you will use a digital camera

Before you go hunting for a digital camera, you must determine how you intend to use it. To make this determination, first read this book to learn more about what you can do with a digital camera. This will give you a more educated view of what you will want to do with your digital camera after you get it. Then, follow the six easy steps for selecting a digital camera that are provided in the upcoming section.

Things to consider when purchasing a digital camera

Experts who study the psychology of buying have found that most people make an emotional decision rather than a rational decision when making a high-dollar-value purchase. When I bought my digital camera (I'm embarrassed to confess), I did exactly as those experts say—I bought mostly on emotion. As you might expect, I searched and read everything I could find on the Internet about digital cameras. I visited a few digital camera forums and asked questions, and I visited the vendor's Web page to read its technical support notes. Having completed this basic research, I made a list of three camera models that I was going to choose from— then off to a retail store I went. The unfortunate salesperson had to spend more than two hours educating me and answering my endless list of questions. In the end, I bought a camera that was not even on my list!

My choice was a Nikon CoolPix 950, because it was only slightly out of the high end of my price range, and because the salesperson was able to show me a printed photograph that was taken with the 950—the picture quality was excellent. More important, though, it simply felt better in my hands than any of the other cameras and had a few unusual features that

I had not even considered. One such feature is the camera's design, which allows the camera to be placed flat on the ground while the LCD is rotated so that it is parallel with the ground and easily viewable (see Figure 1.10).

Figure 1.10
Nikon CoolPix 950
digital camera.

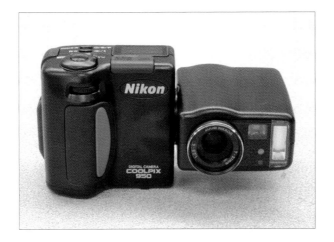

I have always loved the "worm's-eye" view shot, which is very hard to get if you have to lie flat on the ground and try to look through a viewfinder or LCD that is perpendicular to the ground! For an eye-level view of a turtle, see Figure 1.11.

Figure 1.11
Worm's-eye view of a
turtle, taken with a
Nikon CoolPix 950.

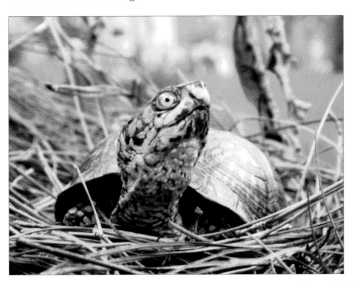

Finally, I bought the Nikon CoolPix 950 because it had a valuable feature for shooting digital panoramas that can be converted into 360-degree virtual-reality videos, which I enjoy making. You'll learn about these videos in Chapter 10, "Doing Extraordinary Things with Images."

Six easy steps for buying the right camera for you

If you want to make a good decision on which digital camera to buy, I suggest following the six easy steps listed next.

Step 1: Decide how much you want to spend

Image quality and digital camera features all cost money. The more money you are willing to spend, the more you will get. As a rough guide to digital camera prices, as of Fall 1999 (and I truly mean "rough"), see Table 1.1.

Table 1.1
Digital camera price and image size

Digital Camera Resolution	Largest Printed Photo-Quality Print	Approximate Digital Camera Cost	Number of Pixels	Remarks
320×240	2×3	Under $300	76,800	Useful for Web page images
640×480	4×6	Under $400	307,200	
1024×768	8×10	Under $500	786,432	
1152×864	8×10	$500 to $700	995,352	Megapixel digital camera
1280×1024	8×10	$700 to $1,000	1,310,720	Megapixel digital camera
1600×1200	11×14	$1,000 and up	1,920,000	2-megapixel digital camera

Step 2: Decide how large you want to be able to print "photo-quality" prints

"Photo-quality" means that the image can be printed at 300 dpi, at least, because the number of pixels is the major determinant of picture quality—the more pixels, the larger and clearer the picture is likely to be. Use Table 1.1 to determine the resolution required to print the size of prints that you desire.

Step 3: Find a camera that feels good in your hands and that is well designed

You might not think this is important enough to be number three on a list of six things to consider when buying a digital camera, but it is. Digital cameras can be rather small and lightweight. Using a camera that is uncomfortable to hold can make it hard to hold on to. Several digital cameras that I have used were so hard to hold that it scared me—they were too expensive to drop. Also, take a few pictures to determine whether you can hold the camera level. The shape and size of some cameras makes it hard to shoot pictures that are horizontal, which might require you to edit each one to straighten it. To straighten an image, you not only lose some pixels, but you also have to store the image again, which decreases the quality if you store it by using a compressed format, such as JPEG.

Besides considering the shape and size of the camera, you'll also want to make sure that you are comfortable with the camera controls. Often, photo opportunities come and go quickly. If you can't quickly turn on your camera, set the flash on or off, and make sure that you have the right image resolution and quality, you'll miss pictures that you want to take.

Step 4: Learn which features will help you to shoot the kinds of pictures that you want to take

Digital cameras can have hundreds of features. Eleven of the more important standard features that substantially differentiate cameras are listed next. Once you decide how you want to use your camera, make sure that your camera has the features that you need to shoot the pictures that you want.

▶ **Point-and-shoot (fixed focus) or autofocus**—Fixed focus attempts to focus everything in the image, whereas autofocus gives you a little more control over what is and isn't in focus. Autofocus cameras generally produce a better-quality image.

▶ **Lens focal length and speed**—Focal length determines both the magnification and angle of view that can be taken with a lens. Lenses are categorized as wide-angle, normal, telephoto, or zoom. A zoom lens enables the focal length to change within a specific range. Lens speed determines how much light is needed to take a picture. A fast lens enables you to take a better picture in a lower light environment than a slower lens.

▶ **Optical versus digital zoom capabilities**—Optical zoom enables you to zoom in on an object by using the lenses. Digital zoom enables zooming through the use of software. Optical zoom provides a far better image than digital zoom.

▶ **Macro capabilities**—Enable you to take close-up images.

▶ **Viewfinder and/or LCD**—A viewfinder is an optical window that enables you to point the camera. It does not, however, accurately represent the image that you are taking. In contrast, an LCD is a television-like screen that shows you what your picture will look like.

▶ **Image storage media (CompactFlash, SmartMedia, floppy disk, or other)**—CompactFlash and SmartMedia are the most common and have the most storage capacity—ranging from 4MB to 96MB or more.

▶ **Type of interface between the PC and digital camera (serial, USB, or FireWire)**—The interface enables you to hook a digital camera directly to a PC. Serial cables are the slowest by a relatively high factor. Universal serial bus (USB) and the new FireWire connections are fast and easy to connect.

▶ **Image file format, file compression options, and capacity**—Digital camera vendors all offer a variety of file formats and compression technologies, which impact the overall capacity to store images. Different formats also have implications on quality and the capability of the file to be used and viewed by software applications. See Chapter 5, "Getting Images into Shape," for further information.

▶ **Flash capabilities**—A built-in flash is useful, but not very powerful. If you need more powerful flash capabilities, find out whether the camera can be used with an external flash.

▶ **Capability to add lenses**—If you need telephoto or wide-angle capabilities outside the range of your camera, check whether the camera you are considering supports the use of additional lenses.

▶ **Capability to output to a television**—A nice feature that enables you to connect your digital camera directly to a TV screen by using a cable that plugs into the VIDEO IN port in the TV or VCR. Often, digital cameras that have this feature also offer slide show capabilities.

After you investigate these major features, you're likely to find "surprise" features. Generally, you find out about the surprise features only after you have purchased your camera, shot a hundred or so pictures, and finally have decided to sit down to read your user's manual. Such features typically are neither written up in the comparison tables or included in the feature lists on the retail packaging, and you probably won't find a salesperson that will be able to tell you about them.

When I purchased the Nikon CoolPix 950, for example, I was astounded by the number of additional features it has. A small sample of those are as following:

- Flash settings
- Self-timer
- Film-sensitivity adjustment
- White-balance adjustment
- Continuous-shot mode
- Image adjustment for brightness/contrast
- 1.25 to 2.5 times digital zoom
- Capability to create folders on image disks
- Capability to turn sound off
- Automatic sequencing of image file names
- Printing settings

- Focus settings
- Variable image quality
- Multiple exposure modes
- Three exposure meters
- Three-shot mode
- Best-shot selection
- Choice of black-and-white images
- Adjustable LCD brightness level card format
- LCD slide show capability
- Many more features not listed here

The moral of the story: If you want to know all about the features offered by a particular model of camera, visit a retail store and ask to see the user's manual. Sometimes that is even hard to do, because some vendors assume that you have a PC and, thus, provide the user's manual to you on a CD-ROM to be read on a computer!

Step 5: Select a brand and model

As promised earlier in the chapter, this section provides resources to help you compare cameras and make a choice of the best camera for your use. One of the most valuable online resources for comparing technical specifications and prices of most models made by the major vendors is the ZDNet site at **www.zdnet.com/computershopper/index1.html**.

Once you are there, find the Shop by Category section and click Digital Cameras. Besides offering an excellent Shop and Compare by Price Range feature, you'll find the Experts Pick and How to Buy features valuable. If you have decided on a specific vendor, there is a useful Shop and Compare by Manufacturer section. If one of the Ziff-Davis journals has reviewed a specific product, then you'll find a place to click and read the review in detail.

The most compelling reason to visit this site is that it is linked to most of the major merchants' Web sites, so with a single click, you'll find yourself, at say, Beyond.com, MicroWarehouse, or PCZone. Also visit the HP Shopping Village, where you can waltz down the electronic aisles and order photographic paper for your ink-jet printer. The ZDNet site is an excellent site; but be careful of the "Buy It!" buttons—they make it so easy to buy online! If you visit just one Web site, this should be the one.

Usually, you can find the most up-to-date information and news on products at the manufacturer's site. This is the best place to go for pictures of the cameras, detailed specification sheets, and product brochures, which are frequently available in a format that you can print. The easiest way to get to the various manufacturers' sites is by using the Digital Camera Resource Page at **www.dcresource.com/links/links.html**.

If you'd like to join a digital camera forum so that you can ask questions and learn firsthand how users of a particular camera like it, then I again suggest a visit to the Digital Camera Resource Page at **www.dcresource.com**.

Finally, if you have an appetite for yet more information, visit the Photonut site, **www.photonut.com**, where you'll find lots of links and real-time chat. If you are prone to sign up for mailing lists, try Photoforum by subscribing to **listserv@listserver.isc.rit.edu**.

That just about completes the information that you need to determine what camera you want to buy—now it's time to figure out where to buy it.

TIP

If you want a real bargain on a digital camera, bid on a new or used one online at **www.ebay.com**, **www.egghead.com**, **www.amazon.com**, or any other online auction Web site. Egghead.com enables you to sign up for an e-mail service that notifies you of specials.

Step 6: Decide where to buy your digital camera

Should you buy a digital camera and accessories at your local "brick and mortar" store, or should you buy online? Good question! If price is all that matters to you, then it is an easy answer—buy online. A $1,000 camera will cost as little as $800 at some of the online stores, plus you'll save a few dollars on sales tax (but pay a few more for shipping and handling). In the end, you might save as much as 20 percent, or $200! However, I must raise a caution flag here. Beware of online merchants who offer discounts substantially lower than most of the other merchants. Anyone selling electronic components of any kind must compete in a highly competitive marketplace, and it's hard to sell too cheaply for very long. Ask them if the model you want is in stock and if it will be shipped immediately. Ask them about their return policy, and make sure you get a comparable product. To make prices look lower, some less-reputable vendors will charge you extra for an image storage card or batteries that are normally shipped with the camera.

If service is an issue to you, as it is to me, then you should support your local retail store. If that is where you go to get a "hands-on" feel for the camera of your choice, then, in my opinion, that is where you should buy it. Knowledgeable salespeople can add substantial value, and they need compensation for their efforts.

The two dominant national retail camera chains are Ritz Camera and Wolf Camera. They both have more than 900 stores or photo-processing labs spread across most of the states, and both offer a considerable range of digital cameras and digital film-processing capabilities. To find a store near you or to learn more about these stores and what they offer, visit their Web sites at **www.ritzcamera.com** and **www.wolfcamera.com**.

Another advantage of some of the national chains is that they can offer you unusually good warranties that you cannot get from the online stores or from some local independent stores. For example, for about 10 percent of the purchase price of your new digital camera, Ritz Camera will sell you a renewable one-year Expanded Service Policy (ESP). The written agreement states: "With ESP you never need to worry about: mechanical malfunction, accidental damage, water damage, even damage caused by your own negligence!" Now you know where I bought my digital camera! If you are incredibly careful and don't intend to use your camera much, buying an extended policy might not be worthwhile. If you shoot pictures outdoors, on ski trips, near the beach, from horseback, or in other risky environments, then get one.

If you decide to buy online, you will find that the ZDNet site lists all the large (and some small) mail-order and online merchants. One of my favorite online camera merchants is cameraworld.com at **www.cameraworld.com**.

Other things you'll need to buy

Once you have purchased a digital camera, plan to also buy the following:

▶ **120V AC battery charger**—Because digital cameras consume so much power for lens focusing, flash, and the mighty power-sucking LCD, you will drain more batteries than you can believe. Some digital cameras consume four AA batteries in an hour or two, which is the amount of time it takes to shoot twenty or so pictures. The following are the three types of batteries to choose from:

—**Alkaline:** The least expensive, but doesn't last as long as the other two. The advantage to these batteries is that they are available everywhere and cost $1 or less. The disadvantage is that they cannot be recharged.

—**Ni-Cd:** Last longer than the alkaline and can be recharged.

—**Ni-MH:** Last even longer than the Ni-Cd and can be recharged. And, as you might expect, they are the most expensive.

In simplistic terms, there are two basic types of battery chargers—fast ones and slow ones. The less-expensive slow chargers for AA batteries are about $15 or less and take twelve hours to recharge Ni-Cd or Ni-MH batteries. The faster chargers cost $30 or more and can recharge both Ni-Cd and Ni-MH batteries in less than an hour. The obvious advantage here is that if you purchase two sets of four rechargeable Ni-MH batteries, you can charge them faster than you can use them! With the slower charger, you undoubtedly will have to wait for your batteries to recharge, unless you have many, many sets of batteries.

TIP

Radio Shack sells an excellent "fast" charger for less than $30 that can charge both Ni-Cd and Ni-MH batteries. It also offers a four-pack of Ni-MH batteries for $10.00, or $2.50 per battery. Buy two or more sets of batteries, and for less than $70, you can have the best batteries and charger on the market.

▶ **Padded carrying case**—There is not much to a digital camera except a lens and a tiny computer that is exceptionally good at compressing large graphics files—consequently, digital cameras are fragile and won't survive bad bumps or a drop to the floor or a hard drop to a desktop. A padded carrying case is worth the money, plus you'll have a place to store your extra batteries and image storage media.

▶ **CompactFlash or SmartMedia drive**—To get your images from your digital camera to your PC, you have two options. You can either buy an inexpensive storage media card reader, or you can connect your digital camera directly to your PC with a connector cable supplied by your digital camera vendor. If your PC has a USB port, consider getting a card reader like the one made by SanDisk (Figure 1.12). It not only is easy to connect but is as easy to use as any other hard drive.

Figure 1.12
SanDisk storage media
card reader.

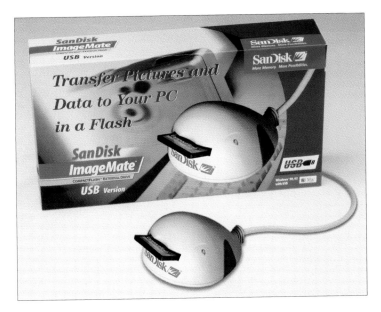

▶ **AC power supply**—If you decide that you want to connect your digital camera directly to your PC, or if you expect to connect your digital camera frequently to your TV, then I suggest that you buy an AC power supply adaptor. Otherwise, you will drain your batteries faster than when you shoot pictures, because the power-draining LCD remains on as long as you are using the camera.

▶ **Extra "digital film" or image storage media**—The number of images that image storage media can hold varies widely depending on image resolution, image file format, and the level of compression used. When purchasing a digital camera, you should check the documentation to see how many images you can save on the size of media that comes with the camera. If this is not sufficient for your use, purchase additional cards. Image media storage cards typically come in 4, 8, 10, 16, 20, 32, 48, 64, and 80MB and 96MB versions.

▶ **Image storage media PCMCIA card adaptor**—CompactFlash or SmartMedia disks can be inserted into a PCMCIA card slot like those typically found on notebook computers, providing you have an adapter. Once the media card and adapter are inserted into the PC PCMCIA slot, it will be recognized by the PC's operating system as just another drive.

▶ **Software**—Depending on what you intend to do with your images, you will need one or more software applications to manage, edit, enhance, and share images. Most of the following chapters cover applications that help you get the most from your images.

Do you need a PC to use a digital camera?

Do you need a PC to use a digital camera? When I first started writing this book, the answer was close to being a definitive "yes." Within the few months that it took to write this book, that answer rapidly became "maybe not," as many vendors and service companies rapidly created new offerings. One of the most startling innovations came from Kodak—the PM100 Kodak Personal Picture Maker by Lexmark, which is shown in Figure 1.13. Its onboard digital camera card reader allows photo-quality prints to be made without a PC—all for less than $300. It offers some photo editing capability, including framing, cropping, and creating text messages, and it prints at a 1200×1200 dpi resolution. Even more exciting is its capability to connect to an external parallel port storage device like the Iomega Zip 100 or 250. This solves the long-term image storage problem, which was the really compelling reason to have a PC if you have a digital camera.

Figure 1.13
Kodak Personal Picture Maker PM100 by Lexmark for the "PC-less" environment.

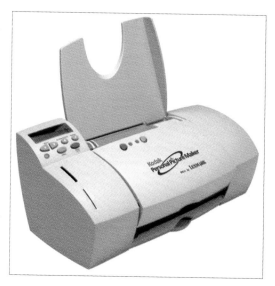

With photo-printers that work in PC-less environments and solve the long-term storage issues—what is it that you can't do without a PC? You can't easily upload and share your images on the Internet or via e-mail. However, that, too, is changing rapidly as Kodak and Fuji begin to introduce kiosks to the market and as photo labs get connected to the Internet. Before long, you will be able to step up to a kiosk like the one shown in Figure 1.14 and insert your digital image storage card. From there, you can select the images that you want to print and the ones that you want to upload to the Internet to be shared. You can add text, restore color, and copy images from your digital camera's storage media card to a CD-ROM to mention just a few of the many features offered.

Figure 1.14
Kodak PictureMaker helps you "Take Pictures Further."

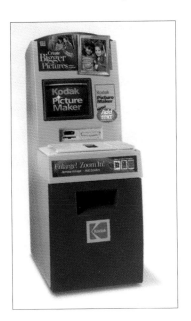

Well then, you might ask, how do you, *yourself,* enjoy images from others without a PC? I don't have an answer to that question, and so I still suggest that you own a PC—but you can bet that there are many companies working hard to solve that problem as well! I guess the safe answer to the question is that you no longer have to have a PC to enjoy using a digital camera—you can just do more with your digital images if you have one.

The next obvious question: What kind of PC do you need? Manipulating large image files can be very resource-intensive, so naturally, the more power you have, the faster you can do what is needed. Since mid-1998, PC prices have dropped dramatically as their performance has increased exponentially.

The following is a suggested PC configuration geared toward using a digital camera:

▶ 200MHz Pentium or above

▶ 32MB or more of RAM for Windows 95; 64MB or more for Windows 98 (and more if you use a high-end image editing application, such as Photoshop or Corel Photo Paint)

▶ 2GB or larger hard drive

▶ Graphics card and monitor to support 1024×768 resolution or higher images

▶ CD-ROM drive

Although not essential, it is nice to have the following, too:

▶ A high-capacity removable media drive, such as a 100MB Zip drive or a rewriteable CD drive

▶ A USB port, which is a useful feature for high-speed connections to a digital camera

To find out more about current PC configurations and costs, visit Dell (**www.dell.com**), Gateway (**www.gateway.com**), or any other online computer vendor's Web pages.

That concludes the introductory overview of digital cameras. In the next chapter, you'll learn a few tips on how to take better pictures. Good luck shopping, if you are off to buy a digital camera!

2

Learning to
Take Better Pictures

Since you bought this book, it is reasonable to assume that you have a digital camera or are planning to buy one. You are also likely to have a PC, various peripherals, and a variety of software. Statistics suggest that you have access to two, three, or more traditional film cameras plus accessories. Your total investment, then, is likely to be in excess of $3,000. That is a serious investment and, therefore, you ought to learn how to take the best pictures possible. Since every chapter following this chapter is about what you can do with your digital images once you have them, we'll spend one chapter looking at ways to take better and more creative pictures.

More specifically, we'll look at the following:

▶ Deciding why you are taking pictures so that you get the results you want

▶ Ten traditional photography techniques

▶ A starter kit of fifteen digital imaging techniques

▶ Steps to follow to continue getting better at taking pictures

Why are you taking pictures?

When my daughter was three years old, we would spend many of our weekends up in the mountains. We'd sit and watch ants on an anthill for an hour or more. We would throw rocks into the lake or paddle in a small backpacker's inflatable raft, expecting to catch fish—which we never did. I would watch her walk across a stretch of water on a narrow fallen tree trunk, wondering all the time if she were going to fall into the ice-cold water. In the evenings, we would make dinner and then just sit. We'd listen to the outdoor sounds and make up stories before we would climb into the tent for the evening. Those were wonderful and rare hours, which, sadly, vanished too quickly. Luckily, photography has kept those memories alive for all of us forever in photographs like the one shown in Figure 2.1.

Figure 2.1
A memory saved with a digitally enhanced photograph.

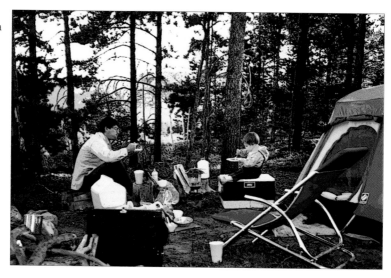

I also have experienced indescribable joy at watching the expressions of youth soccer players or lacrosse players as they eagerly paw their way through piles of photographs to find themselves in a perfectly captured action shot. I've listened to the lacrosse players argue over which of their digitally edited pictures that I had posted on a Web site were the best ones. Professionally, I have benefited from my skills at creating business proposals, product brochures, slide presentations, and newsletters with digital images that make them compelling business and sales tools. I enjoy displaying my digital artworks on the Internet and getting an endless supply of comments—both good and bad. Many family members and friends make year-round comments about the images that we send out on a Christmas letter each year. Others enjoy photographs that are taken and shared throughout the year. Those are just a few of the reasons I enjoy taking pictures. Why do you take them? What is it that you want to shoot?

Deciding what to shoot

Sometimes the question of what to shoot is an easy one to answer and other times it is not. If you don't know, just think for a moment about your family, friends, or business colleagues. Where can you provide the most benefit or enjoyment? When you answer that question, you'll know what to shoot. Maybe your kids' grandparents have not seen their grandkids for several months, and you ought to send some pictures to them. Are you working on a new project team that could use a boost in morale? Does your small business need a new sales tool—either a print version or an online version? As you read more of this book, you'll begin to see how many possibilities exist to use digital images.

Choosing how you will present and share your images

Okay, you have your camera in hand. It is loaded with fresh film or an empty digital image storage card. Now what? Stop and think for a minute. Before you begin shooting, decide what it is that you want to shoot. Decide what your final output will be, if you can. Do you need images for a Web page or large prints for a product brochure? Are you going to create a digital slide show or a screen-saver? Will your images be used to create a photo album? Will you want to create a panorama? Are the images to be used in a business or school class report? Will your images be printed on a high-resolution printer?

The more aware you are of why you are taking pictures, the more likely you will be to take the pictures that you will need. Without having some idea of why you are shooting, you won't be able to choose the right film, the right images, the right digital camera resolution, or the right compression format. You'll just be shooting to shoot. Sometimes that is okay, too—other times, you won't have the images that you need if you don't know in advance how you are going to use them. So, think! Plan—then shoot. You'll be better off, because you'll have all the right equipment, film, lenses, flashes—all things will be in order. Success will follow.

Picture-taking is easy, but getting outstanding pictures is hard

Before we look at some techniques for taking better pictures, let's be realistic about what we can accomplish. Photography unquestionably is a form of art. Great art takes hard work, talent, and persistence. Not many people are able to take pictures that are considered works of art, or at least considered sufficiently good that buyers will pay money for them. However, almost everyone—with some thought, applied knowledge, and creativity—can create photographs or digital images that will be lifelong, valued treasures or that are indispensable business-building tools.

If you've ever taken up a new sport, you might recall the difficulties that you had early on. If it was golf, you probably experienced some painful times learning to drive or putt—I still feel that pain! If you've taken up tennis, it probably was difficult to learn to serve successfully. Even a weight-loss program or piano lessons start with the proverbial "uphill" battle. The fact is that you can learn to take photographs that you will be pleased with—provided that you work at it. Nothing valuable comes easily!

Seeing the "light"—
photography is the art of capturing light

Photography is the art of capturing light. To be considered a photographer (as opposed to a picture-taker), you have to be able to see the "light" and capture it correctly. To capture light correctly, you need to learn how to control all kinds of variables with each shot. Besides choosing the appropriate lens aperture, shutter speed, and film speed, you also need to learn about adding flash and controlling metering, depth-of-field, focus, adding exposure corrections, and choosing lens length, to name just a few of the more important variables. Some of the new digital cameras have as many as 200 functions just to help you capture the light. When you consider all the possible combinations of these variables, you can understand why it is hard to get the "perfect" picture. It can be done, though—sometimes with luck and sometimes with skill.

Realistically, learning to take good pictures in just a few different types of environments takes years, and sometimes even a lifetime, which is why so many professional photographers specialize, at most, in one or just a few types of photography. They might shoot landscapes, portraits, wildlife, sports or action shots, available light, close-up, or underwater photography. They might specialize even further by doing only weddings, building interiors, product shots, or maybe just insects. The point is that photography taken seriously is like any other kind of art. Creating outstanding work requires a focused, persistent effort, the right equipment, and the right subjects.

Just as most tennis players never play at Wimbledon, most photographers never become professional photographers. However, many good tennis players, golfers, and photographers get tremendous joy and value from their respective pursuits. Work hard and you'll be one of those who gets enjoyment and value from your interest in capturing the light!

Ten traditional film-based techniques that always work

Libraries and bookstores have many shelves filled with wonderful books on photography. However, because this book isn't a book about learning how to shoot pictures, that subject is best left to those other books. Within the next few pages, however, we can look at ten time-honored techniques for taking better pictures. They are invaluable tips that you should know.

Shoot with the best possible light

Generally, if you are shooting pictures outdoors, there are good times and not-so-good times to take pictures. Early morning and late afternoon offer the most dramatic lighting effects. Those times of day not only allow the sun to come in at a low angle, providing the best angle of light to ensure both highlights and shadows, but also can offer exceptionally warm and colorful light, which rarely exists at other times of day. The twenty minutes before sunset and the twenty minutes around sunrise are "golden" times for taking outstanding photographs. You can see the warm coloring in the faces of the two children shown in Figure 2.2.

Figure 2.2
The warm "golden glow" of sunset.

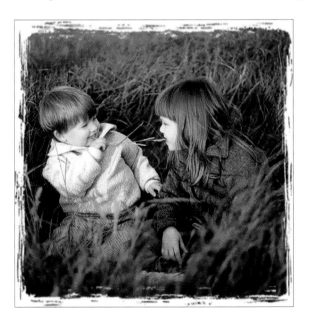

Rule of thirds

Symmetry might be comfortable to many, but it generally isn't as interesting as some alternatives. When you shoot a picture, do you frequently aim your camera to center the subject in the middle of the viewfinder? If so, try taking pictures with the subject centered on any one of the intersections of the interior lines of a 3×3 table, as shown in Figure 2.3. This composition technique is known as the "rule of thirds."

Figure 2.3
"Rule of thirds" composition technique.

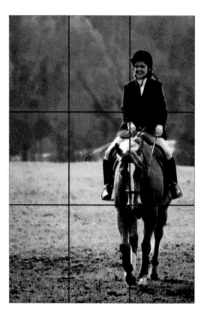

Low camera angle

Taking pictures with your camera at eye-level or five to six feet above ground is common and, consequently, you'll get ordinary or common images, because we are used to seeing the world from that vantage point. Try shooting a few pictures with your camera as low to the ground as you can get it—almost at a worm's-eye level. Figure 2.4 shows how effective that viewpoint can be.

Figure 2.4
A "worm's-eye" view
offers an unusual
perspective.

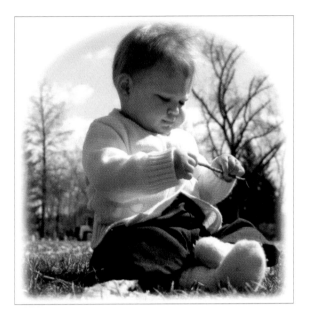

Include appropriate foreground or background

While you might want to take a picture of a specific subject, try to
include some interesting foreground or background to help set your
subjects in the context of their environment. Figure 2.5 shows how the
old English hotel adds to the character of the two children. If you look
carefully, you'll also notice that a digital filter has been applied to the
background, which helps bring the children into focus.

Figure 2.5
A background can add
character to the subject.

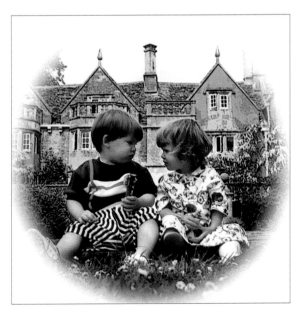

Silhouette a backlit subject

One of the more difficult techniques to master is the silhouette shot. To shoot a silhouette, you need to shoot at an object that has a strong light source coming from behind. If you set your exposure to the light source, the object that you wish to silhouette will become black, or silhouetted, as shown in Figure 2.6.

Figure 2.6
Palm tree picture taken as a silhouette.

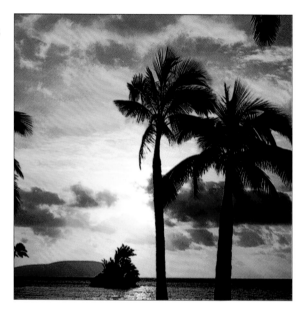

Bright subject on black background

This technique is the opposite of the preceding technique. Instead of shooting a backlit subject and making the object in front turn into a black silhouette, you make the subject bright and colorful and the background completely black, as shown in Figure 2.7. Obviously, you need the light source in front of the subject instead of behind it. You'll find that images like this will look exceptionally good displayed on a computer screen in a slide show, screen-saver, or as wallpaper.

Figure 2.7
Dramatic effect created
by a black background.

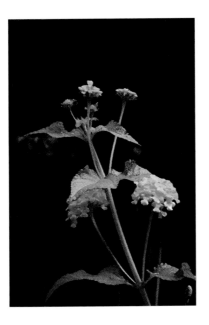

Frame things

Often, you will have the option of stepping behind a few tree branches or
to the side of a building to add a frame to your subject. Alternatively, you
can shoot an image that has a frame around it, or you can shoot a picture
of a frame and digitally include it in another image, as shown in Figure
2.8. Besides framing the image, it offers realism and depth to your image.

Figure 2.8
A framed subject can be
more interesting than an
unframed one.

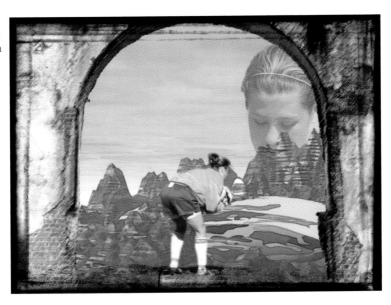

Crop or shoot for "partial images"

You do not have to shoot your entire subject to make an interesting image. Often, you can compose a picture that includes only a small portion of the subject, and the picture will be more interesting than if you had shot the entire subject. In Figure 2.9, the decision was made to fill the entire picture with just part of a cat's face. The effect is powerful— you almost feel like you are face-to-face with the bright-eyed fur ball! You can just about see the reflection of your face in her eyes and feel her whiskers.

Figure 2.9
Cropping can create interesting images.

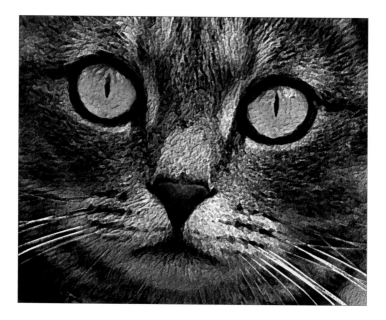

Reduce depth of field

Controlling the depth of field, or the area of the picture that is in focus, is another valuable technique. It takes practice and a good understanding of your equipment to be able to get the pictures you want. The results often can be outstanding. For example, Figure 2.10 shows a picture of a crab on a beach. You might have seen the holes that these crabs make, but rarely will you see the crabs, because when they see you with those big eyes— down the hole they go. This particular crab had his picture taken with about a four-inch depth of field. The two inches in front of him and the two inches behind him are in focus. Everything else is blurred, which helps bring him into sharp focus and makes him the center of attention.

Figure 2.10
A four-inch depth of
field around a crab.

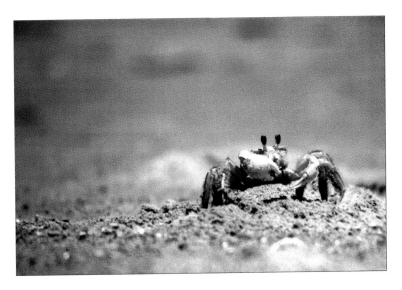

Look for strong geometry

One way to create an interesting picture is to shoot subjects that offer
strong lines or shapes. The lily pad image in Figure 2.11 is interesting not
only because of the flower but also because of the geometric shape of the
flower and the circular pads surrounding the flower.

Figure 2.11
Strong geometry attracts
attention.

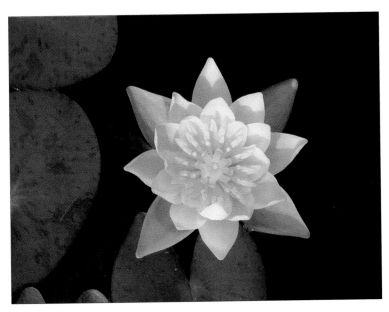

These ten techniques are some of the more basic techniques for taking
better pictures, although they don't even begin to touch on the knowledge
base that is available for learning how to take pictures. Most bookstores

and libraries have large sections on photography and learning how to improve your picture-taking skills. If you want a good basic book on taking better pictures, I suggest *Kodak Guide to 35mm Photography— Techniques for Better Pictures* (Silver Pixel Press, ISBN: 0-87985-613-0). It is an inexpensive yet well-written book filled with more than 400 excellent color photos that "teach, explain, and illustrate." You also might want to look at Web sites that offer tips and techniques for taking better pictures such as:

www.dastcom.com/lop/glossary.html
www.fodors.com/focus/
www.fujifilm.com/home/faqsfact/tips.htm
www.kodak.com
www.photosecrets.com

If you are interested in online discussions, you should consider subscribing to an e-mail discussion group (also known as an electronic mailing list or listserv) on digital imaging or photography. About 50 of these mailing lists are included at:

www.rit.edu/~andpph/photolists.html

That concludes this short overview of ten useful techniques that you can use to take better pictures. I know they will help you for as long as you take pictures—either with a traditional film camera or a digital camera. Now let's look at some techniques for taking better pictures when they will be used in the new world of digital photography.

A "starter set" of 15 digital imaging techniques

Once you leave traditional film-based processing and move into the world of digital editing, you enter a new realm of possibilities. Your power to control size, shape, color, light, and almost every aspect of any part of any image will enable you to do dazzling things. This is especially true if you learn to shoot images specifically for digital editing and then begin combining images. Therefore, to take advantage of the many features of the endless supply of new digital imaging software and hardware, you need to begin thinking differently about how to take photos. How do you think differently? The easiest way is to learn the following 15 techniques and then begin inventing your own.

Shoot objects

When I first started digitally editing images, I was thrilled to see what could be done. I could place any kind of object in an image—it could be scaled, the perspective could be altered, and the colors and lighting could be changed to match that of the scene that it was being placed in. One object can be placed in front of, or behind, another object. Objects can be removed as well as inserted. They can be duplicated, blended, transformed, and manipulated in an endless number of ways. After a few of these sessions, I became very aware of the importance of shooting objects for the objects themselves.

Once you learn how much effort it can take to remove an object from one image to place it in another image, you'll start thinking about ways to diminish that effort as much as possible. Chapter 6, "Performing Digital Imaging Magic," covers masking for those of you who want to get into object creation. After reading that chapter, you'll know how to shoot objects—just for the objects themselves.

You'll also learn to pay close attention to light sources and the resulting highlights and shadows. For example, if the light is coming from the left and it leaves a shadow on the right of one object, and another object has a shadow on the left, you'll have a lot of work to do to remove one shadow and create another one to make the image look correct. Complex objects often make correcting shadows and highlights difficult, if not impossible. The solution to this problem is to shoot with the correct lighting.

I keep a separate file directory just for objects. In it are butterflies, seagulls, people, cats, turtles, mushrooms, moons, boats, flowers—even LEGO models. Figure 2.12 shows the results of combining a North Carolina turtle (the Loch Ness monster), a South Carolina seagull, and an old wooden boat from Portugal into an image off the coast of Scotland! You might call this a very international image.

Figure 2.12
Inserted objects from all over the world.

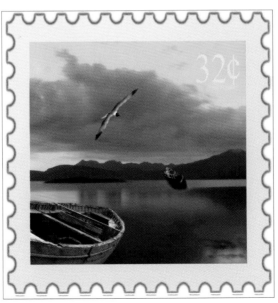

Shoot poses

Several years ago, I watched as my kids jumped up and down on a trampoline. At the time, I noticed how cool they looked just as they reached the highest point in each jump. For just an instant in time, they were suspended in air—they looked as though they were floating. I quickly fetched my camera and took two photographs of them jumping, as shown in Figure 2.13. Several years later, I was able to remove the floating kids, find a moon object from my object collection, and create the magical image shown in Figure 2.14.

Figure 2.13
Kids jumping on a trampoline.

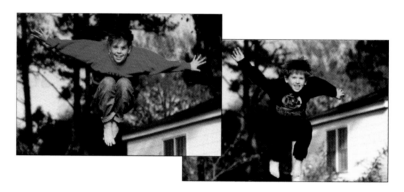

Figure 2.14
Inline flight at dusk with the seagulls.

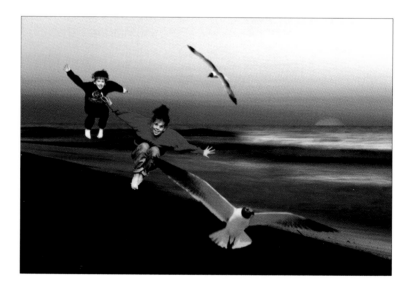

The second technique, then, is to shoot people while they are posing in the right way. Think about the angle you'll want later. Perspective is a very important and sometimes difficult thing to show correctly. Our eyes are good at spotting image fraud if the perspective is not correct.

Shoot backgrounds just for a background

Deep inside a cavern, I found a most amazing place, which is shown in Figure 2.15. The colors were incredibly rich and the shapes were out of this world. I took a few time exposures (sadly, without the luxury of a tripod), knowing that someday I would want the images just for the backgrounds they might provide. Then one evening, with a few moments to spare, I created the even stranger world shown in Figure 2.16. On a more serious note, look for backgrounds that are more ordinary and take pictures just to be used as background images at a later time. After a few years of shooting such pictures, you'll find that your collection of backgrounds is quite valuable as you learn to combine them with images from other pictures.

Figure 2.15
The unusual world of stalactites and stalagmites.

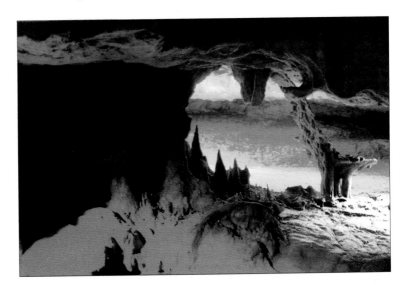

Figure 2.16
A strange world made even stranger with a few odd subjects added.

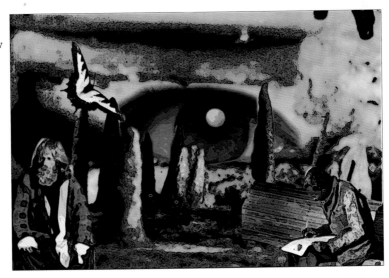

Shoot to create fantasy

Every now and then, shoot images that you know will just be fun to use. Figure 2.17 is a low-angle view of a few lily pads. I'm not sure what I'm going to do with this image yet—but I took the picture simply because I know that, someday, I'll have the inspiration to do something cool with it. When I took the picture, I could imagine a few cats lying in the sun on several of the lily pads. Since my object collection has many sports objects, I might even create a practice area for lacrosse or soccer players on each pad. The point is that you have to use your imagination and think differently to create unique and creative images.

Figure 2.17
Lily pad land waiting for...?

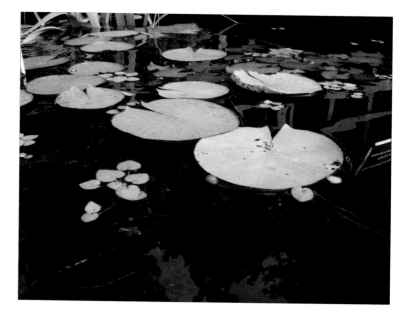

Shoot just for color

This might seem like an odd technique at first. Why would you want to shoot a picture just for the colors in the picture? It turns out that some digital editing applications enable you to create a color palette based solely upon the colors contained in an image. If you take a picture that has outstanding colors, such as the rich brown colors of a decaying log shown in the inset in Figure 2.18, you can then use it as a palette for another image such as the soccer player that has been transformed into a graphic for a T-shirt.

Figure 2.18
This image was colored by using colors from the inset image.

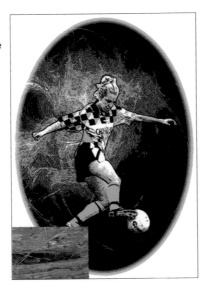

Shoot sequences of images

Once you see a series of photographs that has been taken in sequence for a digital slide show, you'll love this technique. By reducing the image size, you also can use the right kind of image series as animation on a Web site. A sequence you might want to try is to shoot a whole series of pictures of a person's face while they talk, laugh, and make faces. Played back as a slide show with an appropriate slide transition and speed, the series can be very lifelike—almost as if you were there.

If you want to shoot pictures of an old home that you have lived in for years, you could shoot a series of pictures as you walk up to the front door from the street. You could pause at the door, walk in, and take more pictures as you walk about the house. When you create the slide show, you could add sound files that add a doorbell sound, kids running around the house, or other sounds that make you feel like you are there.

Standing on the sidelines of a final state-wide, year-end soccer match a few years ago, I watched in complete suspense as the ultimate winner was to be decided on the last of ten penalty kicks. Methodically, I took a picture of each penalty kick and later created a slide show. Now, anyone watching that slide show can relive that winning event—one kick at a time! It is even more exciting for me, because my daughter was the keeper that made the stop! Yes, good pictures help you brag more convincingly!

Shooting sequences taken specifically for use with the appropriate digital presentation software can make a few ordinary shots become a fantastic show or album. You can view several sequences at **www.reallyusefulpage.com/dcs/02-01.htm.**

Shoot panoramas

One of the real limitations of traditional film photography (and of most cameras and lenses) is that it does not represent life as we see it. We have peripheral vision of nearly 180 degrees, which can make our surroundings incredibly beautiful. How many times have you just sat on the beach with your toes in the sand and looked out over the sea at the spectacular view? Maybe you've looked at a snow-capped mountain range in amazement at the beauty of the wide expanse of mountains along the horizon. To record those views, you shoot a few photographs that represent a very narrow slice of the world that you see with your eyes. When you get the photographs back showing only the partial scene, you wonder why you wasted the film. I have surely done that more times than I'd like to admit.

Now, you can capture those wonderful panoramas just by shooting a series of overlapping photographs and digitally "stitching" them together to create a panorama all the way up to a full 360 degrees! You can learn more about creating panoramas in Chapter 10, "Doing Extraordinary Things with Images." To see how they look, you can view several QuickTime Virtual Reality movies at **www.reallyusefulpage.com/dcs/02-02.htm.**

Shoot images for a photomontage

A *photomontage* is a composite picture made by combining more than one separate image. This technique can result in wonderful images—but it is a complex technique that requires one of the more advanced digital editing applications, such as Adobe's Photoshop, and sufficient memory and processing speed to manage multiple files. If you are willing to invest in a product such as Photoshop and want to create photomontages, consider buying a book written by Gregory Cosmo Haun titled *Photoshop Collage Techniques: Visual Guide to Creating Collages and Montages with Photoshop 4* (Hayden Books, ISBN: 1-56830-349-1). Gregory discusses in detail each of eight elements of composition that you need to learn to control to create a successful photomontage. These eight elements are size, shape, form, texture, space, value, color, and line. Figure 2.19 is a photomontage showing that a good soccer goalie can be in more than one place at the same time. A true "no-goal" goalie!

Figure 2.19
A photomontage
showing five images of
the same goalie catching
a ball.

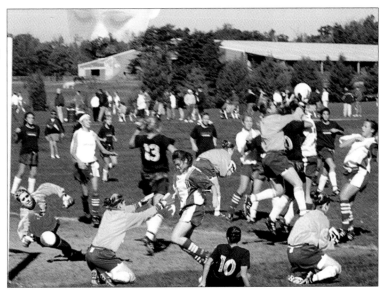

Shoot for specific filters

Most of the time, we do all that we can do simply to shoot pictures that are
in focus and as sharp as possible. However, a sharply focused image that
has edges is not necessarily a good image for a soft, no-edge watercolor
image that will be printed on fine-art watercolor paper. You can digitally
edit the image to blur it, but an image intentionally taken out of focus (see
Figure 2.20) can produce a very nice effect, as shown in Figure 2.21.

Figure 2.20
Soft focus image of
a cat.

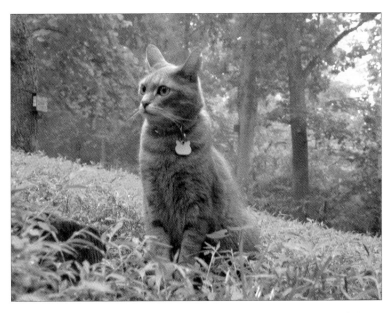

Figure 2.21
Watercolor filter applied to image shown in Figure 2.20.

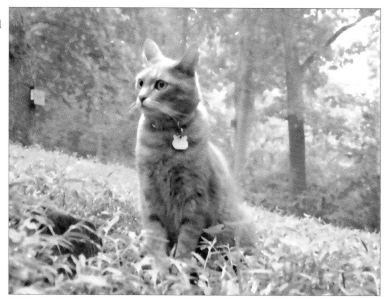

Shoot personality

Not too long ago, school children were required to have a stern look on their faces when they had their school pictures taken. Sadly, right about the time they were allowed to smile and look normal, portrait galleries popped up all over the country and began shooting "canned" portraits. Sure, they allowed their subjects to smile, but they all looked the same and showed no character. When you shoot pictures of people, shoot them in a natural environments and let their personalities and characters show through. When you look at the kid in Figure 2.22, there is no question that she has character! Capturing character will make you a favorite photographer to all of your subjects.

Figure 2.22
A cool kid with lots of
character.

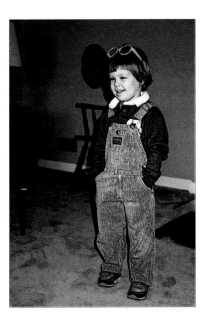

Shoot to create Web page images

Keep your eyes open for interesting things that can be used as images on
a Web page. Web pages need backgrounds, buttons, images, and textures.
It is surprisingly easy to take pictures that can be turned into fast-loading
artwork for Web pages—especially if you use a digital camera. Figure 2.23
shows a photograph taken of a real art gallery door in Charleston, South
Carolina. That same door was slightly modified and turned into the door
for the digital art gallery at **www.reallyusefulpage.com**, as shown in
Figure 2.24.

Figure 2.23
Real art gallery door in
Charleston, South
Carolina.

Figure 2.24
Digitally edited door
for online digital art
gallery.

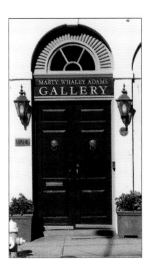

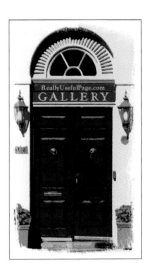

Shoot knowing that you can fix it

Often, a shot that you want to take might be obstructed by a telephone pole and lines, a billboard, or some other object that ruins the scene. Or maybe the picture is perfect, except that you are there at the wrong time of day and the lighting is bad. You cannot fix everything that is bad, but good digital editing software, knowledge of what can be done, and some skill can fix quite a lot. As an example, you can see how the image of downtown Chapel Hill shown in Figure 2.25 was fixed and turned into the fine-art image shown in Figure 2.26. You can learn how this "fixing up" was done in Chapter 5, "Getting Images into Shape."

Figure 2.25
This is not a very good picture—it needs lots of fixing up.

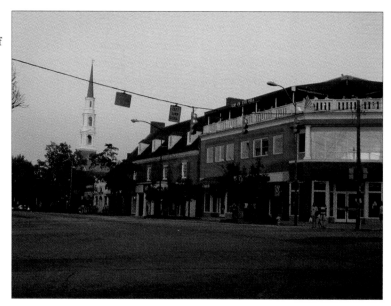

Figure 2.26
Figure 2.25 fixed up and turned into fine art.

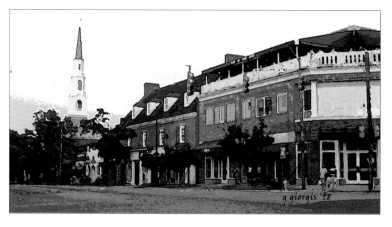

Shoot for varying length-to-width ratios

Have you found that the 8×10-inch ratio of width to height sometimes just doesn't suit a particular image? Once again, the magic of working with digital images and the fact that you have control over the printing process enables you to print the image as you choose. Figure 2.27 shows how a single 4×6-inch photograph taken with a normal lens can be cropped, enlarged, and enhanced to create a panoramic view. Likewise, you can create an equally tall and narrow image of a few white-barked birch trees basking in bright sunlight. Have it your way—you now have a choice.

Figure 2.27
An Iowa farm in full panoramic view.

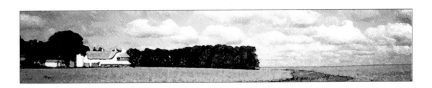

Shoot for intrigue, conflict, mystery, action, or...

What makes a novel or movie good? You're right. It is intrigue or conflict. The same concept can apply to your images if you want. Figure 2.28 shows an ordinary hole in the base of a tree trunk. When I first saw the black hole, I was intrigued as to what might be in it. As you look at it, what is looking at you? Can you tell? Besides adding intrigue, you can add conflict, mystery, action, or all kinds of other feelings by using a variety of digital imaging tools and techniques.

Figure 2.28
What is looking at you?

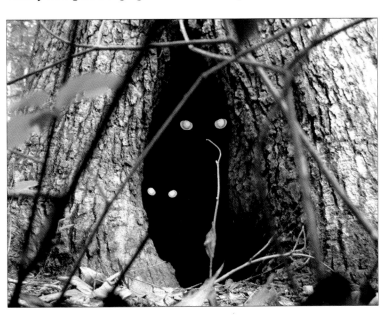

Shoot to maximize black for a dramatic effect

I have always liked high-contrast images. Yet getting good images with that classic black background can be hard. Figure 2.29 shows a cat face with a black background that helps to make this cat look unusually fierce.

Figure 2.29
Cat with dramatic look.

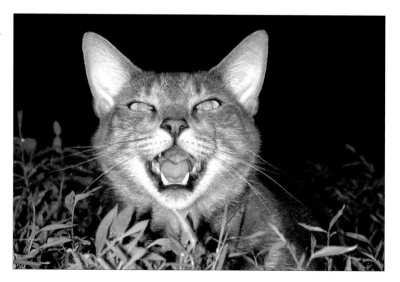

You are now familiar with a "starter set" of 15 digital imaging techniques. This set is by no means exhaustive. It is not unique to me or to you. It is just a starter set to help you begin to think differently about how you take pictures so that you can ultimately create wonderful digital images that you will be pleased with. Practice using these techniques and even create your own techniques, and you'll be destined to have success!

Ways to get better at taking pictures

We've now covered twenty-five techniques to help you take more creative and better pictures. Learning these techniques unquestionably will help you, but there are more "pieces to the puzzle" than just learning those techniques. Here are a few more things that will help you take better pictures.

Know thyself and thy equipment

Whether you shoot with a digital camera or a film-based camera, it will have user-controlled features that have been designed to help you take better pictures. Many of the more expensive and feature-rich cameras can offer well over 100 features. Read your camera manuals. Read them again. Then, periodically read them again, until you understand how you can use your camera to capture all of those moments and scenes that you want to capture. There simply is no substitute for knowing all about your equipment.

The Saunders Group in Rochester, New York, publishes an excellent series of books for most popular cameras called the Magic Lantern Guides. I have one for my Canon EOS A2E (ISBN 1-883403-00-6). I have learned much more about my camera with this book than I did with the camera's user manuals. I highly recommend that you find a Magic Lantern Guide or similar book for your camera—they are well worth the money.

Know your films (or know your digital camera settings)

One of the most important factors in getting the right image for your needs is the film. All film is not created equal and all film is not appropriate in all shooting conditions. Film speed, brand, and grade must be carefully selected. Likewise, when you shoot with a digital camera, you need to know what image resolution and file compression to choose. Some digital cameras enable you to make adjustments for lighting conditions, such as when it is sunny or cloudy or when you are shooting in a room with incandescent or fluorescent lighting. If you use the wrong setting, you might not be able to correct the image. Some digital cameras also have exposure compensation settings and other settings that can dramatically improve (or degrade if improperly used) your images. Learn about them and use them to your advantage.

Nothing is worse than thinking that you got the perfect shot of something and later finding that it was stored in a high-compression format and at a 640×480 resolution or that you used a grainy, low-quality roll of film. Know your films and your digital camera settings!

Visit art galleries and digital photography Web sites

If you are truly serious about developing an eye for art or photography, then you need to spend time looking at the works of great artists and photographers. The best place to do this is at art galleries or museums, where you can look at the originals in full living color. When you do visit such a place, look at each piece that you like and ask yourself: "Why do I like this piece? What makes it a good piece?" The more you do this, the more you'll develop your own personal view on creating fine-art works with your camera and your digital editing tools.

Shoot over and over until you get it right

Practice makes perfect. I'll bet you've heard that one before. The real advantage of a digital camera is that you can shoot repeatedly—with no additional cost. When a specific image is important to me, I usually take five, ten, or more images with different settings and light conditions just to get the perfect one. Unfortunately, with film-based cameras, we don't enjoy that luxury without the expense of film, processing, and printing.

Create for, and share with, others

The single most important thing that you can do to learn more about how to take great pictures is to enjoy taking them. If you develop a passion for taking the pictures and digitally editing them, your work will improve rapidly. You can take that idea one step further by creating and sharing your images with others. The more others enjoy your images, the more you're likely to enjoy creating them. If you have a neighbor who is greatly attached to a dog or a cat, try creating a frameable, fine-art-like image of their pet. Create a photomontage of the members of a youth orchestra for the conductor. Send a continuous supply of digital images to friends or family members of those things that interest them. Document the work done on a new project for the benefit of the team members. Doing these kinds of things will create joy for everyone, including you—and that is what life is all about.

The next chapter, "Turning Photographs into Digital Images," is for those of you who shoot with a film-based camera.

3

Turning Photographs into Digital Images

After you turn your photographs into digital images, you can do many things with them. In fact, the remaining eleven chapters of this book are devoted to showing you what you can do with your digital images. The purpose of this chapter is to help you turn your photographs into digital form so that you can use them as you read the rest of the book. The good news is that the options available for turning your pictures into digital images are more numerous and cost less than ever before. In this chapter, we'll look at the following five approaches:

▶ Using a flatbed or film scanner to create digital images

▶ Using the digitization services of a local one-hour photo lab

▶ Visiting a local photo-processing retailer and using a photo kiosk to scan your photos or negatives

▶ Using the digitization services of a mail-order photofinisher

▶ Using the services of a custom photo lab to get the files that you want

The basics of digital image files

This is supposed to be a fun book that provides you with an understanding of what you can do with digital images—not a deep technical "bits and bytes" kind of book. However, you need to know certain digital image file fundamentals. Therefore, we'll cover these fundamentals here and now. If you already know about color depth, image resolution, file compression, and other related terms and concepts, skip this section if you'd like. If you do not know these concepts, you ought to read this section—it covers most of what is considered to be fundamental and essential content for even beginning digital image users. After you understand the content of this section, you'll have more success purchasing appropriate products and services, end up with better images, and be able to make your images more accessible to others. If you are not technically oriented, not to worry—we're just going to cover seven terms and concepts.

Image and print quality are based upon a number of interrelated factors, including, but not limited to, image size, resolution, color depth, file type, and level of file compression. Some of the more important terms that will help you understand these factors are defined next.

Pixels

A *pixel* is the smallest unit used to make an image on a computer screen. Most PC monitors display between 72 and 120 ppi (pixels per inch)—usually 72 or 96 ppi. The actual display resolution is dependent upon the video card, the monitor resolution, and the software settings that have been selected. The higher the ppi setting that you use, the larger the image that you can see on your monitor and the smaller that image will be.

Surprisingly, many PC users are not aware of the fact that they can change the display resolution of their monitors. If you are going to be working with digital images, you should learn how to change settings when needed. Sometimes you will want to use a higher resolution so that you can see all of, or at least more of, an image. For example, if you have an 800×600-pixel image, such as the one of the chameleon shown in Figure 3.1, you cannot see the bottom one-third of the image when your display resolution is set at 800×600 pixels. When you resize your desktop to 1024×768, you can see the entire image, although the image (and text) will be smaller, as shown in Figure 3.2.

Figure 3.1

An 800×600-pixel image displayed in a browser maximized on an 800×600 desktop.

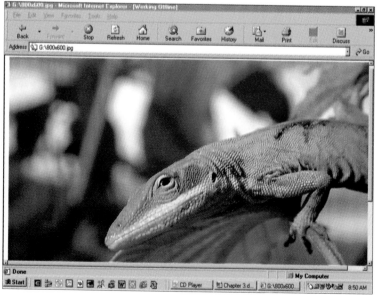

Figure 3.2
An 800×600-pixel image
displayed in a browser
maximized on a
1024×768 desktop.

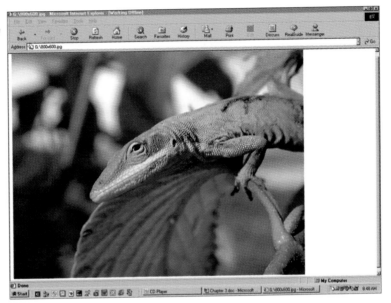

To change the resolution setting, click the Start button and select Settings>
Control Panel. Click the Display icon and then the Settings tab, and you
will see the Display Properties dialog box, as shown in Figure 3.3. To set
the screen resolution, simply click and move the Screen area slider. To the
left of the Screen area slider is another important setting control—Colors,
which is the color depth setting. You might notice that when you select a
higher resolution, the color depth is automatically reduced. If this
happens, your video card might not have enough memory for some of the
higher resolutions and color depth settings.

Figure 3.3
Using Windows Display
Properties dialog box to
change display
resolution.

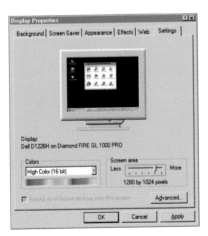

When surfing the Internet, especially on image-intensive pages, you might have noticed the notes that recommend the page be viewed with a 16K or 24-bit color setting—the Display Properties dialog box is where you go to change that setting. Setting your monitor to the appropriate setting enables you to view images optimally, and it minimizes having to scroll up and down or left and right to view an entire image.

Dots per inch (dpi)

Dots per inch is a simple term that tends to be confused with image size. Dots per inch is an important characteristic of both output and input devices. If you have a photo-quality inkjet printer, you might know that it prints at 300 dpi or even higher. This means that for each square inch of print, 300 times 300-or 90,000-dots are in each square inch. Why do we care? We care because, up to a certain point, more dots per inch will make a better-looking image. Gradations will be smoother, with no banding, and they will look more like a continuous tone image than one composed of fewer dots. Generally, a 600 dpi print looks more realistic than a 300 dpi print.

Image color depth or number of color bits

Image color depth, or number of color bits, refers to the number of *bits* (a technical term meaning a single digit) used to describe the smallest unit in a display (a *pixel*), a printer (a *dot*), or a scanner (a *sensor*). The more bits you have to describe each unit (pixel, dot, or sensor), the more colors you will be able to display. Obviously, being able to display more colors will improve the quality of the image. The total number of available bits needs to be divided among the red, green, and blue color channels. So, for example, a 24-bit image is represented by 8 bits of red, 8 bits of green, and 8 bits of blue (8 + 8 + 8). Likewise, 30-bit images have 10 + 10 + 10 bits, and 36-bit images have 12 + 12 + 12 bits.

The complicating factor is that nearly all imaging software works with up to 24-bit images only. You might wonder, therefore, why it is important to have a scanner that can scan more than 24 bits of information. Scanner vendors claim that this technique, called *over-sampling*, enables scanners to provide more details in the shadows than you would get with a lower-bit scan. If you are interested in an especially high-quality scan, look for a 30- or 36-bit scanner. Many of the scanners in the $100 to $200 price range now offer 36-bit scanning capabilities.

Image size

Image size is usually expressed in terms of inches or pixels. Generally, when we speak of images that are to be output on paper, we use inches. When we speak of digital image sizes, we refer to their sizes in terms of pixels. For example, the Web page shown in Figure 3.1 displays an 800×600-pixel image that takes up the entire screen when the monitor is set at 800×600 pixels. If we printed this same large 800×600-pixel image on a 300 dpi printer, we would get a print that would be only 2.7×2 inches (800 pixels/300 dpi printer resolution equals 2.7 inches, and 600 pixels/300 dpi printer resolution equals 2 inches).

An important point concerning image size is that every time the resolution is doubled, the resulting file size of the image quadruples. A 4×6-inch photograph scanned at 300 dpi results in a 6.48MB file. The same photograph scanned at 600 dpi will consume four times that amount, or 25.92MB. To compute image file size, simply multiply the image width in pixels by the height in pixels and then multiply by a factor of three—one for each of the three color channels (red, green, and blue). In case you are wondering, an 8×10-inch photograph printed at 300 dpi consumes 21.6MB, and the same image at 600 dpi requires 86.4MB! This important mathematical relationship will affect just about everything you do with digital images, including storing, transporting, editing, printing, and scanning.

Relationship between scanning resolution and output resolution

Ideally, the scanning resolution should be equal to the output resolution. When you scan at a lower resolution than you output to a printer, the software must interpolate between points (that is, the software is forced to guess and fill in), which degrades image quality. As long as your scan is equal to or greater than the output resolution, you will have enough image information to get a good print. In those cases in which you have an image that has been scanned at a higher resolution than you will be printing, simply use a digital image editor and scale down the resolution to match that of the printer. Sometimes, too much information can also produce a sub-optimal image.

Density range

Density range is used to describe the capability of a scanner to differentiate brightness (tonality), or density, and is expressed on a scale of 0 to 4. Let's reduce all of that jargon to something meaningful—the closer the density range is to 4, the more detail that will be shown in shadow areas in your scans. For example, when scanning an image with very subtle clouds in a sky, a scanner with a lower density range simply won't be able to pick up all of the cloud detail. When comparing two scanners—with all other features and specifications being equal—if one scanner has a density range of 3.4 and the other has a density range of 3.6, choose the one with the 3.6 rating. By the way, many lower-priced scanners will not have density ratings, and there is probably a good reason for this: They have low ratings.

Image compression

Image compression is used to reduce image file size so that the image file will consume less space and can be transported (e-mailed or downloaded from the Internet) more quickly. Brilliant mathematicians using complex mathematics and creative techniques create all kinds of compression algorithms that generally provide a tradeoff between image file size and image quality. The most common compression technique is JPEG, because it is the most widely used method of compression on the Internet. Other common compression formats include TIFF, GIF, PNG, Photo CD, FlashPix, PIC, and EPS. TIFF and JPEG are platform-independent and can be viewed on Macintosh and Windows machines; in addition, all imaging applications recognize these two formats.

The two kinds of compression formats are lossy and lossless. *Lossy* compression loses image quality, and *lossless* compression reduces the file size as much as possible without degrading the quality of the image. The TIFF file format is a good example of a lossless format. However, TIFF files are often not much smaller than an uncompressed file, unless parts of an image are nearly identical.

Figures 3.4 and 3.5 show the same image with and without JPEG compression. The 800×1066-pixel image shown in Figure 3.4 is a compressed JPEG format file and is a mere 50K—or about 2 percent of the 2.5MB uncompressed BMP file shown in Figure 3.5. The compressed image in Figure 3.4 shows how using compression can degrade image quality.

Figure 3.4
A 50K image saved as a
compressed JPEG file.

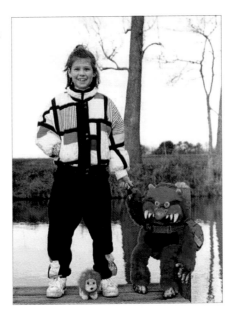

Figure 3.5
A 2.5MB image saved
as an uncompressed
BMP file.

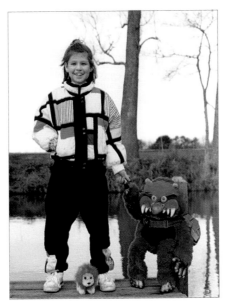

You now should have a good understanding of how color depth (number of digits to describe each display unit), image size (width and height of image), scanner density range, dpi (number of dots per inch), and image compression all contribute to or degrade the overall quality of an image. The moral of the story—bigger files contain more image information, and they look better both in printed form and on a computer screen. The downside—they also consume more space and are more difficult and time-consuming to transport.

Just to make sure that you understand the material just covered, try answering the questions in the next section. You will be faced with problems like this one often when you start turning your photographs into digital images and printing them.

Pop quiz: Can you answer the questions correctly?

Assume that you want to create a greeting card featuring a favorite photograph. The embossed greeting card paper that you plan to use has space for a 4×7-inch image. The photograph that you want to use has been developed and printed as a jumbo 5×7-inch print. Your scanner can scan up to 1200 dpi, and your color inkjet printer prints at 300 dpi. See whether you can fill in the following blanks.

1. Existing photograph size in inches: _____

2. Image should be cropped to what size in inches: _____

3. Optimal dpi setting for scanner: _____

4. "Best quality" image file format: _____

5. Required image size in pixels: _____

6. Bonus question: Finished image file size (assume 24-bit color depth in BMP file format): _____

The previous example shows why you need a good understanding of the basics of digital image files. Without this knowledge, you will not be able to set your scanner correctly, order the most appropriate digitization services, or print quality prints. You will be faced with many choices, and to get the correct answer, you need to know the basics; otherwise, your work will not be as good as it can be. Incidentally, the correct answers to the questions are as follows:

1. 5×7

2. 4×7

3. 300 dpi, to match the printer's capability to print at 300 dpi

4. An uncompressed format, such as TIFF or BMP, or a high-quality JPEG

5. 1200 (4×300 dpi) × 2100 (7×300 dpi) pixels

6. Bonus: 7.56MB (1200 pixels × 2100 pixels × 3 bytes per pixel)

Congratulations if you answered all of the questions correctly!

Using a scanner to get digital images

In many ways, a scanner is similar to a camera, but instead of taking pictures by using natural light to expose film, the scanner's light bar exposes the image to diodes. The *diodes* sense the image and convert it to digital information that is saved to a digital file that can be read by a PC. Similar to the settings that you have on your camera to control how your photographs will turn out, scanners offer controls that you can use to help you get the images that you want.

There are more reasons than ever to have a scanner of your own:

▶ Scanners are getting less expensive, almost on a monthly basis

▶ Each new generation of scanner can scan faster and produce a better scan

▶ The number of ways to use digital images is increasing rapidly

▶ Having your own scanner makes getting digital images easy and convenient when you need them

If you don't own a scanner, this section will help you decide whether you should get one, how to select it, where to buy it, and what you can do with it once you get it.

Should you buy a scanner?

Deciding whether or not to buy a scanner is easy. Owning your own scanner can be very convenient. When you need a digital file made from a photograph, simply scan the photo, and you have a digital image. You don't need to take film or prints to a photo lab to have the work done. You also have control over the quality of the scan and the size and resolution of each scan.

If convenience alone does not compel you to buy a scanner, consider the costs of paying for the use of a scanning service. How many images will you need to scan in a year? Most scanning services are most cost-effective when you have scans made at the same time that you have your film developed and prints made. The cost to scan a roll of film ranges from $8 to $25, depending on the service that you use and the resolution that you require. Assuming a cost of $12 per roll for scanning, having twelve rolls of film scanned costs about the same as a $150 scanner.

Another good reason to buy a scanner is to scan things other than photographs. Most new scanners take up much less desk space than the older scanners. They connect more easily, and with the benefits of a universal serial bus (USB) connection and plug-and-play, they are easy to install and use. If you need scanned images, you really ought to consider buying a scanner.

Six easy steps for buying the right scanner for your needs

Now comes the fun part. You've decided that you want a scanner, and you have to decide on a specific manufacturer and model. The following are six steps to take to get the right scanner for your needs.

Step one: Decide how much you want to spend

Like color printers, digital cameras, and other electronics, scanners vary dramatically in terms of features, capabilities, and price. Your challenge: Find one that suits your needs and fits your budget. Although some scanners cost well over $2,500 (all the way up to about $40,000 or more), many home scanners are available at just about any price point in between $80 and $2,500.

For the majority of people wanting to use a scanner, some of the newer scanners in the $150 to $500 price range are sufficient. They produce good scans, and they definitely create more than adequate images for use on the Internet. Microtek is one of the many scanner manufacturers that makes a wide range of scanners. Figure 3.6 shows the Microtek ScanMaker V6UPL, which costs around $100. The Microtek ScanMaker 4 scanner, shown in Figure 3.7, costs around $500 and enables you to scan both prints and film. If you want a professional-quality scanner, you'll need to spend $800 or more for a flatbed scanner and $1,700 or more for a film scanner.

Figure 3.6
Microtek ScanMaker V6UPL features 600×1200 optical resolution and 36-bit color depth, plus a 35mm slide adapter.

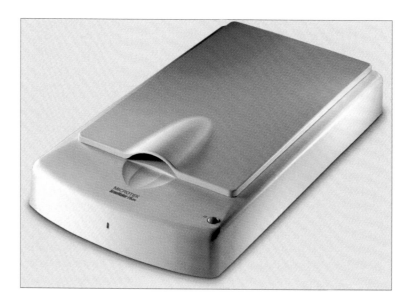

Figure 3.7
Microtek ScanMaker 4 dual-media scanner scans photos and prints on the upper bed and scans film and transparencies in the lower bed.

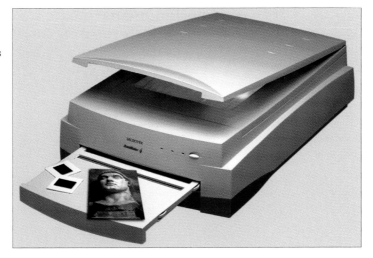

Step two: Determine which type of scanner you want

What do you intend to scan? Besides being able to scan photographs, you can scan other flat "things," such as book pages, artwork, newspaper or magazine clippings, and more. Some scanners even make good images from things such as leaves, pressed flowers, jewelry, or other small 3D objects. If you shoot slide film, you might want to be able to scan slides or even negatives. After you decide exactly what you want to scan, you can decide which kind of scanner to buy.

The following are three kinds of scanners:

▶ **Flatbed scanners**—Scan flat, printed materials such as photographs and printed pages

▶ **Film scanners**—Scan film (photographic negatives), slides, and transparencies

▶ **Combination scanners**—Scan film and slides as well as flat, printed materials

If you need to scan film, make sure you get a scanner that enables you to scan film in the format that you need to have scanned. Some film scanners scan just 35mm film or slides, whereas others also scan APS film or wide format, such as 120 or 220 film. If you've spent years shooting slide film, as many photographers have, you will most likely want to get a scanner that can scan slides or one that at least has an optional slide adapter that you can purchase.

Until recently, combination scanners did not do a very good job with slides or film. Now, several scanners on the market produce reasonably good film and slide scans in addition to high-quality scans from the flatbed part of the scanner. One particularly good example of a high-end combination scanner is the Microtek ScanMaker 5, shown in Figure 3.8, which costs around $1,800.

Figure 3.8
Microtek's ScanMaker 5 offers an 8.5×14-inch scanning area plus a pullout transparent media adapter for slides and film.

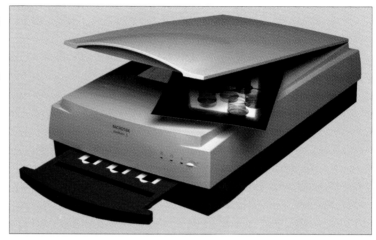

If you want the best scans from film or slides, you need to get a film scanner, such as the Nikon CoolScan III, shown in Figure 3.9. The CoolScan III offers 30-bit color depth and 2700 optical resolution and can scan 35mm film or slides (or APS film, with an optional adapter). It costs around $800.

Figure 3.9
Nikon CoolScan III.

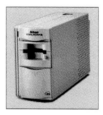

Two other excellent scanners to consider are the Nikon Super CoolScan 2000, which costs around $1,700, and the new Polaroid SprintScan 4000, which is a 36-bit film scanner that has 4000 dpi optical resolution and costs around $1,800.

Step three: Consider features that impact image quality

Although many factors affect the quality of a scanned image, three of the most important factors are optical resolution, color depth, and density range.

Optical resolution

Optical resolution not only determines the overall sharpness of an image but also is the major determinant of how large an image can be. Optical resolution varies from 300 dpi up to more than 4000 dpi for some of the high-end film scanners. Consider scanners with at least 600 dpi or higher. Also, make sure that you are looking at the optical resolution rating and not the interpolated dpi rating, which is achieved with software.

Earlier in this chapter, we looked at how dpi and image size are related. For example, if you plan to make digital images that can be printed as 14×20-inch prints, then you need to make sure that you buy a scanner that has an optical resolution that enables you to create an appropriately large digital image file. Assuming that you scan a 4×6-inch photograph and will use a 300 dpi printer, you need a scanner that can scan at 1000 dpi or greater.

Color depth

Color depth was covered earlier in this chapter. A 24-bit scanner might be adequate for your needs—a 30-bit scanner is better, and a 36-bit scanner is even better. Although color depth is an important determinant of image quality, often the more important factor is the quality of the scanner— some expensive 24-bit scanners produce a better-quality scan than an inexpensive 36-bit scanner. As usual, you get what you pay for.

Density range

You might recall that the density range is a measurement of the breadth of the tonal range that a scanner can capture. This is the single-most important value for film scanners and professional scanners. Most consumer-level scanners do not offer density-rating values. If you want image quality, look for a density range above 3.2; preferably, find a scanner within your budget that has a density rating of 3.4 or even 3.6 or higher.

Step four: Other things to consider

Depending on what you intend to scan and how you intend to use your scanner, you might want to consider these other factors:

Scan speed or time

Scan speed is the amount of time that it takes to scan a single page at a specific resolution. If you plan to scan many images or large images, scan speed might be very important to you. Scan speeds depend greatly on the interface and sometimes on the software.

Interface

The choice of interface (the connection between your scanner and your PC) is an important issue to consider. Generally, a SCSI interface is the fastest, followed by USB, and then parallel interfaces, although this is not always true. If you intend to use your scanner with several PCs, and each PC has a USB connection, USB might be your best choice. Although SCSI interfaces are fast, they also can be difficult to install.

Scanner software

Scanner software varies greatly between different manufacturers. If scan speed or image quality is especially important to you, it will be worthwhile for you to look closely at the scanner's software. Some software enables you to scan an image with a single button click, whereas other packages force you to look at an image preview after the image has been scanned and then wait again while the final scan is made. Likewise, some scanners offer software that gives you lots of control over your scan to optimize the resulting image, whereas others offer little control. In the latter case, you have to manually adjust your images with image editing software.

Bundled applications

More often than not, scanners come with a bundle of software applications. Sometimes, these applications are demonstration versions or are one version older than the most current version. In other cases, you get terrific software that makes the bundle a "good deal." Some of the more common bundled applications include optical character recognition (OCR) software, document management applications, and various painting or digital image editing applications.

Special features

Many scanners offer special features that might be very valuable to you. For example, many Nikon scanners enable batch scans and come with proprietary software called Digital ICE (Image Correction and Enhancement,) which automatically removes dust and scratches. Some scanners come with automatic document feeders or transparency adapters, whereas other scanners do not offer such features or offer them only as add-on components that must be purchased separately.

Step five: Selecting a brand and model

After you decide what you want to scan and decide on the type of scanner and features that you need, you must then select a specific brand and model. As explained in Chapter 1, "Introducing Digital Cameras," even attempting to provide detailed and specific information on electronic products such as scanners isn't worthwhile, because these products change much more quickly than a book can be written and printed. However, there are many excellent online resources with all the up-to-date information and pricing that you can possibly need.

I strongly recommend that you first visit ZDNet at **www.zdnet.com/computershopper/**. It is the most useful site on the Internet for learning about scanners or for finding an online store from which to purchase one. Not only can you search for scanners by manufacturer, merchant, computer type, interface, and price, you can also read product reviews and articles on how to buy scanners. It is a "must-visit" site for anyone considering a scanner purchase. You might want to make a quick visit to Amazon.com, as well, because it has a useful *Buying Guide* for purchasing a scanner.

After you visit the ZDNet site and have a few ideas about which scanners might be right for you, you should visit the Web sites of each of those scanners' manufacturers to learn more about their products.

Step six: Buying a scanner

After you know what kind of scanner you want, you have many buying choices. If you want to buy from a local store, try one of the national retail chains, such as CompUSA, Office Depot, Best Buy, or Office Max. If you want to bid for one at an online auction, try **www.ebay.com**, **www.egghead.com**, or even **www.amazon.com**.

If you decide to buy online, I again recommend using **www.zdnet.com/computershopper/**, because it enables you to compare the prices for a specific product at many online merchants. It makes your online shopping about as easy as it can be. If you are interested in a high-end scanner, you might want to visit **www.publishingperfection.com**.

Using Kodak digitization services

Kodak products and services enjoy widespread use in the traditional film market. Kodak has positioned itself nearly as well in the new world of digital photography. It offers a wide range of products and services to help you share your images digitally. Many of these offerings are available from more than 40,000 retailers plus a rapidly growing number of Internet-based companies.

Besides its PhotoNet Online service, Kodak provides equipment and supplies to a variety of companies that enable those companies to offer four different disk-based services—Kodak Picture Disk, Kodak Picture CD, Kodak Photo CD, and Kodak Pro Photo CD. Further details on each of these offerings are provided next.

Kodak PhotoNet Online services

If, for one reason or another, you are not interested in getting your images back on a CD or floppy disk and you'd prefer to receive the digital files made from your photographs online, try the Kodak PhotoNet Online service. You simply drop off your unprocessed 35mm or APS film to any of the 40,000 retailers or mail-order photofinishers in the U.S. and ask for PhotoNet Online service.

When your film is processed, the photo lab will scan your images and upload them to the Internet, where you can access them. Your images are saved in high-resolution (1024×1536 pixels), medium-resolution (768×512 pixels), and minimum-resolution (384×256 pixels) formats. You can download both medium- and minimum-resolution format files free of charge. There is a $1 charge for each high-resolution image that you download, with a minimum charge of $3 for all online orders.

Kodak Picture Disk

The Kodak Picture Disk service is the entry-level digitization service. Digital images are created and written to a 3 1/2-inch floppy disk, which can store up to twenty-eight images. Acceptable film formats include 35mm and APS. APS processing can take up to a week, whereas Picture Disks for 35mm film can be done in one hour or up to two to three days, depending on where you get your film processed.

The image files are delivered in JPEG format at a 400×600-pixel resolution. This makes the images good for using on Web pages or for displaying on a computer monitor. Because of the small file size, you will not be able to print prints that are particularly good unless they are very small.

NOTE

A novice to digital photography who did not have a PC, a scanner, or any digital image editing software wanted to try using digital images. After shooting a roll of film at a company party, he dropped it off at his regular local photo lab for processing. He requested prints as well as a Kodak Picture Disk. Using the 400×600-pixel JPEG images that came on the floppy disk, he uploaded them directly from his PC at work to an Internet-based, photo-sharing site so that he could share the photos with his coworkers. After receiving many positive comments about his images, he made plans to buy a PC and a scanner for home use.

Kodak Picture CD

Picture CD is the consumer-level offering for 35mm and APS film. It takes about three days for processing, and the files are returned on a CD. When you get your prints and negatives back, you also get an index print, along with a CD that contains digital versions of each of your pictures. All of the images are 1024×1536 pixels and are compressed in the JPEG file format. A file-conversion program and viewing software are included on each disk. Each CD contains images from only a single roll of film.

A roll of 36 pictures will take about 13.5MB, with each file ranging in size from 275K to 550K for a 1536×1024-pixel image when stored in the JPEG file format. Using a 300 dpi printer, the optimal print size is 3.4×5.1 inches. Many of the advanced printers that are used by photo-processing labs print an exceptionally good print using only 200 dpi. This enables them to print near-photographic quality prints for up to a 5×7-inch print.

If you don't have a scanner and want digital images, using Kodak Picture CD services is an excellent way to get good scans done inexpensively. Most services offering the Kodak Picture CD require you to have prints printed when you order a Picture CD.

NOTE

A schoolteacher wanted to get digital images made of her students' science projects. After taking pictures of each science project with a film camera, she dropped off the film at a local photo lab and ordered a Kodak Picture CD. She was then able to use the digital images for school reports, for her annual class report, and for the students. She saved the Picture CD so that she could show the projects to students in her classes in subsequent years.

Kodak Photo CD

The Photo CD is the professional version of the Picture CD. Pictures are stored by using a special proprietary image file format developed by Kodak that stores data at five different levels of resolution. This format enables you to get images from a single PCD (.pcd extension) file at resolutions of 2048×3072, 1024×1536, 512×768, 256×384, and 128×192. When you open a PCD file with an application that accepts PCD file formats, you will see a dialog box like the one shown in Figure 3.10, which enables you to choose the resolution that you need.

Figure 3.10
Selecting an image
resolution when
opening a PCD digital
image file.

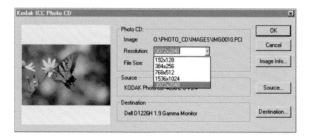

Kodak Photo CDs can take up to a week or more for processing.
Acceptable film formats include 35mm and APS, as well as slide film.
Using Photo CDs is a very handy way to store and manage your digital
images. Each Photo CD is placed in a standard CD music case with a
cover that displays small thumbnail images of each image on the CD, as
shown in Figure 3.11.

Figure 3.11
Kodak Photo CD master
disc and case.

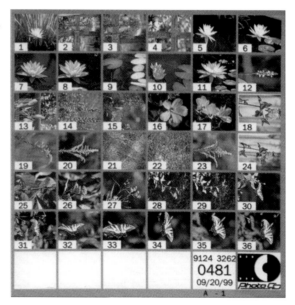

A roll of 36 pictures in the Kodak PCD format requires 145MB, and the
file size typically varies between 3.5MB and 5MB. Seven rolls of 36-
exposure film stored in the PCD format consumes about 1GB of storage
space. Although this seems like a lot, it would take even more space if
the files were stored in almost any reasonably uncompressed format.

It is also possible to have your already-developed negatives or slides transferred to a Photo CD. There are some variations in service, depending on the service provider. Not all will do Photo CDs from already-developed film. Prices can vary between $.50 per picture to $4 per picture. You will need software that supports images on a Kodak Photo CD, such as Paint Shop Pro, Adobe PhotoDeluxe, Microsoft Picture It!, Photoshop, ThumbsPlus, or one of the many other applications that support the PCD file format.

Kodak Pro Photo CD

The Pro Photo CD is very similar to the Photo CD except that it adds an optional sixth level of resolution—an enormous 4096×6144-pixel image! Acceptable film formats include 120/220 film, 4×5-inch film, as well as 35mm. Depending on the film format and the images, the CDs can hold up to one hundred images. The Pro Photo CD is also a rewritable CD, so you can continue to add images to the CD until it is full.

With four choices of Kodak digitization services, which one is best for you? Table 3.1 will help you answer that question. After you decide how you are going to use your images, you can select the right service.

Table 3.1
Kodak Digital Image CD
Image Sizes

Print Size at Image Size		Print Size at 200 dpi in Inches		300 dpi in Inches		
Pixel Height	Pixel Width	File Size	Height	Width	Height	Width
128	192	72K	0.6	0.96	0.4	0.64
256	384	288K	1.3	1.92	0.8	1.28
512	768	1.1MB	2.6	3.84	1.7	2.56
1024	1536	4.5MB	5.1	7.68	3.4	5.12
2048	3072	18MB	10.2	15.36	6.8	10.24
4096*	6144	75MB	20.48	30.72	13.65333	20.48
Available only on Kodak Pro Photo CD						

Getting digital images from a local photo lab

In the prior section, you learned about five Kodak services that you can use to turn your photographs into digital images. These Kodak services, and other services similar to them, are available at most camera stores and at thousands of mass merchants, such as drug stores, supermarkets, and discount stores. Using these services is easy. Just drop off your film, fill out the film-processing envelope as shown in Figure 3.12, and place a check in the appropriate box to order the digital images that you want.

Figure 3.12
Film-processing envelope used for ordering Kodak services.

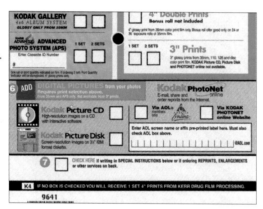

If you intend to use these services frequently, you might want to check prices and offerings from several different companies, because the scan quality, price, turnaround time, and service can differ substantially. Chapter 13, "Turning Digital Images into Prints," offers more information on many of the companies that offer these services. You can also learn more about them by visiting any of these sites:

▶ **www.kodak.com**
▶ **www.ritzcamera.com**
▶ **www.wolfcamera.com**

Using a photo kiosk to get digital images

If you don't have your own scanner and you need to make just one or a few scans from existing prints or negatives (as opposed to a fully undeveloped roll of film), then one of the photo kiosks might be the perfect and cost-effective way to get what you need. *Kiosks* are self-serve photo labs that you can operate. You will typically find these kiosks in camera stores. (Figure 1.14 in Chapter 1 shows a Kodak Picture Maker kiosk.) Another excellent photo kiosk is the Fuji Pictrography kiosk, shown in Figure 3.13. Many of Ritz Camera's retail stores have Fuji Pictrography kiosks.

Figure 3.13
Fuji's Pictrography photo kiosk enables you to scan, print, and upload images to the Internet.

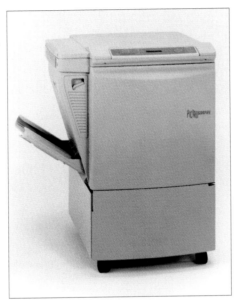

Although the plan is to have all of the photo kiosks be capable of scanning an image and writing it to a variety of media, including CDs, floppies, and, in some cases, Zip drives, not all of them currently have such capabilities.

In the long term, kiosks will become a key part of digital photo networks that tie many retail stores into photo labs and the Internet. When you get an image scanned, you will have the option of writing it to removable storage media, printing it, or uploading it to the Internet. Images uploaded to the Internet can be shared, and online prints and photo gifts can be ordered. Eventually, anyone who has the correct access code can view your images and print copies at any of the kiosks that are networked.

To find a Kodak Picture Maker near you, visit **www.kodak.com**, click the Service & Support button, and then select "Where to find Kodak products and services." Then, select Picture Maker and fill in your city, state, or ZIP code to get a list of Picture Makers near you. Fifteen thousand Picture Makers are installed worldwide, so you are likely to find one not too far away.

Using mail-order photofinishers

Besides using the services of local photo labs, you can use the services offered by mail-order photofinishers. You can request mail-in envelopes for your film from a mail-order lab by visiting any of the following sites:

- ▶ **www.agfanet.com**
- ▶ **www.clubphoto.com**
- ▶ **www.filmworks.com**
- ▶ **www.ezprints.com**
- ▶ **www.mysticcolorlab.com**
- ▶ **www.wolfcamera.com**
- ▶ **www.yorkphoto.com**

Using a mail-order service can save you the aggravation of dropping off and picking up your film at a local photo lab. Simply put your film in a pre-addressed, stamped envelope and put it in your mailbox.

NOTE

When traveling in Europe for two months, a retired couple used mail-in envelopes to have their film processed, scanned, and uploaded to the Internet. Doing this eliminated the possibility that they would lose their film while traveling, plus they could view the images online while they traveled. Their children and grandchildren also were able to view the places that they visited while they were away.

Getting scans from custom photo labs

Occasionally, you might need a particularly good or large scan. In this case, you should look for a local custom photo lab where you can visit in person and discuss your requirements. Custom photo labs are used to meeting the higher expectations of professionals and generally have high-end scanners and software that enable them to create superior image files.

NOTE

An aspiring artist wanted to turn a picture she had taken on slide film into an 11×14-inch print. Using a high-end scanner, a custom photo lab scanned the slide at 3600 dpi, resulting in a 45MB image. The 3226×4849-pixel image was perfect for making an 11×14-inch print on her 300 dpi color inkjet printer. After some digital image editing, she produced an image that she was proud to display on her wall.

At this point, you should have a good idea about how you can turn your photographs into digital images. Before your image collection grows too large, you ought to learn how to manage and store your digital images—which is the topic of the next chapter.

4

Managing and Storing Images

How do you store your photographs? Are they in shoe boxes or plastic containers stuffed in the bottom of a closet or pushed under a bed? Are they in unorganized drawers? Do you catalog them in any meaningful way, or does the order change each time you go through them? If you want a few specific photographs and their negatives, can you find them?

Recognizing the wide range of user requirements for storing digital images, this chapter:

▶ Provides tips for storing and managing image file collections of any size

▶ Shows how Windows Explorer can be used as an image management tool

▶ Presents a few simple, powerful, and inexpensive utilities that make it easier to manage digital images

▶ Provides overviews of several powerful consumer-level digital image editing and project applications with image management capabilities

▶ Shows the capabilities of advanced image management tools

What do you want to be able to do with your images? Will you need to access every one of them by multiple keywords, such as subject and date? Do you want to be able to print contact sheets or upload HTML-based image catalog pages to the Internet? Do you need to catalog images on lots of removable media? Is it important to you to be able to group images together for various projects and share them with other team members? Or do you simply need to find a few images every now and then and are happy to browse a few CD-ROMs to find them?

After completing this chapter, you'll be able to select the appropriate tools to do what you want to do, effectively and efficiently.

Odds are good that you take pictures and then store them without taking time to add a date or subject title to the envelopes or to file them in any organized way. This lack of organization makes it difficult and time-consuming to use and share pictures. Are digital images any easier to store and manage than traditional pictures? I wish that I could answer this question with a definitive "Yes," but I wouldn't be telling the truth. With a digital image collection, there is both good news and bad news about the storage issue.

The good news is that if you set up a system for handling your digital images and you religiously follow this system, several software products are available that can make it extremely easy for you to store and manage all of your images. Figure 4.1 shows how images can be organized into folders, cataloged, viewed with thumbnails, and found by searching with keywords.

Figure 4.1
Using ThumbsPlus 4.0 to manage and organize digital image files.

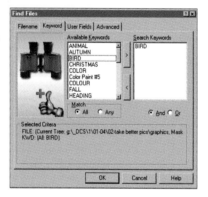

The bad news is that having an unorganized digital image collection is just as easy as having an unorganized traditional picture collection. It might even be easier, because digital image collections can grow very fast—it doesn't cost much to take the pictures, so you might have far more pictures than you imagine!

Ultimately, you'll have to take time to organize your images and transfer them to removable storage media, because you will run out of hard disk space.

In this chapter, you will look at software that makes it a pleasure to work with your digital image collection. With a good filing system and the right software tools, you'll be able to store, organize, and manage your digital images so that you can find the images that you need when you need them. In the end, you'll get more enjoyment and value from your digital image collection.

How much storage will you need?

By now, you probably are thinking that you are going to have to buy several new hard drives and a truckload of CDs to store your images! Before you begin considering ways to store images, get a better idea of how much storage space you will need. To estimate storage requirements, you need to make a few assumptions. First, you need to decide on the probable image resolution and level of file compression that you will use.

Because you have purchased this book on digital imaging, a reasonable assumption is that you are serious about your pictures—that is, the quality of your images is important to you. With that assumption in mind, you need to base your calculations on a 2-megapixel image, which is an image resolution approximating 1600×1200 pixels. It takes a 2-megapixel image to make near-photo-quality 8×10-inch prints. Before long, 2-megapixel digital cameras will become standard, especially as image media storage technology improves to the point where inexpensive memory cards can hold fifty or more images.

The next important variable to consider is the level of file compression that you plan to use. Unless you are shooting images for exclusive use on a Web page, it makes little sense not to always shoot with the least possible compression and enjoy the best image quality, providing you have enough image storage. Based on this assumption, a 1600×1200 image stored as a low-compression, high-quality JPEG file will be approximately 700KB in size.

To make a rough estimate of your storage requirements, you will have to make a guess about how many images you will take in a year. It's not unusual to shoot three to five times as many digital pictures as you would film pictures. After you have made an educated guess, multiply the number of digital pictures per year by 700KB to determine the total storage requirement.

Counting only the images I take for personal use, on average I fill about two 80MB image storage cards per month. That totals about 160MB of images (about 225 images) or about 2GB per year. Assuming I continue to take pictures at that rate over a three-year period, I would have about 6GB of images. Following some of the suggested storage strategies I recommend later in this chapter, I will need twelve CDs, which will cost about $12, to store three years' worth of digital images. Assuming 500MB of images are stored on each disk, there would be about 350 images per disk or about 4,200 total images—the equivalent of 175 rolls of 24-exposure film over three years. That is less than five rolls per month! That might seem shocking to you, but that is the reality of having a digital camera; it doesn't cost anything to take images except the cost of CD storage, if you decide to keep the images.

Part I Good Digital Images

You now should have a good idea about how much storage you'll need for the images that you'll create with a digital camera; but what if you don't use a digital camera and instead scan your photographs with a scanner? Again, you need to make a few assumptions. First, assume that you'll scan to optimize the images for a 4×6-inch, 300 dpi print. Because image storage is not as limiting a factor on a PC as it is with a digital camera, also assume that your images will be saved in a lossless format (such as TIFF or BMP) instead of in a lossy format (such as JPEG or a proprietary digital camera format). To estimate your storage requirements for scanned images, you will again have to make an educated guess.

A 4×6-, 5×7-, and 8×10-inch photo-quality, uncompressed digital image file for a 300 dpi printer requires 6.5MBs, 9.5MBs, and 21.6MBs respectively. After making an assumption about how many images you might have of each size, you can multiply them by the size of the file and determine your overall storage requirement. After you start editing the compressed images that you get with a digital camera, you'll want to keep not only the original compressed file but are likely to also want to store the file that you are editing in a lossless format, such as BMP or TIFF. The reason for this is that your original compressed file will contain the most image information that you'll ever have for that particular image. Any filters that you use on it or adjustments that you make to it might make it look better, but you will lose part of the image. Then, each time you store your image in a lossy format, such as JPEG, you will again lose some of your image. This is very similar to what happens when you make a photocopy of an original. Each time you copy a copy, the copy becomes a little less clear. In contrast, if you save your image to a lossless format, you can edit it and save it repeatedly with no additional loss—but you will need a much larger file.

To get the total disk space requirement for a three-year period, you need to add the space required for the initial images you took with a digital camera and then add space requirements for the converted digital camera images and scanned images. If you frequently use a digital camera and often digitally edit your images, you'll find that you need to store and manage several thousand images across one or two dozen CD-ROMs and a hard drive—that is roughly the magnitude of your storage requirements.

Tips for storing and managing image files

No matter what your requirements are, and no matter how many images you need to store and manage, you must have a plan—or even several plans. You might choose to have one plan for digital image files made with a digital camera, another plan for scanned images, a third plan for images that you have digitally edited, and a few other plans for the various projects that you are working on. The following six tips will help you save time, minimize the chances of losing valuable digital images, and enable you to enjoy and share your work more fully.

Create an organized directory system

One of the most important and easy steps that you can take to keep your digital images organized and safe is to create and maintain an organized directory system. As your digital image collection grows, you'll find that it's not hard to delete the wrong directory of files or to misfile an image and not be able to find it. You can also end up duplicating files that consume lots of space if you are not aware that other copies exist. Finding duplicates and deleting them after you have added new files to the same directories can be very time-consuming.

Take advantage of Windows' long file name feature—use descriptive folder and image names that clearly remind you of their contents, like "cats," "wedding," "horseshow98," "chap06-image_magic," or "soccer06-08-99." When you create a second set of images that can be deleted after you use them, add "tmp" to the folder name, so that you know that all the images can be deleted. For example, you might copy twenty images from multiple folders for use in a calendar. Each of these copied images can be placed in a directory called "monthly_images_tmp," indicating that after the calendar is complete, the entire folder can be deleted.

Make and follow a plan for digital camera images

Images taken with a digital camera can create cataloging problems unique to digital cameras. Some cameras sequentially number each image until you download them to your computer. Then, the counter is set back to 1 and the numbering starts all over again. This means that you have to keep each set of images in a separate directory, renumber each image so that the file names are unique and can be stored in the same file folder, or rename them with a meaningful name.

If you use a low-capacity image storage media card, you might find that, over time, you have to create hundreds of directories—each directory filled with images numbered sequentially from 1 to 20 or 30. Such a filing system makes it very difficult to find images when you need them. Other digital cameras have a continuous numbering feature, which causes your images to be sequentially numbered until they hit 9,999 or some maximum number—then the counting starts again at 1. If you place too many images in the same folder, it will be hard to find the ones that you want when you want them.

Another nice feature offered by some digital cameras is that they time and date stamp each image automatically. Providing that you use the right software, you will be able to find images by time and date. If you want to be able to use this feature, make sure you save your images in the right file format. Not all file formats enable time and date stamps to be stored.

Copy images to removable storage media

Over the last five years, the reliability of most hard drives might make you think that your hard drive will last forever—but they often don't. If you have valuable images, make sure that you are writing them to some kind of removable storage media. Remember, the more images that you save exclusively on your hard drive, the bigger your loss will be if you have a failure. On a frequent basis, copy all of your digital images to removable storage media.

Save original digital camera images

When you first start shooting with a digital camera, you might have a tendency to delete images that aren't up to your visual standards in order to save space. If you have the capability to store them, my suggestion is to keep all of your images. As you learn more about what you can do with these images, you'll find that it can be useful to have a soft, out-of-focus image or an image that is too light or too dark. It costs very little to store digital images, so consider keeping them unless they are very bad. Chapter 5, "Getting Images Into Shape," shows how you can turn some poor-quality prints into rather astounding images.

In many ways, your original digital files are like the negatives for traditional film. The original images contain the best information and the most information possible about the image that you took. Any time that you run filters and digitally enhance an image, it might look better, but you are altering and decreasing the original image in one or many ways.

If you store original digital camera images in a compressed format and you edit them, you'll have to store them again. If you store the image in the same format another time, you'll decrease the quality of the image in a manner very similar to the decreased quality of a photocopy of a photocopy. Each successive generation loses a bit more of the original image. My recommendation is to use the Windows file attribute capability and tag all of your original digital camera images as read-only files—treat them as valuable negatives and keep them safe and in their original condition. To set a file attribute to "read-only," right-click on the file name in Windows Explorer and select Properties. Then, on the General tab, click on "Read-only." After you have set a file's attribute to "read-only," you will not be able to edit and save the file without again changing the "read-only" attribute.

Consider implementing a backup plan

If you spend many hours digitally editing images, you'll want to consider keeping them in a separate directory that is set up to be automatically backed up weekly or even daily. In the case of a drive failure, you could save yourself many hours of unnecessary work. Windows 98 comes with a simple, yet useful, backup utility called Microsoft Backup (see Figure 4.2). If this system utility is installed, it can be launched by selecting Start>Programs>Accessories>System Tools>Backup. If this utility isn't installed, you can install it from the Windows Setup tab in the Add/Remove Programs application, located in the Control Panel.

Figure 4.2
Using Microsoft Backup to back up digital images.

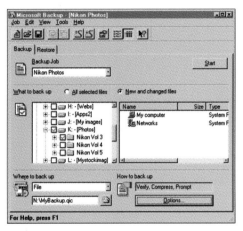

You can also set up Microsoft Backup as a scheduled task by using another Windows 98 system tool called Scheduled Tasks—it, too, can be found on the System Tools menu. This is a good way to make sure that your backups are done routinely. You might want to schedule backups when you are not using your PC, because backups can dramatically decrease the performance of your system.

NOTE

A retired couple spent a considerable amount of time over a four-month period creating a digital photo album for their children and grandchildren. They used digital images from a digital camera and selected images from CD-ROMs that were created by photo processing services and from scanned photographs. To get the best possible images, the majority of images had to be digitally edited. To protect their work, they used an automatic backup utility to copy all of the edited images to two CD-RWs. One was for the first and third week of each month, and the other was for the second and fourth week of each month. The backups were automatically done at midnight. Fortunately, they did not suffer from a hard-drive failure, but on two separate occasions, they did accidentally manage to erase an entire directory of edited images. Because of their backup plan, they did not have to re-edit any images—they just copied the images that they had deleted from their backup files!

Create extra copies of some images on an organized basis

Although extra copies of images can increase your storage requirements, there are good reasons why you'll want to make them. When you begin working on a project that requires the use of valuable images, think about creating a new directory and making temporary copies of those images you need. This will prevent you from destroying the original image, should you mistakenly save an edited image over one of the copied, original images. It's also usually wise to create an extra directory full of copied images when you use batch-processing capabilities. This will, for example, prevent you from ever accidentally converting an entire directory of high-resolution images into reduced-size JPEG files for a Web page. You might not think that you could make these mistakes, but they really do happen—I've made them myself!

Image management with Windows 98

Before you consider purchasing any image management software, first look at what can be done with the tools and features that are available with the Windows 98 operating system. Windows 98 ships with three different tools for working with digital images: Windows Explorer, Quick View, and Imaging for Windows. If your image management requirements are minimal, these tools might be all that you need. Although Imaging for Windows sounds like it could be a great tool, it isn't, and don't even take the time to load it unless you are interested in annotating your digital images and shipping them around like a fax.

Using Windows Explorer

Windows Explorer is the main operating system-level tool for managing folders and files. If you don't already know how to use it, you really ought to learn everything you can about it. It will enable you to move, add, copy, delete, and rename files or folders on your system. You can also set file attributes for archiving purposes or protect the files by setting them to be read-only files. From Explorer, you can select an image or images and send them to a mail recipient, to the Windows Desktop, or to another application such as Microsoft Word. Explorer also enables you to drag and drop files and folders onto other applications. It is a very powerful tool that can do things very quickly—it can also do a tremendous amount of damage if you don't know how to use it and you use it incorrectly.

Now I'm going to show you something that you might not know about Windows Explorer:

1. Right-click a folder in Explorer that contains graphic files, and then click Properties on the shortcut menu.

2. Select the General tab of the Properties dialog box. At the bottom of the tab, click the box to the left of Enable Thumbnail View to put a checkmark in it.

3. Click the OK button. Strangely, you now need to close Explorer to update the folder—even the menu option Refresh doesn't help.

4. Reopen Explorer and select the same folder.

5. Select the menu View and then click Thumbnails.

You now have an Explorer window with thumbnails, as shown in Figure 4.3. What a great way to view a folder with images, right? Well, almost. Explorer suffers from a limited set of file types (BMP and JPEG) that it can preview. It is so limited, in fact, that you might find that it isn't worth using at all.

Figure 4.3
Using Windows Explorer to display thumbnail images.

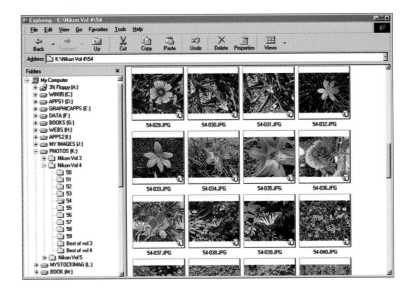

If you want to find a file or folder, you can use the Explorer's Find File or Folder feature—provided that you know something about the name of the file or folder. To find a file, select Tools>Find>Files or Folders and fill in the fields (see Figure 4.4). You can find a file either by looking for a specific name or file type or by searching by date. Windows Explorer is an essential part of the Windows Desktop, and it has made us very comfortable with the familiar directory tree view shown in the left pane in Figure 4.3—learn to use it well.

Figure 4.4
Finding a file with the
Find feature in Explorer.

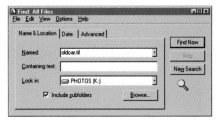

Using Windows Quick View

After you select a file in Explorer, you can double-click it to open it with the default application that is set to read that file type. Alternatively, you can preview the file if you have a viewer that can read the file. To preview a file from Explorer, right-click the file that you want to preview. On the File menu, click Quick View. If you do not see Quick View on the File menu, either no viewer is available for the file that you've selected or Quick View is not installed. After Quick View is launched on your desktop, you also can drag and drop files onto the open application. Alternatively, you can drag and drop files from Explorer to the Quick View file icon if it is sitting on your desktop.

If Quick View isn't installed, you can install it by going to the Control Panel and selecting Add/Remove Programs. Select the Windows Setup tab and double-click Accessories. Click the box to the left of Quick View to put a checkmark in the box. Notice that this is also the place to go to install the Imaging for Windows application, if you want to try it. Click the OK button, and your chosen applications will be installed. Sadly, the Quick View viewer can preview only the same limited set of file types that Explorer shows as thumbnails. It is likely that it can't even preview the files created by your digital camera.

It takes only a short while to go completely crazy when browsing files with Explorer and right-clicking each image file to open a viewer or application to view the image and then closing the viewer, only to repeat it all over again to see the next image. A little of this action and you know there has to be a better way—and there is! The better way involves using image management utilities or applications that are capable of showing *all* digital image files as thumbnails.

TIP

To get a freeware version of one of the best image viewers around, get Ulead's PhotoImpact Viewer 4.0. Anyone interested in easily viewing a wide range of image files should have this utility—you'll find it immensely valuable. You can download it at **www.ulead.com/download/download.htm.**

Using image management utilities

After you see how easy it is to work with directories full of images by using thumbnails, you'll rarely want to do without them. Windows Explorer showed you how useful these thumbnails can be, but you really need to see thumbnails of all images types. It would be nice if we could even see other multimedia file types, such as WAV or MIDI and video files, such as AVI or MOV. Fortunately, our wish is well within the range of possibility.

Midnight Blue Software's SuperJPG Version 4.0

If a picture is worth a thousand words, a directory of thumbnails is worth millions of words! That's my thought, anyway. If you want to view nearly instantaneous thumbnails of your images, SuperJPG 4.0 is a good tool to use (see Figure 4.5). This high-performance utility creates a small thumbnail image file for each file in each directory that you want to view with thumbnails. It then saves thumbnails for all the files in a directory, as a single file in that directory. After you view a directory, the thumbnails open quickly, because they need to be created only once. SuperJPG also enables you to select and view images in a slide show fashion.

Figure 4.5
Using SuperJPG to view images in a folder.

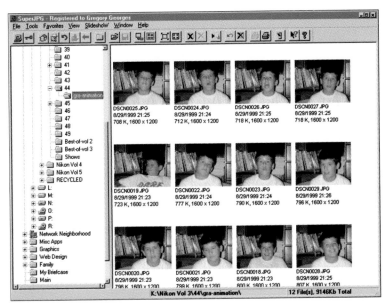

E-Book Systems Inc.'s Flip Album 3.0

If you are an album person, like me, you'll really like Flip Album 3.0. For those of you who use a digital camera, you'll love this application even more. Besides being an excellent tool for browsing directories containing digital images, it also makes an excellent photo album. To learn more about this fantastic tool, read Chapter 8, "Displaying Digital Images Electronically." Figures 8.5 and 8.6 in Chapter 8 are screenshots that show you how you can browse directories by using Flip Album 3.0.

Paint Shop Pro 6.0

If you use or are considering using Paint Shop Pro, you are in luck. It offers a superb directory-browsing feature that can be accessed from Explorer or from the File menu in Paint Shop Pro (see Figure 4.6).

Figure 4.6
Paint Shop Pro 6.0's directory browser.

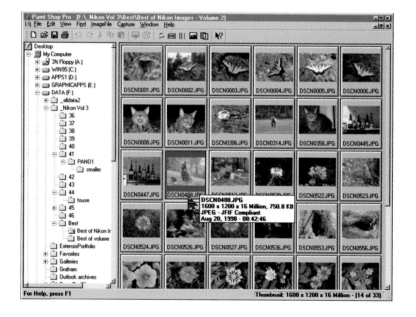

Part I Good Digital Images

Using consumer-level image editors and project applications

For years, the software industry has forced users to be very application-centric rather than task-centric. Recently, some terrific products have been introduced that work the way that you want to work instead of making you work the way the applications make you work. These new products tightly integrate all the functionality into a single interface that enables you to go about your tasks as you want.

MGI's PhotoSuite III

One of the most well-designed products in any software category I've seen in the last few years is MGI's PhotoSuite III, which it calls the "PC & Internet Photography Power Pack"—and it is. PhotoSuite III very tightly integrates file management with image editing and project creation tools. This logical interface makes it very easy to get your work done by selecting from the seven workflow steps shown at the top of the interface (see Figure 4.7). You can easily move between Get, Prepare, Compose, Organize, Share, Print, and Browse with a click of your mouse button. Each time you change steps, all the information, help, and controls that might be needed in each step appear on the left side of the screen, as shown in the Compose step in Figure 4.8.

Figure 4.7
Organizing images with PhotoSuite III.

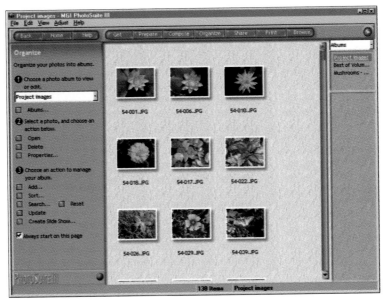

Figure 4.8
Composing an image
with PhotoSuite III.

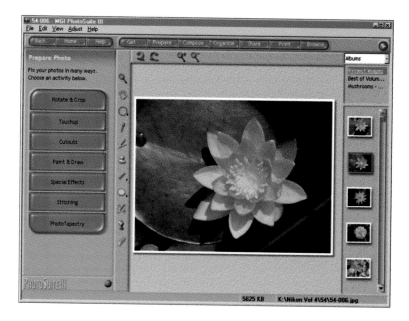

Ulead's Photo Express

Another outstanding product is Photo Express. This product also has
an interface that enables you to get your tasks done quickly without
switching between different applications. You simply click a tab for
Project, Photo, or Album and select from the options that are shown
down the left side of the interface (see Figure 4.9). If you want to create a
twelve-month calendar, for example, you first click the Album tab and
then either select an album that already contains the twelve images that
you need or open one or more directories and select the images that you
want. To make the calendar, you then click the Projects tab and select
Calendars. From there, you click to move to the photo-editing area,
where you edit the image that was placed in the calendar, as shown in
Figure 4.10.

Figure 4.9
Organizing photos into albums with Ulead's Photo Express.

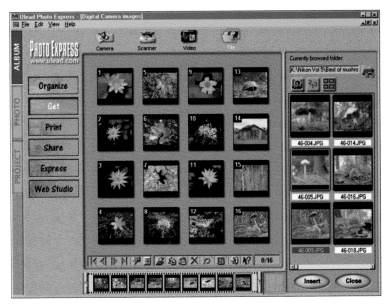

Part I Good Digital Images

Figure 4.10
Editing an image for a calendar project with Ulead's Photo Express.

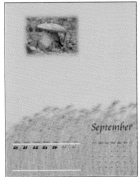

Although these products offer image management capabilities complete with thumbnails and the capability to add and use keywords for selection, they are not intended to be used as image management applications for thousands of images on multiple volumes and removable media. Rather, they are designed to enable you to complete projects easily by building portfolios of images that you are considering using for specific projects. They also can be used to manage a few directories of files quite effectively.

These consumer-level products might meet all of your image management requirements. If not, then consider using one of the more advanced image management applications discussed in the next section. They offer many more features and capabilities, and most of them are built upon powerful databases that enable tremendous flexibility and speed not found in the consumer-level products.

NOTE

A parent took pictures of youth soccer players both on and off the field during the season. He used a film-based camera for most of the action shots and a digital camera for the rest of the pictures. When pictures from the film-based camera were processed, he had his local photofinisher scan them and provide them to him on CD-ROM without regular prints. Using image management software, he was able to view each photo and enter jersey numbers into a keyword field in an image for any players who were prominent in the picture. At the end of the season, he created a CD-ROM with two slide shows for each of the players. The first show was about the whole team and key events as well as a variety of shots of all the players. The second slide show displays slides of that specific player only. These CD-ROM shows were easy to create because he could do a simple search on the image database by player number and then create a slide show with a simple drag-and-drop operation to the slide show software. Using digital images exclusively and inexpensive CD-ROMs, he provided these shows for very little cost.

Using advanced image management applications

So far in this chapter you have looked at using Windows Explorer, several inexpensive browsing utilities, and consumer-level image editing applications to store and manage images. This section introduces you to some more powerful image management applications that have been designed solely for managing large digital file collections.

Advanced image management applications to consider

Although each of these applications has been designed differently, conceptually, they all do the same thing: They enable you to create one or more databases that contain a thumbnail image of each digital file type that you select. With each thumbnail, you can optionally store other kinds of information, such as keywords, a description, or other custom fields. Most of these products are built around sophisticated database engines that offer speed and the capability to manage very large numbers of images.

If you intend to efficiently manage a large digital image collection, consider using one of the products described next.

Cerious Software Inc.'s ThumbsPlus 4.0

Up front, I must tell you that I've never worked for Cerious Software, nor do I know anyone who works there. I'm in a defensive mode because you might feel that my praise for this product is too great—until you try it. The fact is, ThumbsPlus 4.0 is one fantastic program. I have used it in many versions and over many, many years—it just gets better and better. I don't know how I could have even begun to manage all the images that I looked at, created, and used in this book without using nearly all the capabilities in ThumbsPlus.

The ThumbsPlus 4.0 interface looks and works just like Windows Explorer, making it a very easy tool to use from the moment that you install it. The left side has a window that shows your system in the familiar tree style, as shown in Figure 4.11. The right side enables you to view thumbnail images of any graphics file in the directory—in fact, ThumbsPlus supports more than 70 file formats. You can navigate through the folders by clicking them to expand or contract them. The third window at the bottom left of the screen is the Task window, which shows when tasks are running, such as the scanning of a folder or volume or a batch-processing task. Most of these and other tasks can be run in the background while you continue to use ThumbsPlus's other features.

Figure 4.11
Cerious Software Inc.'s ThumbsPlus, showing thumbnails of files in a directory.

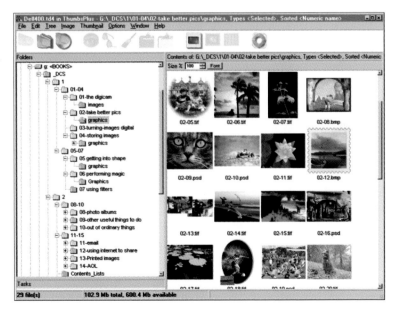

If you have a tendency to scatter image files that you need and use all over your hard drives—which is not unreasonable or uncommon—you can have ThumbsPlus scan your entire system. It will color-code any folders that contain images, enabling you to rapidly browse through all the images on your system.

One of ThumbsPlus's most valuable features is its capability to manage offline CD-ROMs. Figure 4.12 shows part of a list of fifteen offline CD-ROMs. As you click each directory, the appropriate thumbnails are shown, thus enabling you to search for images without having to insert each CD-ROM. After you find the image or images that you want, you can insert the CD-ROM and get access to the images. This is a real time-saver.

Figure 4.12
Managing offline CD-ROMs with ThumbsPlus.

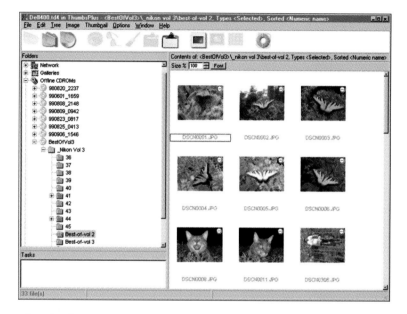

ThumbsPlus's Automatic File Rename feature enables you to automatically rename files in a directory according to the scheme that you choose. This is an excellent tool for renumbering files created with a digital camera. Figure 4.13 shows how each folder of images has been automatically renumbered so that the file name indicates the folder in which an image can be found.

Figure 4.13
Using ThumbsPlus to automatically rename files in a directory.

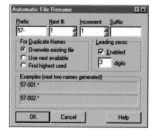

ThumbsPlus offers many other useful features, including the capability to find similar images, perform a thorough search, run batch-processing, build Web pages, create contact sheets, and print catalogs. It also includes a reasonable set of digital image editing tools. I like this application—a lot!

Extensis Portfolio 4.0

Portfolio 4.0 is another exceedingly capable, "industrial-strength" tool. It is designed for use in work groups to manage digital media files, including presentations, movies, sound files, and some other common files, such as Microsoft Word documents. Although you certainly can use Portfolio to successfully manage digital media files as a single user, its real strengths and unique features are most apparent when used in a networked environment by multiple people.

In a work group setting, catalog administrators can control what each user can do with the images in the catalog. Members of work groups can simultaneously search, view, and use images from catalogs whose source files are located on one or many network servers, shared volumes, CD-ROMs, or removable drives. Users can even access the Portfolio Server remotely by using TCP/IP. Portfolio's wide range of features and capabilities is similar to the range of many of the other products in this group. If you work in a group and need to share files among different group members, this might be the best application for you.

Unlike most image management applications that work with directory trees, Portfolio's interface has been designed to facilitate working with images by using keywords. Figure 4.14 shows the keyword palette on the left side, which includes book chapter numbers. To manage the chapters in this book, for example, you could assign chapter numbers to each image. If you want to view, copy, edit, or move images in a specific chapter, you could do so simply by clicking the appropriate chapter keyword. Alternatively, you could use the powerful keyword search facility, also shown in Figure 4.14. This search facility enables you to find all pictures of cats, mushrooms, soccer players, or any other topic across all chapters or across just a few chapters—or whatever else you might want.

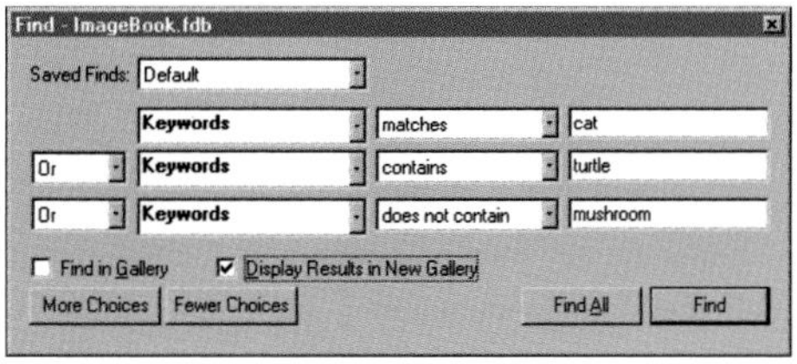

Figure 4.14
Searching for images by keywords, using Extensis Portfolio.

Ulead's PhotoImpact Album 4.0

This is another outstanding cataloging tool. To learn more about
PhotoImpact Album, read Chapter 8, "Displaying Digital Images
Electronically," in which PhotoImpact Album is used to create a photo
album-based asset record of tools in a woodworking shop. Figures 8.1,
8.2, 8.3, and 8.4 in Chapter 8 show screenshots of PhotoImpact. Besides
its image management capability, PhotoImpact is also a very good digital
image editor, especially for Web graphics.

NOTE

I used ThumbsPlus 4.0 to store and manage more than 3,500 images that were
considered for, or included in, this book. Folders were created for each
chapter. Additional subfolders were created for images that were being
considered for use, images that were not going to be used, and images that
were going to be used for each chapter. Additionally, offline CD-ROM folders
were created to display large thumbnails for images contained on seventeen
offline CD-ROMs. These folders made it very easy to search for and find
images for a specific purpose if they were not located on the local hard drives.

One hard-drive volume was dedicated entirely to online storage of images
taken with a digital camera. ThumbsPlus was used extensively in managing
these images, because there were 2GB of images. An image selected to be
used in the book could be dragged, dropped, and copied into the correct
chapter folder. This advanced image management application was also the
tool used to print contact sheets for chapter editing purposes and for selecting
images to be zipped and sent to the publisher's Internet site to be published.
Besides using this application for professional purposes, I also use the tool to
manage images for personal use. Figure 4.15 shows using ThumbsPlus 4.0
to manage images for this book.

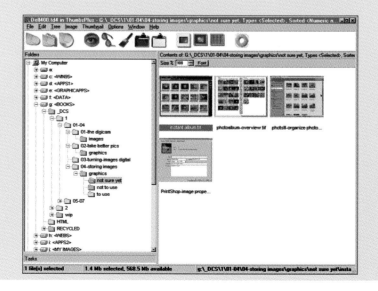

Other useful things that can be done

Some of these advanced image management applications have other features that might be especially important to you. Several of these features are described in this section.

Gallery creation

The capability to create a gallery is a useful way to select a group of images from multiple locations for different projects and to manage them all effectively while avoiding having to have multiple copies of the same image stored in multiple places. For example, when writing this book, I was able to store all the images used in the book in chapter folders. If I then decide to offer a sampling of the images on a Web site, I can create a gallery for images from two or more chapters. By copying the thumbnails into a gallery, I will always be using the same original images, yet I can see all the images chosen for the Web site in its own gallery (or folder).

Export to HTML feature

The capability to automatically export thumbnails and images to the Internet can be a very valuable feature. Although most image management applications enable images to be exported as Web pages, some enable more control over the look of the pages than others. Figure 4.16 shows one of many possible Web pages that can be created with ThumbsPlus 4.0 by using the Webpage Wizard.

Figure 4.16
Web page created with ThumbsPlus 4.0.

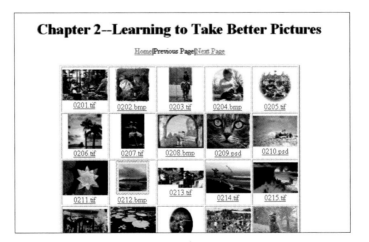

Finding duplicates

Finding duplicates is a useful feature that is not available in all image management applications. If you have a tendency to end up with many copies of the same image scattered about your hard drives and removable media, this feature can help you save disk space. If you have Norton Utilities, you can use the Duplicate File Processing feature in the Space Wizard to accomplish the same task.

Generate slide shows

Another good way to view images in a folder is with a slide show. This is a particularly useful feature if you use a digital camera because it's a fun and practical way to view your images in slide show fashion. You can also select just the images that you want to show instead of all files in a folder by clicking the desired thumbnails.

Saving images to removable media

Even if you have lots of available capacity on your PC's hard drive, you'll want to make sure all of your images are backed up or stored on some kind of removable storage media. The questions you must answer are what media to use and how to go about copying all of those images.

Choosing removable storage media

Deciding which removable media to use to store your digital images is an important decision—even if it does not seem so now as you begin to collect your first few hundred digital images.

Make sure that you store them on the most lasting storage media that you can find. By *lasting,* I mean both in terms of media that will last for a long time and in terms of the technology that you use to store them—and that you will, thus, need to play them back. A quick review of the brief history of the PC recalls the moves from 8-inch floppies to 5-1/2 -inch floppies to 3-1/2 -inch floppies to CDs and now DVDs and a variety of other media, such as Zip, Jaz, Clik, DAT tape, and others. All of these different media serve a purpose; however, most of them are not going to be around for as long as you are likely to need them for image storage and playback.

My educated guess is that CD technology will be one of the more lasting storage media types that we will see for some time. As more of the online and local photofinishers continue to deliver digital images on CDs, this will become an increasingly important storage medium.

My suggestion, then, is that if your digital image collection is valuable to you and will be for many years, you should store your images on CDs.

Invest and standardize on CD technology. A single CD can hold up to 650MB of images, which is a considerable number of images—all for under $1. If you are thinking about any other type of storage media, ask yourself whether such a playback device will be available to enable you to access and view your stored images and multimedia files in five or even ten or more years.

CD technology is ideal for storing digital image files. CDs will not suffer if exposed to most liquids, such as water or even coffee (provided it isn't too hot!). If there is a universal medium, the CD is it. Most computers have a CD drive as a standard feature, and nearly all photo service bureaus can read them.

Writing image files to CDs

To write files to CDs, you will need a ReWritable CD drive that will enable you to write data to a CD as well as read it. Most PCs come equipped with a CD-ROM drive, which will enable you only to read CDs—not write to them. Theoretically, writing image files to a CD with a ReWritable CD drive is as easy as copying files from one directory to another on your hard drive; however, in reality, sometimes it isn't that easy—although it should be soon. With each new generation of ReWritable CD drives and software, it is becoming easier, more reliable, and faster.

When using a ReWritable CD drive, you have a choice of two different kinds of writable CDs—each of them has advantages and disadvantages. CD-Recordable (CD-R) disks enable you to record files on them once and only once. CD-ReWritable (CD-RW) disks, on the other hand, can be written to many times. CD-RWs can function exactly like a regular hard drive or floppy drive. To write to these specialized CDs, you need a CD-RW drive that is capable of writing to CDs, and you need specialized software. You should also be aware that a CD-RW disk can be read only by a CD-RW drive—not a standard CD drive. CD-Rs, however, can be read by both CD-ROM drives and ReWritable CD drives.

Adaptec's Easy CD Creator 4.0 is one of several products that can be used to write files to CDs. It offers two basic methods of writing files. You can use an Explorer-like window to select files that you want to write to a CD and then have them written in one session (see Figure 4.17). Alternatively, you can set up a CD to function just like a new drive on your PC. This method enables you to write and delete files to the CD as you choose.

Figure 4.17
Using Adaptec's Easy
CD Creator to write
digital image files to
a CD.

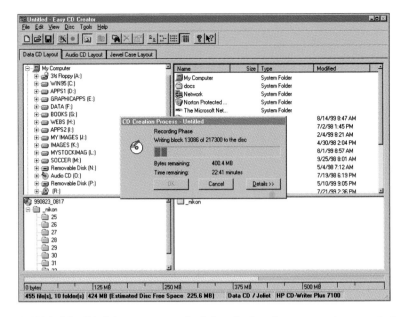

ReWritable CD drives are wonderful tools, but I must caution you to be
both wary and careful when writing files to CDs, especially when you
plan to copy them and then immediately delete the originals from your
hard drive. Stuff happens! You might think that the files have been
copied, but they really weren't. As with any new technologies, there
are "gotchas" that can cost plenty. I once copied about 500 images to a
CD-RW disk. I then upgraded to a new version of CD-writing software
and attempted to write more files to the disk. The new software (from the
same vendor) damaged all the files that I had previously stored. My only
choice was to reformat the CD-RW disk and use it again! The moral of the
story: Be careful!

Tips for storing images on CDs

After you begin writing digital image files to a CD, you might want to
consider following one or more of the following tips. These tips will not
only minimize the chances of losing images but also make it easier and
more enjoyable to use and view your images from CDs.

Save thumbnail images in each folder for quick browsing

To enable quick browsing of CD-ROM directories with thumbnails,
consider using a utility such as Midnight Blue Software's SuperJPG
Version 4.0. If you write thumbnails to each directory when you write the
files to the CD-ROM, you will not need to wait for thumbnails to be
created each time you access the folders. This tip can save a considerable
amount of time, especially when you have large image files, full CDs, or a
slow CD drive.

Use a combination of CD-RW and CD-R to save images

As your digital image collection grows in size, you might find that that your images are most easily found and used when they are categorized into subjects like birds, landscapes, seascapes, family, or other appropriate categories. Then when you need a bird, for example, you can load the CD with a bird directory and choose from all of the bird images.

The problem with this approach is that it takes a long time to get enough images to make a whole directory of birds, frogs, landscapes, seascapes, or whatever categories you choose. One solution to this problem is to use a combination of CD-RWs and CD-Rs. Initially, use the more expensive CD-RWs to collect images. After you have filled several CD-RWs with images, you can then organize all the images into certain categories and write them to a CD-R disk for permanent storage. These "stock albums" sorted by subject can become exceedingly useful for years.

Make more than one copy of each image

A CD can hold more than 900 700KB images (like those from a 2-megapixel digital camera). If you generally fill your CDs and something were to happen to one of them, you would lose all 900 images. Obviously, one way to help prevent this from happening is to make one or more copies of your images on additional CDs. If you have a ReWritable CD drive plus an additional CD drive, you can simply copy one CD onto a second CD.

Alternatively, you can duplicate 50 percent of the images on one disk onto the next disk that you write. For illustration purposes, assume that you sequentially number your directories and that directories "101" through "130" contain about 900MBs of images. On the first CD you would copy 600MBs of images from directories "101" to "120." Next, copy directories "111" to "130" to a second CD. Directories "121" to "140" would be copied to a third CD and so on. This approach minimizes the number of images that you need to leave on your hard drive, and it enables you to have two copies of each of your images—one on each of two CDs. Using this approach, you won't need to have two CD drives to successfully make copies of your files.

Make multiple copies of your "best images"

Each time you write a collection of images to a CD, make a new directory on your hard drive for the best images from that image collection. Then, on each successive CD, add several of these "best of volume" directories to the new CDs. This strategy not only protects your best images by having multiple copies of them on different CDs but also makes it easier for you to access these images. Using an image management application that creates thumbnail images, you can very easily browse through a large collection and create a "best of volume" collection.

Label each disk with a unique label and write it on the face of the disk

Before you write images to a new CD, make sure that you label the disk with a unique disk label. This must be done with your CD writing software. Unique labels enable you to catalog offline CDs in an image management application. Without these labels, you won't be able to differentiate one CD from another, so you won't be able to store the thumbnails as an offline image collection.

Using photofinishing services

One of the easiest ways to get your images written to a CD is to use one of the many digital image-processing services offered by a wide variety of photo labs. Many of these services not only provide you with a CD with your images but also come with a paper-based color printout showing each image on the CD, as well as software with thumbnails (see Figure 4.18) that enable you to browse all the images easily and quickly.

Figure 4.18
Viewing thumbnail images on a Ritz Camera Big Prints photo CD.

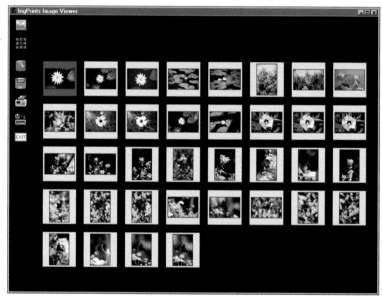

Some of the more expensive services, such as the Kodak Photo CD service, provide multiple resolutions of each of your images. To learn more about these services see Chapter 3, "Turning Photographs into Digital Images."

The end of this chapter also concludes Part I, "Starting with a Few Good Digital Images," in which you learned about digital cameras, how to take better pictures, ways to convert photos into digital images, and how to manage and store images. Part II, "Transforming Ordinary Images into Extraordinary Ones," begins with a chapter on how to get your images into shape.

Part II
Transforming Ordinary Images Into Extraordinary Ones

5
Getting Images into Shape

Each time you take a picture, you usually endeavor to take a "perfect" picture. However, the moment you enter the world of digital imaging, you will soon realize that the "perfect" picture is a relative term, and it will take time and work to get one, no matter how you take your pictures. A digital image that makes a perfect print on a color ink-jet printer will not make a perfect image for a Web page, nor will it make a perfect image for use as an attachment to e-mail. So exactly what is the perfect image, you might ask. Besides showing the perfect subject that is well composed, our elusive "perfect" picture ought to:

▶ Be free from dust, scratches, tears, wrinkles, stains, smears, or other defects.

▶ Look good—that is, it should have a wide tonal range, the colors should be correct, and the image should be sharp, if that was the intent.

▶ Be the right size, both in terms of the aspect ratio (i.e., horizontal or vertical orientation) and the physical size, which can be expressed in inches, pixels (or dots per inch) or even a combination of the two.

▶ Be saved in an appropriate file format so that it can be viewed or used in the intended applications.

▶ Be saved in a file that is the right size. If the image is to be downloaded from a Web site, it might require file compression, which involves a trade-off between image size and image quality so that an optimal size must be chosen.

In summary, we will consider a digital image to be in shape when it looks good *and* the file is the right size and in an appropriate format. When considering all of these variables, you can understand why this chapter is titled, "Getting Your Images into Shape." The tools that you use to do this work all loosely fall into the category of digital image editors. Not only are there a tremendous number of these tools, but they also vary in their capabilities and in the quality of the results that they produce. The two-fold purpose of this chapter is, first, to give you an idea of the kinds of tools that are available and how they can help you get your images into shape and, second, to help you find one or several tools that will suit your purposes.

Correcting imperfect images

To learn about digital image editors, we'll walk through the process of getting three sample images into shape. The three images we will work on are very different—in both their subject matter and their original form.

The first image, shown in Figure 5.1, is of downtown Chapel Hill, North Carolina. It was taken with a digital camera while waiting for the streetlights to change. The light level was low enough to require a tripod, but one was not used. The image was taken out-of-level. It is underexposed, and it is hard to see much of the detail in the buildings. Sadly, a few of the more dominant features of the image include the traffic lights and the wires that hold them up. We'll refer to this poorly taken picture as the "Chapel Hill" image. Incidentally, the digital camera was set at a 1600×1200 resolution and at the lowest compression setting, which resulted in an 865KB file.

Figure 5.1
A poorly taken picture of downtown Chapel Hill.

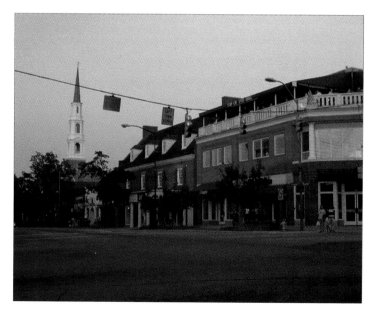

The second image, shown in Figure 5.2, was made by scanning a 6×6-inch photograph that was taken with a medium-format camera in typical English weather with heavy, gray, overcast lighting. We will refer to this image as the "castle" image. The intent is to turn this image into a high-quality image that will make an 8×8-inch print on photo-quality paper. If we are successful, it'll turn out to look like a professionally taken photograph that we will be pleased to frame and hang on a wall. We want to see more detail in the shadows of the castle wall, more of the bright green colors in the plants, and the golden yellow glow of sunset that existed when this picture was taken.

Figure 5.2
A "not-quite-right" print of Warwick Castle in England.

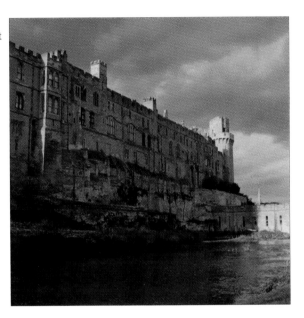

Part II Transforming Images

Our final picture is of a beloved grandmother taken in 1924. Figure 5.3 shows the classic, old-time, hand-printed, hand-signed, sepia-colored print. Besides a few spots and crinkles, the 5×7-inch print is in relatively good shape, with the exception of a horrible tear near her forehead. Because this was a special lady, we want to make a fine-art print of this image on high-quality art paper, if we can repair and improve the image. Because we have a 5×7-inch print, we'll plan to scan it and then make an 8×10-inch print so that it will fit in a standard frame. You still aren't sure what we are going to do with that tear near her forehead, are you?

Figure 5.3
A damaged picture of a grandmother, taken in 1924.

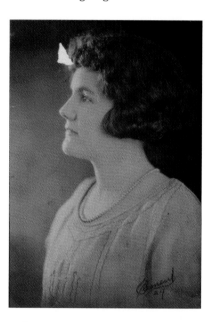

Before we get started on the images, we need to select a tool to do the work. Just as all photofinishers are not created equal, neither are all digital image editors created equal. For years, Adobe's Photoshop has been, and still remains, the ultimate digital image editing application. It is such an exceptional product that it can command a price approaching $600. If you want the best digital image editor and the best results, this is the one to get.

In the same league as Photoshop are Corel's PHOTO-PAINT 9, MetaCreations' Painter 6, and Jasc Software's Paint Shop Pro 6, all of which sell for several hundred dollars less than Photoshop while offering many of the same features, plus many very different and useful features.

Part II Transforming Images

TIP

For years, Jasc Software's Paint Shop Pro has stood out as one, if not the very best, of the shareware products in the software industry. Since release 6, Paint Shop Pro has become a very powerful image editor (it also includes Animation Shop) that compares well with many of the capabilities offered by Photoshop 5.5, PHOTO-PAINT 9, and Painter 6.0, and it is much easier to use. Even more significantly, many of the Photoshop "plug-in" vendors are now making sure that their applications work with Paint Shop Pro, as it dramatically lowers the cost of using their products by about $500. Paint Shop Pro, which costs around $100, can be downloaded as a fully functioning evaluation version at **www.jasc.com**. It is also available as a shrink-wrapped product at major retail stores and most Internet and catalog retailers. It is an excellent product and a great value for digital camera owners.

An even lower-priced group of editors includes MGI Software's PhotoSuite III, Ulead System's PhotoImpact 5, Microsoft's PhotoDraw 2000, and The LivePix Co.'s LivePix 2.0 Deluxe. Any of these tools will enable you to do a great job on all three images we are about to work on and most of the images that you will work with in the future.

The common characteristic of all of these packages is that they are professional tools that enable you to do many things to your digital images—if you know how to use them. They are not all easy applications to learn to use, but once you learn how to use one of them, you will be able to get excellent results from your images.

A third group of digital editors, perhaps one step below those just described, includes those designed for the consumer market—as opposed to advanced users or professionals. Streetwise Software's Professor Franklin's Instant Photo Effects, Broderbund's The Print Shop series, Ulead's Photo Express 3.0 and Xaos Tools' FlashBox are just a few examples of the tools in this group. They are easy to use and can do some amazing things in an automatic fashion—but often not with all the control offered by the tools in the first two groups.

For each of the three imaging examples, I will refer to generic tool features that are typically available in all of the applications in the first group and in some of the second group mentioned so far. If I use any unique feature or filter to perform an action, I will tell you what application I used to do it. For those of you who are curious, I happen to be a Photoshop addict and use it on practically every image that I work on. However, I use many, many other tools when they offer something unique or can produce a better result than Photoshop.

Fixing an image taken with a digital camera

Let's start on the Chapel Hill image first:

1. First we need to straighten the photo. We'll correct the tilt, by using Image>Rotate Canvas>Arbitrary, and rotate the image counterclockwise about 2.5 degrees. Now the horizon is level, and the steeple no longer leans like the famed Leaning Tower of Pisa.

2. Using a constrained aspect ratio of 10×8 (this is the ratio of width to height of our intended final print), select the part of the picture that you want to appear in the final image, as shown in Figure 5.4. Then crop the image and save the file in an uncompressed format, such as BMP or TIFF.

Figure 5.4
Selecting a region of the straightened image for the final print.

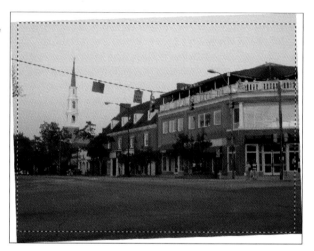

3. To add some depth to the image, we need to adjust the highlights and shadows. We'll do this with the Curves tool, shown in Figure 5.5. The Curves dialog box enables you to adjust the tonal range of an image with great precision. In this case, we will brighten the face of the building so that we can see more detail. We also want the street to be a bit lighter gray than it is.

Figure 5.5
Adding tonal range with
the Curves tool.

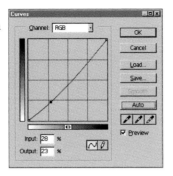

4. Next, we must get rid of the streetlights and wires. To do this, we use
    a simple tool called the Rubber Stamp tool. It is like a clone brush,
    which allows you to paint one part of an image onto another part. In
    other words, you simply copy sky over the streetlights and wires.
    When you get to the buildings, you copy bricks over the top of the
    streetlights and wires that you want to remove. You can see this
    being done in Figure 5.6.

Figure 5.6
Removing the ugly
streetlights and wires
with the Rubber Stamp
tool.

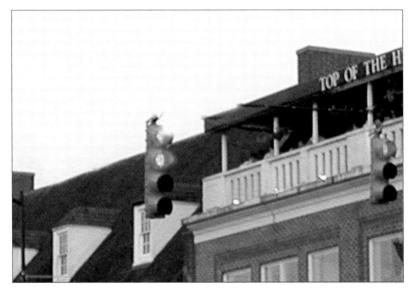

Part II Transforming Images

5. As the sky is overly light and void of much character, we'll select it with the Magic Wand tool and then use the Curves tool again to add tonal range to the sky.

6. To enlarge the image so that it can be used to make a high-quality 8×10-inch print, we need to select Image>Image Size and then fill out the fields in the dialog box, as shown in Figure 5.7. You can see our original image was only 4.48MBs and to print on an 8×10-inch print on a 300 dpi printer, we will need to increase print size, which will make the file 20.6MBs. Normally, you do not want to increase the file size this much as it will degrade image quality—in this case, however, we'll run a filter on the image, which will sharpen the image.

Figure 5.7
Increasing image size so that it can be printed as an 8×10-inch print.

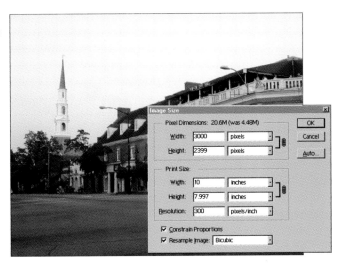

We have a nearly perfect image—one that would print on photo-quality paper on a good inkjet printer in a way that would rival a one-hour photo lab print. That wasn't so hard, was it? Now we need to transform this image into something more artsy. That is the subject of Chapter 7, "Filtering for Special Effects," so for now we are just going to apply a filter, the result of which will look like Figure 5.8. The whole process took less than ten minutes, the printing took another five minutes, and we have a fine-art print on watercolor paper that is suitable for framing! If you'd like the image to look more like a painting, refer to Figure 2.26 and its description in Chapter 2, "Learning to Take Better Pictures."

Figure 5.8
Completed image with
Poster Edges filter
applied.

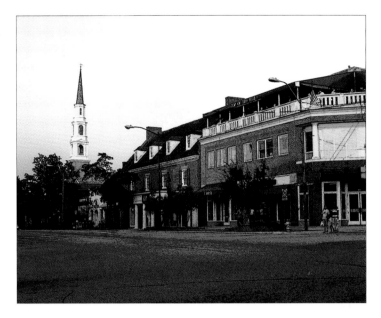

Fixing a scanned image

Okay, that's one photo fixed. Now, let's start on the castle image. This
image was shot in the "golden" glow of sunset and, thus, it has a very
warm glow that we need to be careful to bring back into our final image
along with additional detail in the castle wall.

1. To see more detail in the castle wall, we need to adjust the image so
    that it shows a wider tonal range in the shadow areas. To do this
    automatically, we'll select Image>Adjust>Auto Levels; suddenly we
    can see the texture of the castle walls, window details, and even
    more of the plants.

2. To put the warm golden glow of the sunset back into the image,
    select Image>Adjust>Color Balance and adjust it for the golden glow,
    as shown in Figure 5.9.

Figure 5.9
The Color Balance
slider is used to put the
golden color of sunset
back into the image.

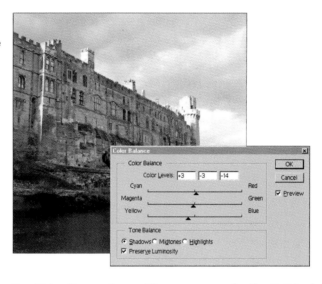

3. Using Image>Image Size, we can make the 5×5-inch image into a
    10×10-inch image for printing.

4. Finally, because we have lost some detail by enlarging the image,
    we'll strengthen the definition of the edges by selecting
    Filter>Sharpen>Sharpen Edges, which results in the final image
    shown in Figure 5.10.

Figure 5.10
Final corrected castle
image—better but not
great!

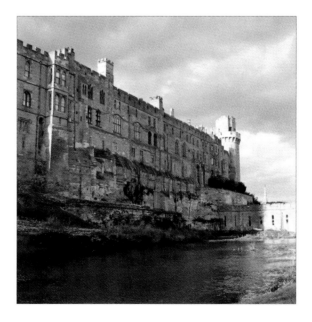

At this point, we can see the detail in the castle wall that we wanted, and we've returned some of the "golden glow" from the sunset that we had hoped to get. What do you think of the image now? There is no question that it is better than it was—but it is surely not going to be one of my favorite images. Our lesson here is this: Not all images can be turned into good images. Our initial objective of turning this into a print that is good enough to frame and hang on a wall is not likely to be met, especially since we had to double the size of the image. You have now learned that there is a limit to the magic that can be performed with a digital image editor. If you want a really good image, you need to begin with a really good photograph or digital image!

Fixing a damaged photograph

Now, let's see how we can grow some hair back on Grandmom's head. Believe it or not, this will be the easiest of the three images to fix.

1. First, let's get rid of that awful tear in the photograph surface. Use the magnifier to enlarge the area of the tear, as shown in Figure 5.11. Then, using the Rubber Stamp tool, select a part of the image that matches the area that needs to be filled in. Carefully copy one part of the image over the tear until most of the tear is gone, leaving a part of it where we need to put hair. While we are at it, let's cover up all the other spots and imperfections on the image in both the light and dark areas until no flaws remain. We'll also replace a few dark spots on her dress with part of the clean dress.

Figure 5.11
Fixing a tear in the photo with the Rubber Stamp tool.

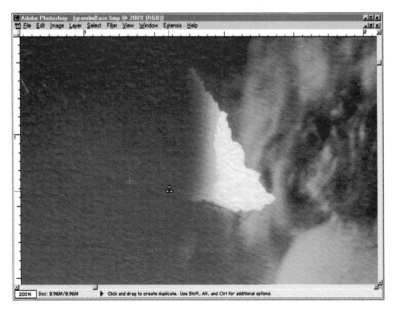

2. Next, let's put some hair back where it needs to be. Once again, we'll use the Rubber Stamp tool. In this instance, select part of her hair that looks like it could work where the tear was. Copy and mix the hair with the Rubber Stamp tool until her hair looks like it did in 1924 (see Figure 5.12). Looks better than her beautician could have done—don't you think?

Figure 5.12
The hair replacement completed.

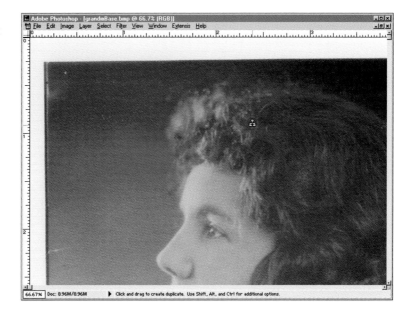

3. Now we need to clean up the edges by selecting an area within the photograph that is rectangular and then by copying that selected part onto a new white image that is a half-inch wider and taller so that we have a quarter-inch border all around, as shown in Figure 5.13. As one final detail, select the border with the Magic Wand tool and then use the Eye Dropper tool to select an almost-white color to use as a fill for the border, because the pure-white border is too bright.

4. As an optional step, you can elect to give her a little warmer color by applying a pre-set duotone color scheme, like the one shown in Figure 5.14. I like this result better than Figure 5.13, don't you? By the way, I printed this image on a piece of Digital Art Supplies' canvas paper. It looks wonderful framed.

Figure 5.13
Restored grandmother
image shown at left.

Figure 5.14
The result of applying a
pre-set duotone color
scheme shown at right.

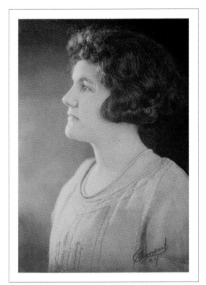
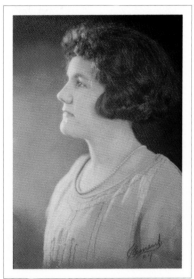

At this point, you are probably becoming a believer in the awesome
capabilities of digital image editing software to make an image look better.
You have also learned how important it is to have a good image to start
with. Now, if you recall, at the beginning of this chapter we agreed that
an image is not "in shape" until it both looks good *and* the digital file is
the right size and in an appropriate format. To get the file itself into
shape, we have to know how the image is going to be used, which will
determine the file format, file size, image resolution, and other
characteristics. We'll cover all of that in the next section.

Selecting the proper file characteristics

Why do we care so much about getting digital files into shape if the
image looks good on our computer screen? That is a good question, and it
is worthy of a complete answer. Honestly, in many cases, you won't care,
whereas in many other cases, you'll care a whole lot!

Suppose that you have selected twenty digital images that you took with
a digital camera. You want to use those images to create a PC-screen-
based slide show. The reason for the show and the importance of the
images compels you to try to make this the best show possible. Knowing
that you are going to be presenting on a high-resolution (1280×1024
pixels) projection device, you might want to use very carefully edited,
uncompressed images at the full 1280×1024 image resolution. This means
that the JPEG files created by your digital camera will need to be
converted, and you will need to edit each image to make it perfect.

Part II Transforming Images

Now suppose that you want to e-mail that same slide show. Those huge, high-resolution images will overload almost anyone's e-mail—so, you'll have to reduce them and possibly convert them to a file type that allows the file size to be reduced via a compression technique. What if you want 8×10-inch prints of those same images? If you want the best possible prints, you'd have to work on the images again to create 300 dpi or greater resolution files for use on a color printer. How about taking those same images and putting them on a Web page? You can begin to understand why it can be so important to get your images into optimal shape for their intended purposes.

To get your image files into shape, you might need to complete one or more of the following steps:

▶ If the image is to be digitally edited, it should first be saved to a lossless file format, such as BMP or TIFF. A *lossless* format generally doesn't offer compression, which means that you don't lose any image quality each time you save the image. Conversely, a *lossy* format does offer compression (meaning that the file size can be made dramatically smaller), but a loss of image quality occurs when the image is compressed.

▶ The image should be straightened, if it needs to be straightened, or rotated, if it is in the wrong orientation.

▶ If the image needs to be cropped, it should be cropped.

▶ The bit depth might need to be changed, either to reduce the file size (by using fewer colors) or to increase the quality of the picture (show more colors). *Bit depth* relates to the number of allowable colors. The most common bit depths are 8-bit, 16-bit, and 24-bit images, which allow 256, 65,536, and 16.7 million colors, respectively.

▶ Depending on what is going to be done to the image and how it will be used, the image size, in inches or pixels, needs to be set, plus the resolution or dpi might need to be changed.

▶ After the editing is complete, the image needs to be saved to the appropriate file format. If it is to be a compressed file format, you need to adjust the level of compression for optimal viewing quality and file size.

Sounds easy, right? Well, yes—and no. The subject of graphic file formats is so broad that you could write an entire 850-page book *just* on creating images for the Web. In fact, Ron Wodaski did just that—he wrote *Web Graphics Bible* (IDG Books Worldwide, Inc., ISBN 0-7645-3055-0), which covers interlacing, transparency, image maps, and all kinds of stuff that might or might not be important to you, depending on how you intend to use your images. If you are using Paint Shop Pro, which is an excellent image editor, you might find *Creating Paint Shop Pro Web Graphics,* by Andy Shafran (Muska & Lipman, ISBN 0-9662889-0-4), to be the perfect book for you—and much more readable at a mere 384 pages!

So far in this section, you've learned about the *kinds* of things that you might need to do to get your image files into shape. Now we'll look at *how* you might actually go about doing this. Before spending money for more software, look carefully at the software you currently own to see whether it can do what you need to do. Most graphics applications enable you to convert file types simply by using either File>Save As or File>Export. This makes saving a JPEG file as a BMP (or vice versa) easy. To change bit depth, you need to look for menu items such as Image>Size. Once you find the right menu item, you simply need to fill in the fields in a dialog box, like the one from Paint Shop Pro 6, shown in Figure 5.15. This is also the place to change image resolution.

Figure 5.15
Paint Shop Pro's Resize dialog box.

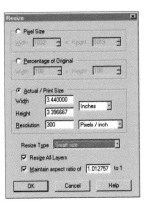

Changing bit depth is equally easy. Just look for a menu item that says something like Bit Depth or Image Mode and make the changes. If you are changing from a lossless format to a lossy format, you'll want to be able to see the relationship between file size and image quality. Many applications let you do this, but few do it as well as the Image Optimizer in Ulead's PhotoImpact 5.0. In Figure 5.16, you can see how the Image Optimizer enables you to compare the original image with the compressed image while viewing the exact file size and the amount of time that it will take to download, given a specified Internet connection speed. In the case of the bee image that is shown, the JPEG quality setting

Part II Transforming Images

reduces the 921,600KB file to 30,394KBs with very little discernable degradation of image quality. The Image Optimizer also enables you to save images in GIF and PNG formats.

Figure 5.16
Ulead's Image Optimizer enables you to view image quality and file size for different compression settings.

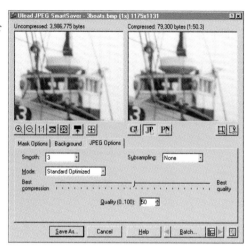

Using software to automate image correction

By now, you should have a good idea how you can use a digital image editor to fix an imperfect image. We have also looked at how a digital image file can be resized and saved to a different file format. In each of these cases, we have done all of the work manually, in a step-by-step fashion—visually checking and refining adjustments in each step. This process not only requires a good digital image editor and the skill to use it, it also takes time—often more time than we want to spend.

Once your image collection grows and you begin to use your images more frequently, you might find yourself with large quantities of images that you'd like to get into shape for a specific purpose. In the next two sections, we will look at two different approaches for getting your work done more easily and quickly. The first approach involves using software with pre-sets, and the second has to do with automatically processing an entire group of digital images.

Using software pre-sets

Once you use Streetwise Software's Professor Franklin's Instant Photo Effects, you will know how exceptionally easy enhancing your photos can be. This inexpensive, consumer-level product does wonders on digital images with ease—all through the very logical interface—which is shown in Figure 5.17.

Figure 5.17
Enhancing an image with Streetwise Software's Professor Franklin's Instant Photo Effects.

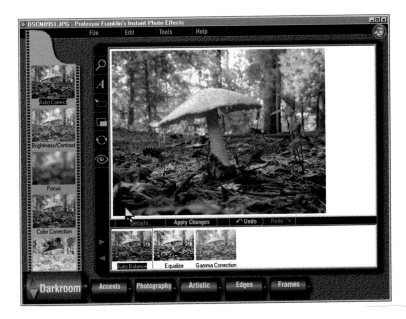

To correct the basic qualities of an image, you simply click on the Photography button at the bottom of the screen. You are then presented with five options on the left side of the window. These options are Auto Correct, Brightness/Contrast, Focus, Color Correction, and Negative. To adjust tonal range, for example, you select the Auto Correct mode, as shown in Figure 5.17. With a click on the pre-set Auto Balance, the tonal range is automatically adjusted. When you are happy with the image that you see in the preview window, click on the Apply Changes button, and you can then correct color by selecting the Color Correction mode. You are then presented with the options for adding more or less of each of the colors red, green, and blue. In each of these six cases, pre-set adjustments are used. If you want the image to be redder than it becomes after clicking on the Add Red button—click on it again. When the image looks like you want it to look, click on the Apply Changes button again.

That takes care of the image—now, how about the file? Instant Photo Effects offers a sophisticated Internet IntelliSave feature that not only enables you to change the file size but also offers a sliding scale that enables you to select the optimal level of compression—ranging from a low level of compression and better image quality to a higher compression and smaller file size. Figure 5.18 shows the IntelliSave dialog box, which shows a preview of the image quality and provides a Download Time Estimator so that you can see how long it will take to download the image at a chosen transfer rate. This is a good place to discover how important reducing file size is when posting to a Web page.

Figure 5.18
Instant Photo Effects' IntelliSave feature for optimizing files for the Internet.

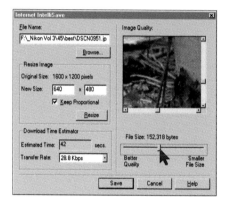

NOTE

A homebuilder needed to provide a progress report to the future homeowners, who lived overseas. Using an expensive digital camera, he took twenty images of the work done on the house and landscape. Some of the images were not as good as he had hoped. Using Professor Franklin's Photo Effects software, he was able to dramatically improve the quality of the images, as well as reduce their file size and change their file format to make them quicker to send via e-mail. The corrected images were sharper, with more tonal range, and the color was improved—all of which made his work look better.

At the opposite end of the spectrum, in terms of software cost and capabilities relative to Instant Photo Effects, is the extremely sophisticated Extensis' Intellihance Pro 4.0. This product is a *plug-in,* meaning that it runs inside another application—like Photoshop, Paint Shop Pro, or Corel PHOTO-PAINT. Intellihance offers more capabilities to fine-tune an image than any other application that I am aware of. You can use Intellihance Pro 4.0 in one of two modes—either as a manual tool, as shown in Figure 5.19, or as an automatic tool by using predefined or user-defined pre-sets, as shown in Figure 5.20. It even offers several pre-sets specifically for images created with a digital camera. If you are very visually oriented, you can elect to have the screen split into multiple windows, with each window showing a different adjustment for comparison purposes, as shown in Figure 5.21. The results with Intellihance are as good as they get, and you can work very quickly by using any one or more of a wide variety of pre-sets.

Figure 5.19
Intellihance Pro 4.0's manual image editing mode.

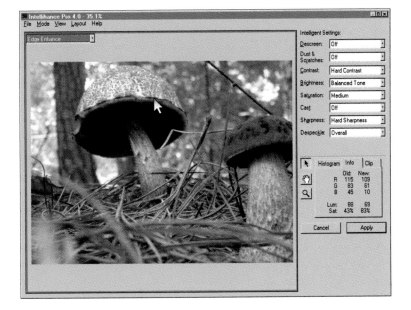

Part II Transforming Images

Figure 5.20
Intellihance Pro 4.0's
automatic image editing
mode.

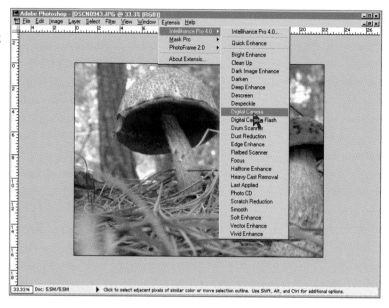

Figure 5.21
Intellihance Pro 4.0's
split-screen view.

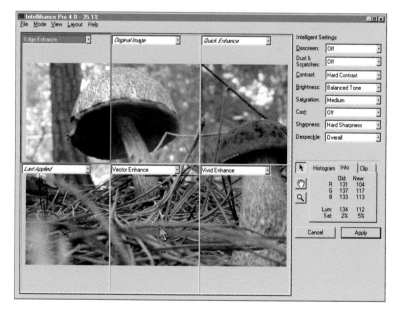

If you'd like to have some of Intellihance's capabilities, but you don't want to be buy Photoshop or another "Photoshop plug-in compatible" application, consider Auto F/X Corporation's AutoEye, which works with Photoshop as a plug-in or as a standalone product.

AutoEye examines and then automatically enhances digital images, providing full-spectrum color correction, increased color vibrancy, contrast and sharpness, and rebuilt detail. AutoEye enables you to work in one of two modes. In the manual mode, you can select from pre-sets and then manually fine-tune those adjustments. Alternatively, you can drag-and-drop a few files from your desktop onto the AutoEye icon and have the pre-selected pre-set enhancement be automatically applied to the images in batch-fashion. This is an excellent product to use to enhance digital images taken with a digital camera. Just be mindful that even with a product like AutoEye, you can make the images look only so good. Digital cameras that store images in a lossy format create images that will have some loss of detail that can't be fully restored. AutoEye will help make most of your images look better, more often than not with very little effort.

Batch processing

In the prior two sections, we looked at a number of applications that enable you to quickly enhance your images and to save them in an appropriate file—one image at a time. In this section, we will look at how you can use Photoshop 5.5 and Ulead's PhotoImpact 5 to batch process selected images automatically.

For example purposes, let's assume that we have a directory of forty images that were taken with a digital camera at a 1600×1200 resolution, and we want to put them on a Web page. We want to reduce all of the images to fit within a 640×640 pixel space, plus we want to digitally enhance each image before saving them as optimized JPEG files in a separate directory. If you had to do this to each of the forty images manually, you would surely go crazy—at least, I would.

With Photoshop 5.5, it is nearly as easy to perform the necessary steps on forty images as it is on a single image. From the Action dialog box shown in Figure 5.22, you click on the triangular arrow and select File>New Action and then type in the name of your Action. Actions are macros— they record all of the steps that you take until you turn the recording off. Once our action has been set up and the record facility is turned on, we perform all the necessary steps to complete the first image—then we turn off the Action recorder.

Figure 5.22
Using Photoshop 5.5's
Action recording
capability.

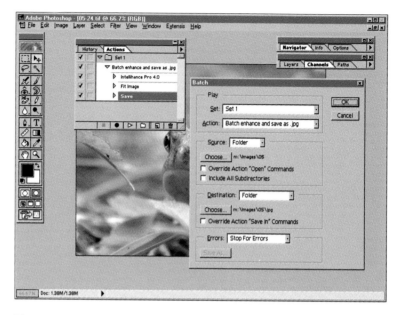

To run our new Action against the other thirty-nine images, we select
File>Automate>Batch to get the Batch dialog box shown in Figure 5.23.
In this dialog box, you select the Action that you want to use, the source
folder containing the original images, and the Destination folder in which
you want the enhanced images to be saved. To start the automatic
processing, you click on the OK button, and the software will do the
work for you—quickly and error-free!

If you work in a production environment, or you have the need to
process large numbers of digital images, there is no equal to the batch-
processing capabilities found in Photoshop 5.5. Not only can you apply
all of the actions that are found in Photoshop 5.5, but you can also apply
any of the actions that might be available with "plug-ins" such as
Intellihance Pro 4.0.

One other application (that costs hundreds of dollars less than Photoshop
5.5) that can help you do more with your images in less time is Ulead's
PhotoImpact 5. In order to accomplish our task of enhancing and
converting forty images for a Web page with Photo Impact 5, we would
have to run the PhotoImpact 5 Batch Manager three times—once for each
step. For example, to reduce each image to fit within a 640×640 pixel
space, we could use the Batch Manager to apply the Format>Dimension
command, as shown in Figure 5.23. Likewise, we would have to again
run the Batch Manager for the Format>Auto-Process command to enhance
the image.

Again, we would need to run a batch process to convert the images to an optimal JPEG compression level. For the conversion step, we would use the Batch Convert dialog box that is shown in Figure 5.24. Unlike the Batch Manager, which can perform actions only on files that are open in the workspace, Batch Convert enables you to select both a source folder and a destination folder. You can also select from a variety of JPEG compression pre-sets or define your own.

Figure 5.23
Using PhotoImpact 5's Batch Manager to change the dimensions of each image in the workspace.

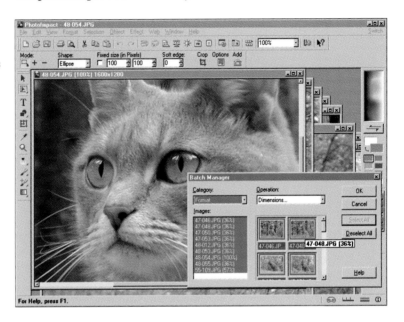

Figure 5.24
Using PhotoImpact 5's Batch Convert to convert a directory of images to JPEG images.

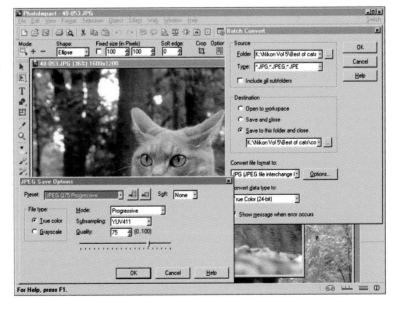

Until you find yourself needing to perform repetitive steps on many digital images, you might not see the value in the batch-processing capabilities discussed in this section. However, when you are faced with such a task, you will want Photoshop 5.5, PhotoImpact 5, or some software that can do the work for you error-free.

NOTE

A photographer who wants to post sixty digital images to a Web site needs to convert high-quality scans of his photographs into good "Web-quality" digital images. To accomplish the work, he needs to reduce file size, change image resolution, change bit depth, resize images, and convert them to the JPEG format with the best balance between file size and image quality for each individual image. To avoid making this a very tedious and time-consuming job, he uses the macro-recording feature in Photoshop 5.5 while he completes the first image. Then, with the batch–processing feature, he simply runs the macro against the selected directory of images and has the work all done automatically. The finished images are written to a second directory. The whole process took just a few minutes instead of hours, and with no errors.

Now that your images are in shape—that means both the actual image itself as well as the image file—you are ready to continue transforming your ordinary images into extraordinary ones. In Chapter 6, "Performing Digital Imaging Magic," you'll learn about many other ways to change your images from ordinary ones to extraordinary ones.

6

Performing Digital Imaging Magic

Welcome to the chapter on performing digital imaging magic. In this chapter, you will not learn how to pull a rabbit out of a hat, but you will learn how you can create a digital image of yourself pulling a rabbit out of a hat. Alternatively, you might want to show yourself pulling an elephant out of a hat, or maybe you want an image of a rabbit pulling you out of a hat! If that is not magic enough, then just wait. We'll also create three images that will leave you thinking that your imagination is the only limit to how you can transform digital images.

Just as a magician must learn the secrets of the trade, you must learn the secrets of digital imaging. To digitally edit an image, you must first have a digital image editor of one kind or another. Many software applications offer digital editing capabilities. Each one has strengths and limitations. Depending upon your skill level and your intended use, one application might be better for you than another. The goal, then, is to determine which product is best for you. To help you make this determination, we'll do three things in this chapter:

▶ Briefly look at four categories of digital image editing tools

▶ Learn eight of the more basic, yet powerful, digital image editing techniques, which will give you an excellent idea of what can be done to an image

▶ Complete all the necessary hands-on work to create three different images with three different image editors

After you finish this chapter, you not only should have significant insight into the magic of digital imaging but also a better idea of which application or applications will be most appropriate for your use. Most important, though, you'll learn what you can do to digitally transform your digital images.

Choosing a digital image editor

First, what is a *digital image editor?* Simply defined, it is a software application that enables you to edit a digital image on a pixel-by-pixel basis to enhance, alter, or transform it into the image that you want it to be. The number and kinds of things that can be done to an image, as you will see, are virtually endless. Most of this digital transformation occurs as a byproduct of running complex mathematical algorithms on the digital image.

One of the major differences between various applications for digitally manipulating images is the amount of control, or lack of control, they provide to the user. To some degree, the more control provided to the user, the more difficult the application can be to learn how to use. The corollary: Applications with less control are generally easier to learn how to use, but they are less capable of doing as much as those that provide more control. Thus, the tradeoff you must consider is the classic case of ease-of-use versus more powerful capabilities.

Let's now look at a few image editors. The following list should *not* be considered to be a complete list of competitive products, nor should it be viewed as a product evaluation or review—rather, it is a list of applications widely recognized to perform well and produce excellent results. The purpose of the list is to show the kinds of products that you can purchase and the wide range of features that these products offer. We'll review applications in the following four categories:

▶ Category I: Professional-level digital image editors

▶ Category II: Advanced consumer or business-use digital editors

▶ Category III: Consumer-level digital imaging applications

▶ Category IV: Professional-level plug-ins

Professional-level digital image editors

If you intend to become a master of illusion and create digital masterpieces, you need powerful tools as well as expertise. The three products in this first group offer you as much power as you will find in any product. These are the "best of the best."

Adobe's Photoshop 5.5

Photoshop is unquestionably the professional image editor's choice. It is the best of all the image editors. It is also the most expensive and the most difficult to learn how to use. Adobe assumes that Photoshop's users are professionals and, therefore, offers few presets for instant success. Expect both a steep learning curve and the best possible results from this product.

Adobe also offers Adobe Photoshop Limited Edition (Photoshop LE), a "lite" version with a street price of under $100. To learn more about this product and how it differs from Photoshop, visit the Adobe Web site at **www.adobe.com/products/photoshople/comparison.html**.

Corel's PHOTO-PAINT 9

PHOTO-PAINT 9 is a powerful image editing and painting application. It also comes with a media asset management tool, textures, 1,500 photos, 1,200 clip-art images, 1,500 floating objects, digital watermarking, morphing software, and more. Besides getting all of these extra goodies, PHOTO-PAINT 9 itself offers the most feature-rich editor in this category, with many presets that enable you to get good results—quickly.

MetaCreations' Painter 6

Painter 6 is known for its capability to faithfully capture the subtleties of an artist's brush strokes and translate them to print or the Web. Painter's Natural-Media digital technology faithfully recreates traditional artists' mediums in unlimited quantities, such as oils and acrylics, airbrushes, colored pencils, chalk, charcoals, crayons, and felt pens, combined with hundreds of papers, patterns, and textures. Additionally, it offers most of the capabilities found in Adobe's Photoshop, as well as techniques not offered by Photoshop. For those with a fine-art background, this tool will both amaze and please you unlike almost any other digital tool on the market. For some of the painting features, a digital tablet is desirable.

You might now wonder which of these three editors is right for you. If you have a limited budget, you might want to consider buying PHOTO-PAINT 9 or Painter 6, as Photoshop has a price around $600. PHOTO-PAINT 9 can be purchased for $300 and Painter 6 for about $400. If you are artistically inclined, Painter 6 is an excellent choice. PHOTO-PAINT 9 is a good mix of the two products. If cost is not a consideration, then get more than just one, as many professionals do.

Advanced consumer or business-use digital editors

This category of tools offers a mixture of the power of the more professional tools and the ease-of-use of the consumer tools. Each of these products offers strong Internet capabilities as well as standard digital image editing features. With a moderate amount of skill, you can achieve excellent results with little effort and in a short amount of time.

Jasc's Paint Shop Pro 6

Arguably one of the best values in terms of features for the money, Paint Shop Pro 6 is a complete solution for creating Web graphics and enhancing digital images. It also comes with an excellent animation tool and a good image browser. This is a good choice for almost any digital image-editing task, especially if the images will eventually be used on a Web page.

Part II Transforming Images

MGI Software's PhotoSuite III, Platinum Edition

A wide range of powerful features are accessible from an exceptionally clean interface with PhotoSuite III. It makes it easy to get, prepare, compose, organize, share, and print photos. Additionally, it offers image management, digital image stitching, and PhotoTapestry features, as well as the capability to create Web pages complete with thumbnails that contain links to full-size images.

Microsoft's PhotoDraw 2000

PhotoDraw combines powerful illustration and photo editing in one easy-to-use program that works like Microsoft Office. If you are not a graphic designer, and you know what you want to create, this project-oriented application might be perfect for you. It comes with more than 300 templates to help you get started quickly on business cards, logos, brochures, Web banners, and more.

Ulead Systems' PhotoImpact 5

PhotoImpact is far more than an image editor—it offers one of the most useful image album tools, Web graphics tools that are considered by some to be the best, and an extensive range of image editing capabilities. Web designers and business users will find the vast number of presets useful for getting projects completed speedily.

Consumer-level digital imaging applications

All five of the products in this category are both fun to use and very simple to use. The strength of this product group is that users do not have to understand fundamental image editing concepts. They just have to be able to follow logical steps and select the results that they want from automatically generated previews or presets.

MGI Software's PhotoSuite III, Platinum Edition

Unquestionably, PhotoSuite III is one of the most highly capable products in this category—so much so that it can be of tremendous use for advanced consumers and business users, as noted in the preceding section.

Streetwise Software's Professor Franklin's Instant Photo Artist

Photo Artist lets you select from one of many predetermined art styles and then paint right over your photos, enabling you to transform them into works of art. After you complete your painting, you can use templates to turn it into a greeting card, a T-shirt, an invitation, a flyer, or any other useful project. For the occasional artist, this is a cool product.

Streetwise Software's Professor Franklin's Instant Photo Effects

This is a wonderfully simple and capable product that produces excellent results. If you want a point-and-click application that does all the work for you, this is a good choice.

Ulead Photo Express Platinum 2000

What a bargain! You get an image cataloging tool, a calendar maker, a Web studio, more than 500 project templates, interactive 360-degree or wide-angle panorama capabilities, a photo assistant, and more than 6,000 graphic elements for your projects. A great interface makes this an excellent product and one that is easy to use.

Xaos Tools' FlashBox

With a little work, this innovative and unique product enables you to turn your digital photos into an endless variety of artistic creations that probably will be unlike work created with other products.

Professional-level plug-ins

A *plug-in* is an application that has been designed to work seamlessly with a helper application, such as Adobe's Photoshop. While most of the plug-ins have been designed to work with Photoshop, an increasing number of them also work with MetaCreations' Painter, Corel's PHOTO-PAINT, and Paint Shop Pro. There is also a trend to make these plug-ins work as standalone applications (in other words, without the help of an application such as Photoshop). If you are buying a plug-in, make sure that you understand what other applications (and specific versions) you might need to make them work properly.

Extensis PhotoFrame 2.0

This product enables you to interactively design border and edge effects in a multitude of combinations. A full-screen preview enables you to create great frames and excellent edges.

Extensis Intellihance Pro 4.0

Intellihance is a plug-in dedicated to image enhancement and color correction. With both automatic and manual controls, this product makes it as easy as possible to make your images look their best. It even offers special presets for digital cameras. You can fine-tune and compare different settings for fast, professional results by viewing up to twenty-five setting combinations or multi-pane previews simultaneously (see Figure 6.1). If you can't fix an image with this plug-in, it can't be fixed.

Part II Transforming Images

Figure 6.1
Multi-pane preview mode for comparing image enhancements in Intellihance Pro 4.0.

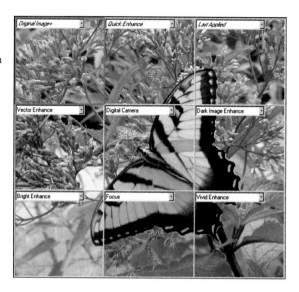

Extensis Mask Pro 4.0

Mask Pro enables you to remove with precision and ease almost any object from its background by using the Magic Brush, Magic Wand, Magic Pen, and Magic Fill tools (see Figure 6.2). Not only does this plug-in save an enormous amount of time, but it also produces cutout objects that will blend seamlessly into new backgrounds as if they were taken with the background picture. If you frequently need to cut out objects, and you use Photoshop, you must have this tool.

Figure 6.2
Using Extensis Mask Pro to remove a butterfly from its background.

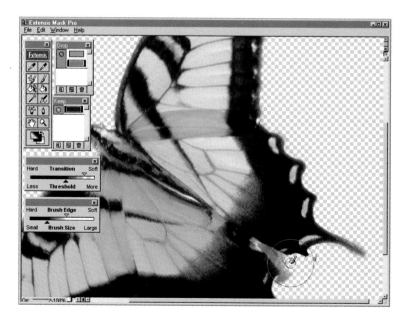

Right Hemisphere's Deep Paint

Although Deep Paint can be used as a standalone product, it was designed to complement Photoshop by adding artistic tools to Photoshop's powerful editing tools. This tool creates very distinctive work that is unlike work created by any other software, with the possible exception of MetaCreations' Painter 6.0. The Artistic Cloning feature enables you to transform digital images into rich oil paintings, delicate charcoals, or any one of many other media types. If you have artistic skills and a graphics tablet, you'll love this product.

Auto F/X AutoEye 1.0

This plug-in was designed to enhance and improve digital images. Significantly, it also can be used as a standalone product. Batch processing and drag-and-drop file launching capabilities make this an excellent product for production workflow.

Auto F/X Photo/Graphic Edges 4.0

Like AutoEye 1.0, this application works as a plug-in and as a standalone application. It creates awesome edge effects for images of any type. Multiple edge portfolios are available that contain thousands of edge effects. If you want edges on your images and you want the greatest control possible over your edge effects, this is the tool to use (see Figure 6.3).

Figure 6.3
Using Auto F/X
Photo/Graphic Edges 4.0
to create an edge effect.

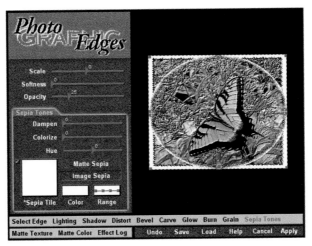

Part II Transforming Images

Alien Skin Software's Eye Candy 3.0

Eye Candy is one of the leading special effects plug-ins, with twenty-one special effects, including Fire, Smoke, Antimatter, Chrome, Carve, Cutout, Drop Shadow, and Bevel filters.

Alien Skin Software's Xenofex 1.0

Xenofex offers 16 time-saving special effects filters for print, Web, or multimedia projects. This tool helps you create lightning, clouds, and stains. Other unique effects include Stamper, Constellation, Crumple, Origami, Rounded Rectangle, and Shower Door.

MetaCreations' KPT5

Pretty-darn-cool tools! Kai's Power Tools 5 is a collection of plug-in applications that includes ten plug-in tools, in addition to the original eighteen KPT3 filters. If you are the creative type and want to do something different with your images, then get KPT5. See Chapter 7, "Filtering for Special Effects," to see some work that was created with a few of the KPT filters.

Xaos Tools' Total Xaos

A bundle of three designer plug-ins: Paint Alchemy, TypeCaster, and Terrazzo. Paint Alchemy transforms images into fine art, with more than one hundred preset paint effects, such as Colored Pencil, Impressionist, or Pastel. TypeCaster turns ordinary type into broadcast-quality 3D titles. Terrazzo creates symmetrical tiled backgrounds.

TIP

Purchasing any kind of graphics software can be expensive, and it's possible to buy something that either doesn't suit your needs or requires more skills than you have. To save money, consider the following.

Visit software vendors' Web sites, where you often find pre-release versions, or *beta* versions, which are available for download free of charge. You can use these programs to learn more about them and to determine whether they will enable you to do what you want to do. The vendors hope that you will report software "bugs" or problems that need to be fixed before the final version is released—it's a good policy for both vendors and prospective buyers. As an example, Jasc Software made a fully functioning beta version of Paint Shop Pro 6.0 available for download for several months on its Web site prior to the final release

Read upgrade policies carefully to see whether you can get a competitive product discount or if you can upgrade from another product from the same vendor. Some vendors provide a good discount for "switching" from a competitor's product to one of their own.

TIP *(continued)*

Some vendors allow you to download (or request a CD-ROM containing) full versions of their products that have been designed to work for a limited time. Other vendors allow you to use "crippled" versions of their products for as long as you want to use them. One of the more popular ways of crippling software is to provide fully working software that will not save files—a big problem if you want to put it to practical use rather than just learn all about it. Extensis is a good example of a vendor that makes all of its products available in fully functioning, time-limited trial versions, which you can obtain either on a single CD-ROM or by downloading them individually from its Web site.

If you want a good-quality product but feel that you won't use all the features that it offers, consider purchasing a "one version older" product. Corel generally makes several different versions of its products available at different price points. When Corel PHOTO-PAINT 9 became available, you could still buy one or two earlier versions for much less money. These older versions are also bundled with other applications and hardware and are considered "lite" versions that can be upgraded.

Visit one of the book superstores and check what software is offered on the companion CD-ROMs that often are included with various graphics books. This is a great way not only to get freeware, shareware, or trial versions of software, but often these CD-ROMs also give you extra goodies, such as photos, presets, or even a few fully functioning features that might be useful to you. Reading the books will also give you a good idea of what can be done with the software and how easy it might be to use.

Sign up for e-mail update subscription services from vendors that you like. You might be offered a good deal every now and then. MetaCreations made a special offer to its e-mail update service subscribers whereby they could get a free version of the newly released KPT-X plug-in, provided that they downloaded it by a certain date.

Never underestimate the value of some shareware software. If you find a product that you like and you use it, then make sure to honor the company's shareware policy by paying the small amount that it requests so that it continues to stay in business and create new products.

Check whether you have any "lite" applications that might have been bundled with hardware or software products. You can often upgrade these "lite" versions to the full product for considerably less money than if you were to purchase the new product without owning another version.

Visit auction Web sites, such as eBay, and discount software Web sites, such as Egghead, to find whether they offer discounted software or older release versions of products that you want. Often, you can find an older version of a product for very little money. This enables you to upgrade to the most current version for much less money than the regular price. Be careful when purchasing from Web sites, though, because not all sites offer legitimate software or software that can be upgraded.

A digital imaging techniques sampler

The previous section provided a quick overview of a wide selection of software products that offer a diverse range of features and capabilities for editing digital images. Now we'll get much more specific about what you can do with these products. In this section, you'll look at eight basic digital image-editing techniques and how they can be performed with Photoshop. While these techniques are demonstrated with Photoshop, please understand that any one of the other editors in Category I will produce equally good results—and always for less money. Applications in Category II and III will enable you to do some of these techniques with varying degrees of success, ranging from equally good to not possible. That is okay, though—we don't want everyone to be an equally magnificent digital imaging master, do we?

To demonstrate seven of the eight techniques, we'll use three images taken with a digital camera and combine them into a single image. For the background image, we'll use an image of two daylilies. This image has already been digitally enhanced to look like a fine-art print. We will also use two images of butterflies that were taken with a digital camera— but in different states! The intent is to combine these images in an interesting and unusual way.

Selecting things in an image

Our first technique, one of the most important, is to be able to select a specific thing or area in an image. Without being able to accurately select those things that we want to select, our magic would be severely limited.

To select an area, you must first select a tool. Photoshop offers the Marquee, Lasso, Polygon Lasso, and Magnetic Lasso tools, to name a few of its available selection tools. After you select a tool—in this case, I used the Magic Lasso tool—just drag the tool around the area that you want to select. If your settings are correct, the selection marquee (the line around the part of the image that you want to select) should snap onto the object that you want to select. It can be that easy, or it might take many adjustments and multiple tries. In Figure 6.4, the selection marquee shows that we have successfully selected the butterfly.

Figure 6.4
Using the Magnetic Lasso tool to select the butterfly.

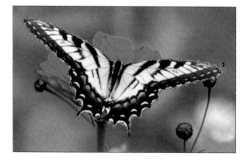

With Photoshop, you also can select by color or color range, invert selections, or use the Magic Wand. You can use the Pen tool and select by drawing a freehand or straight line, or you can use any one of many other methods. With a little skill and practice, you can select practically anything that you want to select with the exact level of precision necessary to meet your needs.

Adding things to an image

Now comes the fun part. Using the previous technique, we selected the butterfly in our first image. Before we open the background image consisting of two daylilies, we first need to copy the selection by choosing Edit>Copy. Now, we can open the daylily image and select Edit>Paste. The butterfly has now been copied onto the daylily image. That was so cool, let's do it again—five more times. Now we have two daylilies and six butterflies in the same image, as shown in Figure 6.5.

Figure 6.5
Daylily image with five added butterflies.

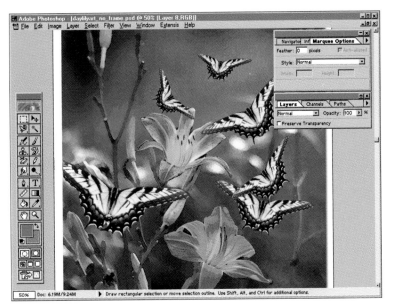

Transforming things

Some of you might have been impressed with the results of the previous three techniques, whereas others of you might have said, "That's cool, but the butterflies all look the same!" Therefore, we'll now learn how to transform things. Our image has two fundamental problems: the butterflies all look identical, and they all are exactly the same distance from us—that is, they are in the same plane. Nearly anyone can see this, and we must be concerned about our audience screaming out, "Image fraud!" and forever ruining our careers as practicing image editors.

The solution is easy. Click one of the butterflies, select Edit>Transform>Scale, and scale the butterfly to look as if it is flying at a distance further away from us than the first butterfly. Then, click another butterfly, select Edit>Transform>Rotate (see Figure 6.6), and rotate that butterfly until you are happy with it. Besides scaling and rotating, you also can use the Skew, Distort, and Perspective features to arrange your butterflies to look like they are part of the original image.

Figure 6.6
Transformation of the added butterflies.

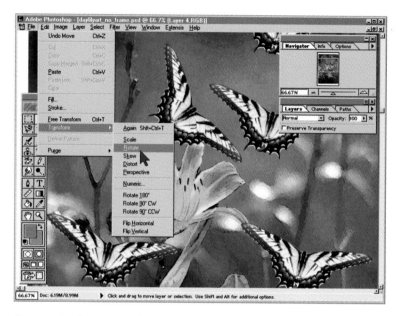

As promised, you now know all that you need to know to make a picture of yourself pulling a rabbit, or even an elephant, out of a hat. All you need is a picture of yourself holding a hat with one hand and have the other hand look like it is pulling something out of the hat. Find an image of a rabbit or elephant and select it; then, copy and paste it into the first image. Size, rotate, and transform the image as necessary. Presto—you are a magician pulling an elephant out of a hat!

Changing colors

Our image is looking good, isn't it? No? I thought we might still have a few skeptics among us. I agree. It would be unusual to have so many butterflies with exactly the same colors all clustered around two flowers. But we are qualified image editors, so let's change the colors of a few of those butterflies.

Select a few of the butterflies, one at a time, and select either Image>Adjust>Hue/Saturation, or Image>Adjust>Replace Color. Use the slider to adjust the colors to suit your taste. Because this is a magical image, I have chosen some rather magical colors, as shown in Figure 6.7.

Figure 6.7
Changing the colors of the butterflies with Adjust>Hue/Saturation.

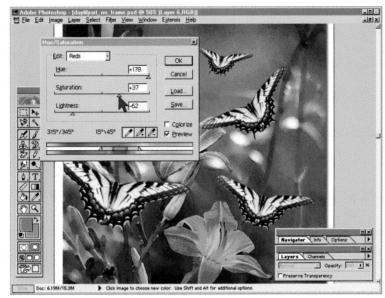

Layering things

Before the skeptics speak up again, let's quickly correct two other problems. If you look at Figure 6.8, you can see that one of the smaller butterflies actually appears closer than a larger butterfly, because one of its wings is on top of the larger butterfly. In addition, one butterfly appears to be further away than the flower size suggests, and yet it is covering part of the flower. We can fix both of these problems by using layers. Each time we added a butterfly, we added another *layer,* which can be likened to a transparent overlay sheet that can hold images. In the end, we have one background and five layers, with a newly added butterfly on each layer. You can see the layers by looking at the Layers dialog box in Figure 6.8. By clicking each of the two butterflies with overlapping wings, you can determine that they are in Layers 5 and 6. Layer 5 is in front of Layer 6—however, it should be behind it; just drag and drop the layer in the Layers box, and the smaller butterfly's wings will now be behind the larger butterfly's wings, just as if you had changed the order of a few transparent sheets containing images.

Part II Transforming Images

Figure 6.8
Using layers to correct image "order" problems.

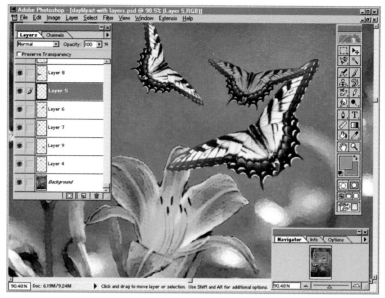

To fix the problem of the flower being covered by the wing that appears to be behind the flower, we have to select a part of the flower, copy it, and then paste it as a copy into the image at exactly the same place. We can now order the layers and have the flower correctly cover the wing of the butterfly. After you have the layer order correct, you can go back and move all the butterflies around until you get them where you want them.

Painting with an image

Our image showing two daylilies and five butterflies is looking good—but what do you think about adding another daylily? There is room for one in the lower-right corner of the image. We can actually paint another one simply by using a clone tool called the Rubber Stamp. Before we use the Rubber Stamp tool, let's create a blank layer for the new flower. To get started on the new flower, first pick a place on the image that you want to copy from—in this case, we'll pick the leftmost petal of the deep-orange daylily. Then, select the new layer from the Layers dialog box and start painting. After we paint the flower and some of the surrounding background, we can once again go to our transformation tools and make this flower look different from the one we copied. This flower looks good just as it is, so we'll rotate it just a little and slide it into the bottom-right corner of the image, as shown in Figure 6.9. You'd never know that the third flower was a copy, would you? That is why this chapter is titled "Performing Digital Imaging Magic"—it's as good as magic!

Figure 6.9
Adding a third daylily
with the Rubber Stamp
tool.

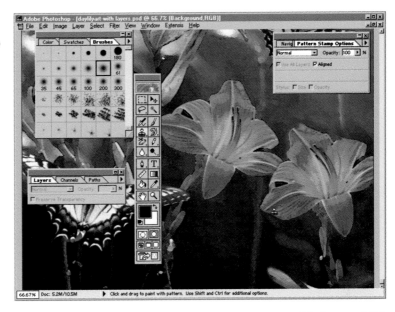

Part II Transforming Images

As one final step, to add a little genetic diversity, I added one additional
butterfly that I cut out as an example of using Extensis Mask Pro, as
shown in Figure 6.2. I also scaled and rotated it just a bit to make it fit
where I thought it should be. The image is now complete, as shown in
Figure 6.10.

Figure 6.10
The completed image.

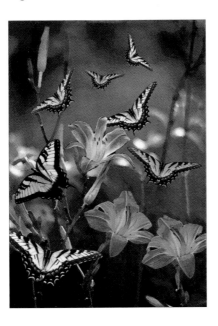

Removing things from an image

In the previous technique, we did quite a bit of adding to images—not removing. Often, however, you need to remove something that is already in an image. Depending on your intentions, there are many ways to remove things. In Chapter 5, "Getting Images into Shape," the downtown Chapel Hill image had some unwanted stoplights and wires. If you recall, we used the Rubber Stamp tool to paint parts of the sky over the stoplights and wires to remove them. In other cases, you can cut and paste one image over the part of the image that you don't want, which effectively removes the part you don't want.

NOTE

One of the better-known and often-used image magic techniques is to paste a new spouse over the top of an ex-spouse to fix an otherwise perfect family photo. You might think that I'm kidding, but I'm not—this is done quite often.

On a more serious note, by using a combination of the techniques already discussed, you can add to a family picture those family members who weren't able to attend a family get-together. It is also fun to add your favorite TV star, sports hero, or politician to an image containing yourself or someone else that you choose. Just be careful which politician you choose to pose with!

Using masks

At this point, this eighth and final technique might not seem particularly useful to you. However, Chapter 7, "Filtering for Special Effects," will make this one of your most used techniques. Masks enable you to do exactly what their name sounds like they do—mask certain parts of an image, which enables you to perform your magic on the rest of the image. Because you can use a wide range of selection techniques to create the masks, you can end up with masks that enable you to perform some awesome feats. Masks also enable you to create vignettes, such as the one shown in Figure 6.11.

Figure 6.11
A vignette created with
a mask.

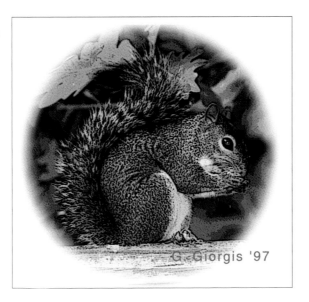

NOTE

A housewife who had successfully published several cookbooks decided to
illustrate her next cookbook herself. Using several inexpensive digital image
editing tools on digital images that she had taken with a digital camera, she
created high-quality images for her cookbook. To complete the images, she
applied several filters that transformed them into distinctive images for her
cookbook. Besides saving the cost of an artist and photographer, she
completed the book sooner and all by herself. To help sell her books, she is
now planning to make some of the recipes, complete with images, available
on a Web site, which is easy to do with her current software.

Creating magical images

In the previous section, we looked at eight of the more important ways
that we can digitally edit an image. In each of these cases, we used one of
the most sophisticated digital editors on the market—Adobe's Photoshop.
To see the difference between the professional products that require
considerable skill and the consumer-level products, we will now perform
our digital magic on three images by using less-expensive image editors
that offer presets for instant success.

Part II Transforming Images

Putting up the rainbow

To get our soccer goalie to "put up the rainbow," we will use Paint Shop Pro 6.0. First, we need to select the goalie from one image, by using one of several available selection tools, as shown in Figure 6.12. After opening the background image, we can copy and paste the goalie into the open image (see Figure 6.13). After the goalie is sized correctly and properly positioned, we can then remove part of the rainbow with a Clone Brush by copying part of the sky just slightly next to the part covered with a rainbow (see Figure 6.14). After these few steps are done, our image will be complete, as shown in Figure 6.15.

Figure 6.12
Using Paint Shop Pro to select the keeper.

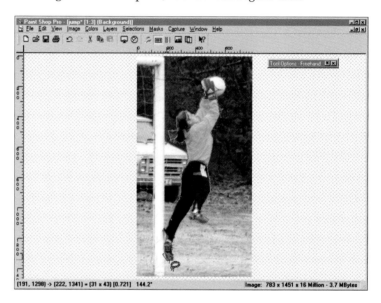

Figure 6.13
Soccer goalie pasted in image at original size.

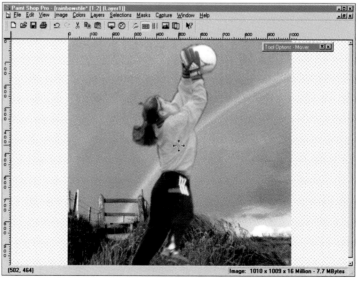

Figure 6.14
Removing part of the
rainbow with the Clone
Brush tool.

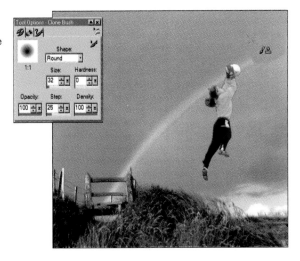

Figure 6.15
The completed image.

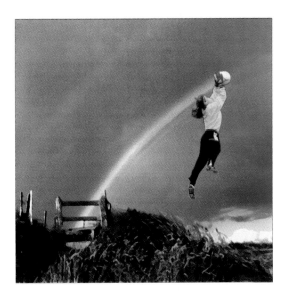

Part II Transforming Images

Paint Shop Pro 6.0 makes creating this image easy, assuming that you
have an understanding of some of the fundamental concepts of digital
image editing. If you don't have this understanding, there are even easier
products to use, as is demonstrated when we create the next magical
image.

The mushroom garden adventure

The daylilies and butterfly image that we created earlier in the chapter required that we be able to select objects, layer them, and transform them into the appropriate size. In this example, we'll do similar things, only this time, we'll use MGI's PhotoSuite III, and we'll create a fun image instead of a fine-art image. This product differs significantly from Photoshop and Paint Shop Pro. Notice particularly how PhotoSuite III has been designed to make it easy to complete this image without having any understanding of digital imaging concepts.

Figure 6.16 shows how we were able to select and copy the image of a boy to be used in our image. On the left side of the application is a list of the steps and a button to click when each step is completed. There is even a Reset button for those of us who have to restart occasionally. We did the same thing to get a butterfly—every image needs a butterfly! After we select, copy, and paste the boy and the butterfly, we need to resize (see Figure 6.17) and position them where they should be.

Figure 6.16
Using MGI's PhotoSuite III to select and copy the boy.

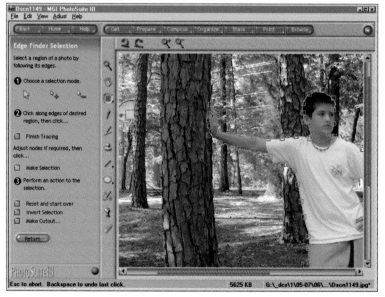

Figure 6.17
Resizing the boy.

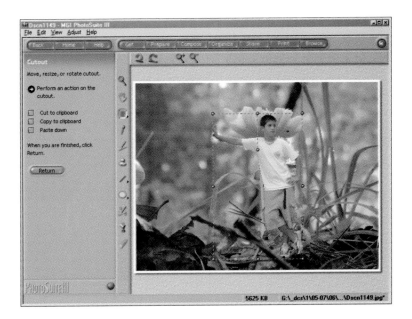

To add a little humor to the image, we can now insert a few of the props that come with PhotoSuite III. We can add a green hat, a shovel, and a soccer ball, as well as a text bubble for adding text. After throwing in one cat face for good measure, we end up with the image shown in Figure 6.18.

Figure 6.18
The completed image.

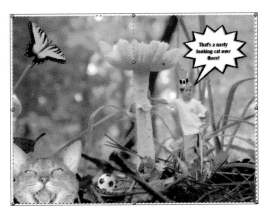

PhotoSuite III is a very good example of how you can accomplish some of the same things that we did in an earlier example with Photoshop. With PhotoSuite III, all the steps were obvious, because there was always a step-by-step process laid out in the left sidebar, which makes it very easy to use. With Photoshop, you have no guidance—you simply must know what you are doing.

Part II Transforming Images

Adjusting light in the North Sea

In this example, we'll get a firsthand look at the value of using presets to change colors. The image shown in the PhotoImpact 5.0 screen in Figure 6.19 is the North Sea with an unusually warm golden glow. Double-clicking the Twilight color adjustment button on the EasyPalette instantly changes the colors to the more dramatic twilight colors shown in Figure 6.20. Alternatively, we can double-click in the EasyPalette, as before, but this time choose from the Season menu and select Spring, producing the results shown in Figure 6.21.

Figure 6.19
Original North Sea image.

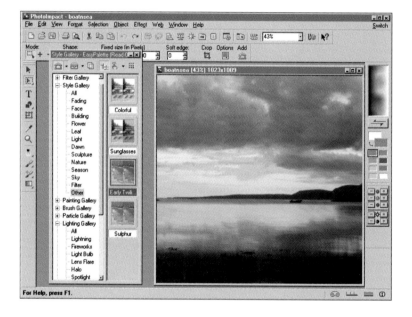

Figure 6.20
North Sea in early twilight.

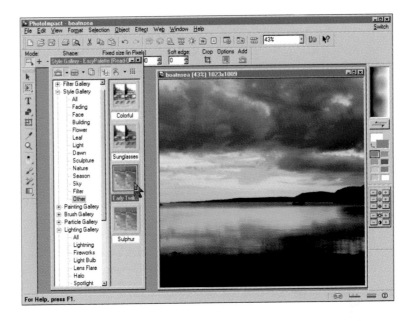

Figure 6.21
North Sea in Spring.

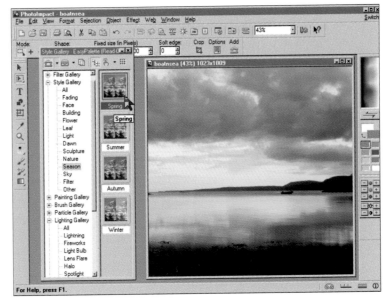

Part II Transforming Images

These are just two of the many presets in PhotoImpact which enable you to make major or subtle changes in an image with a single mouse click. To see a more dramatic change, you can use presets to change a red flower to a blue flower, or you can use one of the Face presets like Sunburned, Heavy Tan, Pale, or even Green to dramatically change the look of a face. These presets might look simple, but if you had to select multiple colors and make the changes yourself in an application such as Photoshop or PHOTO-PAINT, you'd appreciate their value. On the other hand, if you understand the fundamentals of digital colors and how to use selection tools and masks, you can do much more than what is available with just those presets. It's a tradeoff between power and ease of use.

We have now reached the end of this chapter. I hope you enjoyed getting an inside look at what digital image magicians feel is proprietary knowledge. Now, when you look at the images on music CD covers, glossy magazine advertisements, or book covers, you'll be able to see how the feats were performed. Digital imaging brings a completely new meaning to the notion of "trick photography."

In the next chapter, "Filtering for Special Effects," we'll use the techniques we learned in this chapter to create exciting images that begin to look less like photographs and more like works of art or graphics.

7

Filtering for Special Effects

Applying filters to digital images can be one of the most fun and rewarding parts of image editing. An image that was once boring and unspectacular can instantly become fascinating and spectacular. The nearly perfect landscape image with a truly awful sky can suddenly be made into a prized image by selecting just the sky and applying the appropriate filter to it. Applying multiple filters to an ordinary image can transform it into an absorbing, dreamlike image that can entrance the viewer.

Filters can be used to transform a single digital image into an endless variety of entirely different images. The transformed images can look like fine art or like a surreal image from a place that doesn't exist on Earth. Filters can turn a photographic image into a line drawing, transform an okay-looking image into a stunning image, help an image not suitable for the Internet become a perfectly suitable one, or make a black-and-white engraving from a color photo. Filters can add a shadow to an image to make it look more realistic, or they can be used to add fur, lightning, smoke, reflective spheres, and fire where they previously did not exist.

Though they might seem like magic, filters are simply software tools that make it possible for you to apply highly complex mathematics to the digital representation of a picture so that it can be transformed into the image that you want. In this chapter, we will look both at what you can do with filters and at the software that enables you to apply filters to your images.

Part II Transforming Images

What can you do with filters?

First, what is a filter?

In many ways, digital image filters are similar to the glass filters that photographers have used on their camera lenses for decades. The most common traditional glass filter is the skylight filter, which is a protective and UV-absorbing filter that absorbs a significant amount of UV light and also adds a slightly warm tint for better colors. If you have a 35mm camera with a removable lens, you are quite likely to have one. Another common glass filter is the polarizing filter, which helps you to catch a rainbow, enhance subtle clouds in the sky, and reduce reflection and unwanted bright spots on an image. In addition to these two filters, there are many other special effects filters, such as star filters, fog filters, sepia filters, color-graduated filters, color-conversion filters, warming and enhancing filters, and color-compensating filters. Each of these filters is used to make a photograph look more like reality, less like reality, or otherwise alter its appearance.

Photographers who develop their own film in a darkroom have even more opportunities to make a print look different from the negative or the original subject during film processing and printing. They can dodge, burn, control contrast, and intensify color, to name just a few of the many techniques available to them. With digital filters, you can do almost everything that can be done with glass filters *and* with darkroom techniques—plus much, much more!

A "before" and "after" image sampler

Before we begin looking at filter software, let's look at four sets of "before" and "after" images so that we can see first-hand how an image can be changed with the application of one or more filters. Then, we will look at ten additional things that can be done with filters. Figure 7.1 shows an image of an old automobile parked in a garage. The picture was taken with a digital camera and then slightly enhanced to make the colors richer and the image sharper before a final filter was applied.

To make the image look a little more exciting and eerie, a single filter was applied to create the light reflections that are shown in Figure 7.2. You might think that it wasn't that easy—but it was. It was just a matter of selecting the filter and applying it with two mouse clicks. The whole process took under five seconds to complete.

Figure 7.1
Original "old car in a garage" image created with a digital camera.

Figure 7.2
"Old car in a garage" image after a lighting filter was applied.

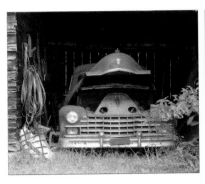
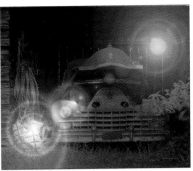

Now let's see how we can take another "not very good" image and make it interesting enough to use as a base image for a Christmas card. The original image shown in Figure 7.3 is an unexciting picture that very definitely would not make a very attractive Christmas card. Once again, we are going to transform this image with two clicks of a mouse. Select a filter and click the Apply button. The result is the image shown in Figure 7.4. With a few Christmas objects placed in the image, it will make a superb card for the holidays. There is even plenty of room for a greeting at the bottom of the picture.

Figure 7.3
Unexciting "before" image of a house.

Figure 7.4
House image after an ink-drawing filter was applied.

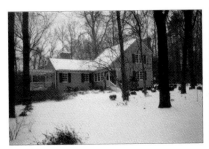
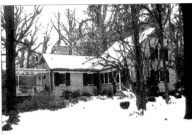

Part II Transforming Images

Now imagine that you need a dozen images for use on the front page of each of twelve chapters in a cookbook that you are writing. All you'll need is some time to arrange a few items on your kitchen counter and a few shots with a digital camera. Figure 7.5 shows one such image of a collection of cooking oil bottles.

After two mouse clicks to select and apply a watercolor filter, you now have the image that is shown in Figure 7.6. Ah, the magic of filters! With the success you've had with this one, aren't you curious to see how a similar image showing a few red, yellow, and green bell peppers would turn out? You might also be able to take a picture of your cook-top showing multiple pots and a skillet with steam rising from one or two of them. Using the same watercolor filter, you can very quickly create the dozen images that you need all in a similar style. As you can see, you can create a dozen high-quality images suitable for printing in just a few hours and with as few as twenty-four mouse clicks to apply the filters. Now imagine what you would have to go through without a digital camera and the magic of filters to get a dozen good images!

Figure 7.5
"Before" image of cooking oils taken with a digital camera.

Figure 7.6
Cooking oil image after a watercolor filter was applied.

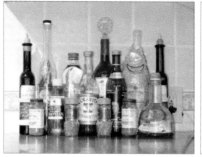 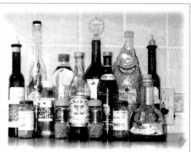

Filters can be wonderful tools to alter the look of an image. They also can be used for other important purposes, which we will discuss later in this chapter. For our fourth and final image, we are going to apply several filters after we have doubled the image size, which is well beyond the point where it will look acceptable. If you have ever enlarged a digital image, you understand how it can get grainy, fuzzy, out of focus, and suffer from the "jaggies." Our goal in this case is to digitally enlarge our original image and then apply a few filters to the enlarged image so that it looks good enough to print, frame, and hang on a wall.

Figure 7.7 shows the original image of a horse and rider jumping a hurdle. Using one of the techniques covered in Chapter 5, "Getting Images into Shape," we will now enlarge the image with an image editor. After it has been enlarged, it will suffer from the "jaggies," as we expected. To improve the quality of the image, in this case we will apply two filters that will once again make it into a print that is suitable for framing. For this specific example, we will apply the Gaussian Blur and then the

Poster Edges filter to the enlarged image. The colors will also need to be adjusted to eliminate the washed-out look caused by doubling the size of the image. The final image, which is shown in Figure 7.8, does not look like a photograph any more. However, it will make an excellent print that is considerably larger than the original—and that was our intent.

Figure 7.7
Original image of a horse and rider jumping a hurdle.

Figure 7.8
Results of applying several filters to an enlarged copy of the image shown in Figure 7.7.

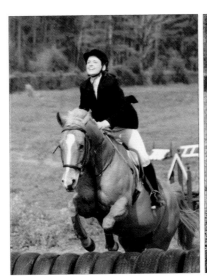 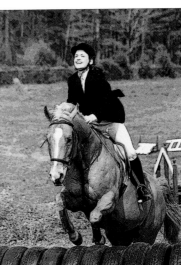

Learning more about what filters can do

We have just looked at four sets of "before" and "after" images to see how filters can change an image. In this section, we'll look at ten additional things that you can do with filters.

Filtering just for the fun of it

At the top of the list of things that you can do with filters is to have fun using them. Those who really enjoy doing what they do—do it better! If you have the luxury of digitally editing images just for the fun of it—then do it. This is the best way to learn how to use filters and explore their possibilities so that you can do what you need to do when you have a specific project to complete. When you have the time, find five to ten images that you like and spend a few hours trying as many filters on them as possible. Try sequentially applying multiple filters on the same image. Adjust and readjust the settings for your filters until you begin to understand how they work and what kinds of images they work best with. You'll be surprised to see how certain filters combine to produce truly amazing (and some not-so-amazing) results.

Part II Transforming Images

Figure 7.9 shows one variation of a "just for the fun of it" image that was made by applying multiple filters. In fact, seven PhotoImpact 5 filters were applied, including one that created the stars and another that made the fancy frame to fit the image. Check out those frame colors—don't you think they fit the colors of the butterfly image perfectly? You might not like this image, but it sure was fun to create, and I know much more about each filter now that I have used them. It is now your turn to create a few images just for the fun of it.

Figure 7.9
Just-for-the-fun-of-it image created with seven PhotoImpact 5 filters.

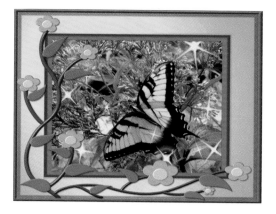

Making an image look better

One of the most common expectations of using filters is that they will make images look better. This is a reasonable expectation, and there are hundreds of filters on the market that will help you improve the look of your images. Easy-to-make improvements include heightening contrast between highlights and shadows, sharpening image focus, and adjusting image brightness. In particular, images taken with many digital cameras can be improved considerably with one of the many varieties of sharpen filters, which help bring images into sharper focus.

Blur, Sharpen, Dust & Scratches, Sharpen More, Sharpen Edges, Auto-level, and Auto-Contrast are just a few of the many powerful image-fixing filters that Photoshop offers to improve the overall appearance of an image. The Darkroom filter category in Professor Franklin's Instant Photo Effects includes single-click filters for Auto Correct, Brightness/Contrast, and Focus. When you begin using these filters or others like them, you'll love seeing how much they can improve almost any image with just a few mouse clicks.

Changing colors in an image

Being able to change colors in an image is another common capability of filters. Filters are available that enable you to change colors in just about any imaginable way. Most of the more powerful high-end image editing applications offer a filter that is similar to the one shown in Figure 7.10. By using the sliders, you can change the color balance of the entire image—or you can individually or in combination change colors in shadows, midtones, or highlights.

Figure 7.10
Corel PHOTO-PAINT 9's Color Balance filter.

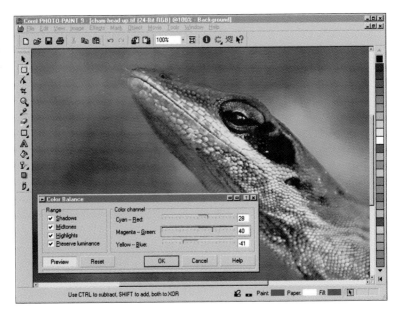

Other filters enable you to change the hue or saturation of a particular color. For example, you can change a red rose into a yellow rose or increase the saturation of the color green in an image to make it look more like a summer image than a soon-to-be winter image. Using an Eyedropper tool, you can even select small parts of an image and change those colors to any color that you want. You might recall that we used this capability in the last chapter to change the color in a butterfly's wings.

Most of the consumer-level products do not give you the fine-detail control that you get with the professional products, but you can still change the color in your images in many ways. Consumer products typically give you color controls such as "more red," "more green," or "less blue." The more times you click these features, the more they apply the same filter, resulting in more or less of the chosen color. You'll also find options for creating *duotones* (an image composed of only two colors) or antiques that not only will change all the colors in an image to sepia tones but also will often add spots, tears, and other signs of old age, as shown in Figure 7.11.

Part II Transforming Images

Figure 7.11
Turning a color photo into an antique print with Instant Photo Effects.

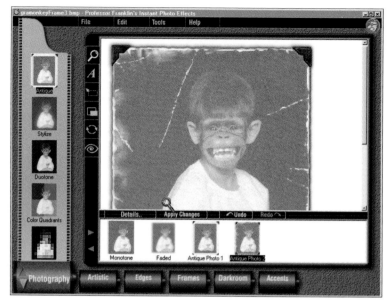

Making an image look like it was painted

In recent years, computers have become powerful enough to quickly perform numerous mathematical computations and enable software developers to offer natural-media painting tools and filters. Several programs allow fine artists to paint with digital paintbrushes, pens, pencils, chalk, or even an airbrush. To create works of art, you must have some artistic skills to use these tools successfully. The best of these real-time painting applications are MetaCreations Painter 6 and Right Hemisphere's Deep Paint.

For those who don't have the time or artistic talent, software developers have created filters that can take a photographic image and turn it into an art-like image with a few mouse clicks. The first thing you will find out about these paint filters, however, is that there are two kinds:

▶ Those that are named after one of the natural-media techniques but don't produce results that look like the intended medium.

▶ Those that are named after a natural-media technique and do create an image that looks like the intended medium.

Sadly, more paint filters fall into the first category than into the second. However, many filters that have a natural-media name can still create an excellent image even though the filter bears little or no resemblance to its natural-media namesake. A good example of this is one of the many filters named "watercolor" that was applied to the image shown in Figure 7.12. Even after a watercolor edge filter was applied, the image bears little resemblance to a real watercolor painting. However, when it is printed on watercolor paper, it makes a fine piece of artwork.

Figure 7.12
A fine-art image
created with a
watercolor filter.

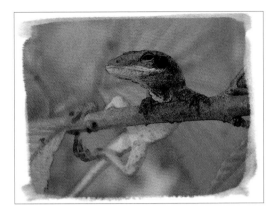

Besides using a single-click art-like filter to instantly create a watercolor painting, you also can apply a variety of filters to get an even better result. Just as learning how to paint a watercolor painting with watercolors and a brush takes time, learning how to create an unusually good digital watercolor painting with filters also takes time.

To make a print that truly looks like a watercolor, you need to begin with a digital image that has certain characteristics. You then need to learn which filters to apply to the image to get it ready for your chosen effect and filter. As a final step, after you have carefully chosen the best watercolor settings and have applied the watercolor filter, you might want to apply one or two more filters or adjust the color saturation before your image will be complete. With experimentation, you can create exceptionally good results, especially when you print your work on real watercolor paper that has been created specifically for an inkjet printer. Chapter 13, "Turning Digital Images into Prints," covers the topic of printers and paper in more detail.

NOTE

After taking a family vacation in Europe, a family decided to create a set of watercolor paintings from some of the photographs that they took. Each member of the family selected two of favorite photographs and transformed them into watercolor-like images.

The set of ten watercolor images was then printed on watercolor paper on their home inkjet printer, framed, and hung on the walls of their home. Over the years, these prints are likely to become a family treasure. The best part about having the digital images is that when the children grow up and leave home, they will be able to easily print another set for themselves to be used as artwork in their own homes.

Part II Transforming Images

Distorting an image

In addition to the filters that are available for fixing or improving images, there are a tremendous number of filters for distorting images. For example, PHOTO-PAINT 9 offers ten filters under the Distort menu. The filters are Blocks, Displace, Mesh Warp, Offset, Pixelate, Ripple, Shear, Swirl, Tile, and Wet Paint. There are also filters that enable you to change the perspective in your image and apply 3D effects. Additional image distortion techniques include Pinch, Punch, Sphere, Zigzag, and Boss.

Many of these image-distortion filters might not seem useful to you now, but as your skills develop and as you begin doing extensive work on your images, you'll find some of them to be immensely valuable—or at least fun and entertaining.

Adding things to an image

All filters do not simply alter what is already in the image. Some filters actually add things to an image. Later in the chapter, you'll learn about filters that create fire, fur, lightning, and other things that you would not imagine being able to create with a few mouse clicks. Figure 7.13 shows a particularly well-executed filter that creates bubbles. The bubbles even reflect the environment of the English countryside at sunset. After the bubbles were added, a second filter was applied to make the entire image look more like a painting than a photograph.

Figure 7.13
Reflective bubbles added with a Ulead PhotoImpact 5 filter.

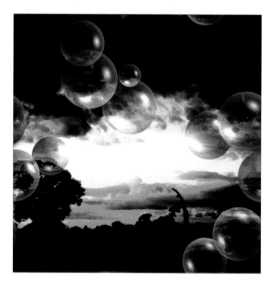

Creating a background image

One of the significant advantages of being able to digitally edit images is that you can put your subjects into the background that you want. When taking a picture with a camera, have you not often thought that the subject was perfect—but the background could be better? After you begin editing your images, you will enjoy having the option of selecting your subjects and carefully placing them into a new background image of your choice.

For some projects, you might just want to create your own background image from scratch. One of my favorite filters for creating background images is MetaCreations KPT 5. Figure 7.14 shows a picture of a youth lacrosse player that was placed on top of an image that was created with KPT 5. After the background image was created, a second filter was applied to smear the clean lines of the original KPT 5 filter. The ability to create your own backgrounds enables you to save lots of time, because you won't have to find an image for or shoot a picture of a background—just create your own and complete your project.

Figure 7.14
This interesting background was created in MetaCreations KPT 5.

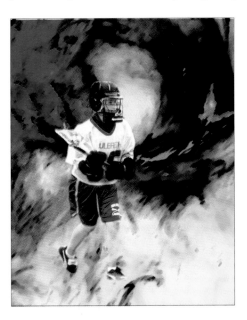

Part II Transforming Images

Transforming a photographic image into graphic art

Some of the filters that can be used to transform a photographic image into graphic art have names like Poster Edges, Poster, Posterize, Cutout, Emboss, and Etching. These filters typically reduce the number of colors and the detail in an image. Figure 7.15 shows an image that was turned into graphic art to be transferred onto a cotton T-shirt. The soccer player was digitally cut from an image that was made from a scanned photograph. She was then pasted into a background image that was created in KPT 5, and the entire image was framed with a frame filter. Finally, a Poster Edge filter was applied after the image was changed to a duotone image to produce the final graphic image. The rich dark-brown color of this graphic image looked terrific on a white cotton T-shirt.

Figure 7.15
A graphic art image created with multiple filters.

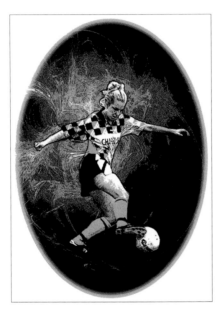

Many of the graphic-art-style filters reduce the total number of colors in an image—this makes them good for use on Web pages, because the file size becomes relatively small and, therefore, will download faster than a comparable photographic-quality image.

Framing an image

After you complete an image, you might want to consider using one of the many frame filters that are available. You'll find frame filters included with many image editors and most consumer-level photography applications plus a few that are "plug-ins" or stand-alone filter applications. Framing images has become very popular, and rightly so. They can make your images look much better, whether they ultimately will be displayed on a Web page, in printed form, or on a computer screen.

There are many variations of frame filters. Some produce good-looking results by creating a rough edge all around the image—the edge might look like brush strokes, torn paper, or even something stranger, such as computer paper or a roll of camera film. Other filters enable you to pick up and merge the colors from your image, such as the one shown in Figure 7.16. The Ulead products even enable you to add frames that look like real wood, plastic, or metal frames, such as you can buy in a frame shop.

Figure 7.16
Frog image framed with an Auto F/X Photo/Graphic Edges filter.

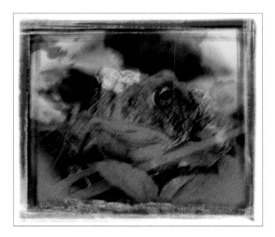

Adding special effects to an image

Now we come to special effects filters. What makes one filter a *special effects* filter and another one just a filter is not clear to me—I think most of them are special, especially when I consider the mathematics behind them! For our purposes, we'll consider any filter that can do something relatively exotic a "special effects" filter.

A few examples of special effects filters include Fragment, Mosaic, Clouds, Lens Flare, Emboss, Electrify, Origami, Puzzle, Motion Trial, Squint, and Star. There are lots more, but you ought to get the idea of what this basic set can do, as their names are indicative of the results that they produce.

Using applications with filter effects

The growth of the digital camera and imaging market has helped fuel the growth of applications that offer filter effects. You can even find Web sites that will apply filters to your images free of charge. Even though there are many available filters, they do vary greatly in three ways. Depending on your skill level and the projects that you want to complete, you should consider the following three items when evaluating filters:

▶ **Ability to control settings**—Some filters are single-click filters, whereas others offer one or more controls that enable you to fine-tune the filter to get results that more closely match your intent.

▶ **Effectiveness of the application's user interface**—If you work on projects such as Web sites or slide shows and need to apply filters to twenty or more images, the ease of accomplishing your task will be important. Some applications offer macro capabilities and are easy to use; others simply make you work hard.

▶ **Output image quality**—The most important aspect of a filter is the quality of output. Some applications or plug-ins offer many filters that simply do not produce output that is very useable. When choosing filter tools, look for filter sets that produce results that match your requirements.

In the next section, we will quickly look at a variety of tools—either applications that offer filters or filter plug-ins. This overview is not intended to be a complete list of filter tools; rather, it provides you with an excellent idea of the kinds of tools that are available.

Adobe Photoshop 5.5 filters

Photoshop has earned its reputation as being the premier image editing tool by featuring a full range of capabilities that help you to efficiently achieve the finest-quality output for Web, print, or online use. Depending on exactly which Photoshop features are counted as filters, there are around ninety-five of them! Photoshop's Help features a Filter Sample Gallery, which categorizes all the Photoshop filters into general categories, including Artistic, Blur, Brush Strokes, Distort, Noise, Pixelate, Render, Sharpen, Sketch, Stylize, Texture, Other Filters, and Digimarc Filters. If you want good filters along with the best image editor, this is the application to get.

TIP

Adobe offers a "lite" version of Photoshop called Adobe Photoshop Limited Edition (Photoshop LE), which is less than one-fifth the cost of the full version. If you want the superb filters offered in Photoshop and a host application to run Photoshop plug-ins, then you can save money by buying Photoshop LE. To learn more about which version is right for you, read a product comparison on the Adobe Web site at:

www.adobe.com/products/photoshople/comparison.html

You can also download a free Photoshop 5.5 product tryout from the Adobe Web site, if you want to try the full version.

Broderbund's The Print Shop

Even though The Print Shop is a consumer-level product, it offers a considerable number of filters that can create fabulous images. If you are interested in a desktop publishing application and an image editor, The Print Shop range of products is a good choice. One of my favorite images ever is one that I created with a filter in the Photo Pro module contained in The Print Shop. The picture, which was taken in a small, abandoned Wyoming town, shows an old car and a suitcase. Figure 7.17 shows the Antique filter being applied to the image in The Print Shop Photo Pro application.

Figure 7.17
The Print Shop Photo Pro being used to create a fine-art image.

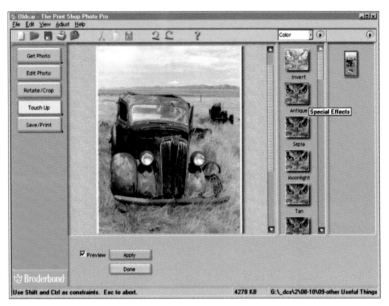

Part II Transforming Images

Corel Corporation's PHOTO-PAINT 9

My bet is that PHOTO-PAINT 9 offers more filters than any other image editing application (with the possible exception of PhotoImpact 5). It offers so many filters that I would not want to have to count them. The Effects menu alone offers sixteen categories of filter effects. Most of the submenus, such as the Art Strokes menu shown in Figure 7.18, list ten or more filters. Additionally, other filter effects can be accessed under the Image menu. Just in case none of these filters creates the look that you want, a User Defined filter enables you to create your own filters, or you can go online to find others.

Figure 7.18
Corel PHOTO-PAINT 9's
Effects menu.

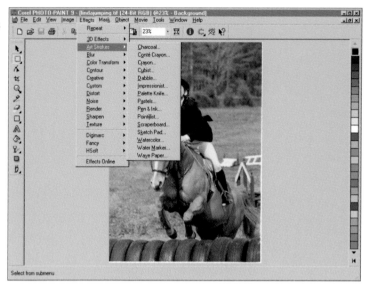

PHOTO-PAINT 9 not only offers many filters, but most of them are also highly configurable and come with a wide variety of presets. A good example of the power of these filters is shown in Figure 7.19. This dialog box is for the Bump-map filter, which has so many settings that it takes three tabbed views to display them all—Bump Map, Surface, and Lighting. The Style preset option at the bottom left of the Lighting tab is for those of you who just want to click and get it done!

Figure 7.19
Corel PHOTO-PAINT 9's
Bump-map filter dialog
box.

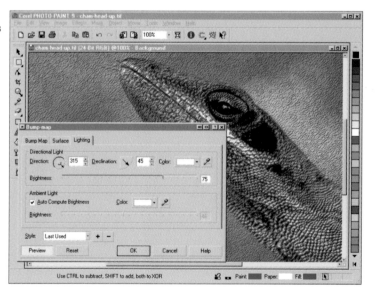

The best aspect of PHOTO-PAINT 9 is not that it offers so many highly configurable filters and presets, but that the final rendered images produced by the filters are spectacular. The filters are as good as they get.

MetaCreations Painter 6

Painter 6 is the ultimate painting tool for fine artists who want to be able to create digital paintings. Besides offering a wide range of excellent filter effects, such as those shown in Figure 7.20, Painter 6 offers tremendous control over an automatic process of applying configurable brush strokes to an image. This technique, or filter, is called Auto-clone. Painter also offers an Impasto painting technique that adds extreme realism to artwork by interactively rendering painted surfaces in 3D.

Figure 7.20
Applying MetaCreations Painter 6's Depth Of Field filter.

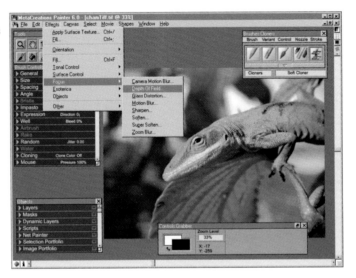

Part II Transforming Images

If you are interested in creating fine-art prints, you also will appreciate the filters that make any other filter that you apply look like it has been applied to a specific kind of canvas or art paper.

Streetwise Software's Professor Franklin's Instant Photo Effects

Professor Franklin's Instant Photo Effects filters create excellent images. I think this product is fantastic. I don't endorse any one product over another, but this is a rare product insofar as it enables you to do exactly the right things in the right way at the right price, without adding too many other features. If you want one product that will enable you to enhance, frame, and filter your digital images with a few mouse clicks, this is the product to get. I don't know of any other product that meets this requirement any better.

Figure 7.21 shows one of the light filters being applied to an image of a chameleon. At the bottom of the screen, you can see the six categories of filters that it offers—Accents, Photography, Artistic, Edges, Frames, and Darkroom.

Figure 7.21
Professor Franklin's Instant Photo Effects filter used to add light to an image.

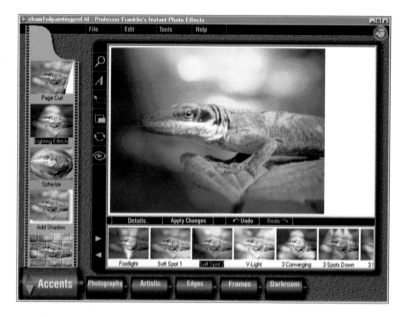

Ulead System's PhotoImpact 5

Figure 7.22 shows PhotoImpact 5's EasyPalette and the many filter galleries that it features. One of the unique strengths of this product is that the EasyPalette enables you to see a thumbnail image of each of the many filters offered instead of just a filter name on a menu. This enables you to get an idea of what each filter does before you take the time to apply it to your image. In addition to the seven categories of filters shown in Figure 7.22, PhotoImpact 5 has filter galleries for Material, Deform, Warp, Type, Button, and Frame, as well as a gallery in which you can put filters that you have created yourself.

Figure 7.22
Using PhotoImpact 5's
EasyPalette to apply
filters.

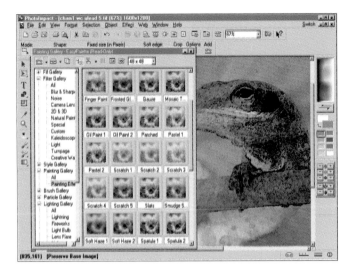

Part II Transforming Images

Besides offering a large number of preset filters, each filter typically has a dialog box in which you can change settings for that specific filter. If you use filters, PhotoImpact probably has one to meet most of your needs—plus it is a top-notch image editor and comes with a fantastic image management application.

Ulead System's PhotoExpress 3.0

PhotoExpress 3.0 is a consumer-level product that is loaded with many of PhotoImpact 5's quality filters. The user interface is one of the best you'll see, which means you can get your work done quickly and easily. Figure 7.23 shows the Effects filter options. The filter categories, shown across the top of the window, include Warp, Artist, Color, Sharpness, Lenses, Special, and Particle.

Figure 7.23
PhotoExpress 3.0's
Effects filter options.

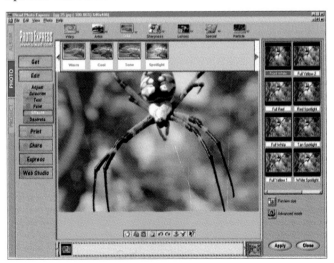

Using plug-in filters

A plug-in application generally requires a host application, such as Photoshop, PhotoImpact, or Paint Shop Pro. When purchasing a plug-in filter, it is wise to carefully ascertain what additional software you might need to use it. In this section, we will look at the capabilities of several filter plug-ins so that you can get a good idea of what can be done to a digital image with a plug-in.

Alien Skin Software's Eye Candy 3.0

Eye Candy offers twenty-one filters, most of which are actually useful (as opposed to being merely cool, meaning that you might or might not ever need to use them for anything practical). Eye Candy's filter collection includes the aptly named filters Antimatter, Carve, Chrome, Cutout, Drop Shadow, Fire, Fur, Glass, Glow, HSB Noise, Inner Bevel, Jiggle, Motion Trail, Outer Bevel, Perspective Shadow, Smoke, Squint, Star, Swirl, Water Drops, and Weave. These twenty-one filters are tremendous timesavers. Many of the things they do can be done with any good digital image editor, but not without lots of skill, knowledge, and experimentation. With these filters, you have lots of control and can get your work done well and quickly.

Each of the twenty-one filters has its own user interface, with plenty of sliders to adjust the outcome to look unique and appropriate for your specific image. An Auto-Preview option enables you to make changes to the filter effects and view the effects that you select in real-time mode.

If you are serious about enhancing digital images, Eye Candy 3.0 offers filters that you probably will need—especially if you create images for use on the Internet.

Alien Skin Software's Xenofex 1.0

Xenofex 1.0, like Eye Candy 3.0, is full of filters that can be used for standard purposes as well as to create unusual and wonderful results when they are creatively applied. For example, with the right adjustments, the Lightning filter can be used to make terrific cracks in marble-like surfaces.

Xenofex 1.0 consists of the following sixteen filters: Baked Earth, Constellation, Crumple, Distress, Electrify, Flag, Lightning, Little Fluffy Clouds, Origami, Puzzle, Rounded Rectangle, Shatter, Shower Door, Stain, Stamper, and Television. The filter names quite accurately describe what each of the filters can do.

Many of the Xenofex 1.0 filters are exceptional, such as the lightning filter. If you need lightning in an image, you can select from seventeen presets. In addition to the presets, ten additional adjustments can be made so that you get just what you want. Each filter has its own user interface, such as the one shown in Figure 7.24. Figure 7.25 shows the outstanding lightning bolts that were added to an image of a place near the Scottish coast. With all of these options, you can create almost as many different lightning effects as you might find in real life—well, almost.

Figure 7.24
Creating lightning with Xenofex's Lightning filter.

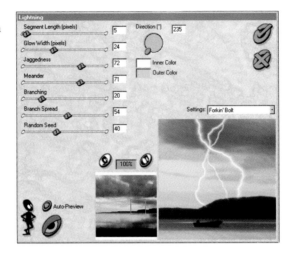

Figure 7.25
Image with lightning added by using Xenofex's Lightning filter.

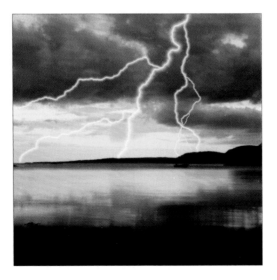

Part II Transforming Images

Andromeda Software Inc.'s Series 3—Screens Filters

Have you ever had the perfect color photograph or color digital image for a project and wondered what you ought to do to it before printing it as a black-and-white image? Although the cost of color printing keeps dropping, and the time that it takes to print a color page keeps decreasing, the vast majority of printing is still done in black and white. Screens Filters is a filter application that helps you get better-looking black-and-white prints.

Screens Filters comes with six categories of ready-to-use presets to help you get your work done quickly. The categories are Mezzotints, Mezzograms, Mezzoblends, Patterns, Special Effects, and Text Effects.

Screens Filters initially starts in Novice mode. When the Novice presets are not enough to meet your needs, you can select the Expert mode, as shown in Figure 7.26. In this example, you can see a mezzotint being created from a black-and-white image of a bronze statue.

Figure 7.26
Andromeda Series 3—
Screens Filters being
used to create a
mezzotint.

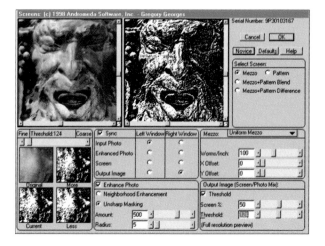

With a good image and some experimentation, you will be able to use Screens Filters to make engravings, etchings, and woodblock prints that will rival those of the masters from centuries past. However, you do have to experiment with this filter to get the excellent results that it is capable of producing.

MetaCreations Kai's Power Tools 5 (KPT 5)

If you want the ultimate creative, innovative, useful, and just-for-fun set of filters, then Kai's Power Tools 5 is an excellent choice. Although most of the KPT 5 filters fit into the special effects category, many are useful for common, everyday tasks.

Blurr, Noise, RadWarp, Smoothie, Frax4D, FraxFlame, FraxPlorer, FiberOptix, Orb-It, and ShapeShifter are the ten filters that compose KPT 5. When you buy KPT 5, you also get KPT 3, which includes another nineteen filters, which are aptly named Gradient Designer, Interform, Spheroid Designer, Texture Explorer, 3D Stereo Noise, Glass Lens, Page Curl, Planar Tiling, Seamless Welder, Twirl, Video Feedback, Vortex Tiling, Edge f/x, Gaussian f/x, Intensity f/x, MetaToys f/x, Noise f/x, Pixel f/x, and Smudge f/x. KPT filters have been used on many images in this book, including figures 7.14 and 7.15.

Xaos Tools' Segmation

The Segmation filter transforms images into vectors, contours, and patterns that will make your work look like line art. One of the benefits of this filter is that it makes your images easily editable by vector-based applications, such as Adobe Illustrator, CorelDRAW, or Macromedia Freehand. Figure 7.27 shows the Segmation screen and a preview of an image of a tractor being converted to line art. This is one of the all-time great timesaving tools if you want to be able to edit photographic images as graphic art.

Figure 7.27
Segmation filter being used to transform tractor image into line art.

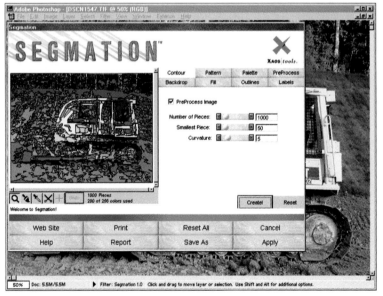

Part II Transforming Images

Xaos Tools' Terrazzo 2

When you need the effects that Terrazzo 2 creates, there is no substitute for this filter. Figure 7.28 shows the results of applying the Terrazzo 2 filter. To reduce some of the repetitiveness of the filter, small portions of the image were altered with the Rubber Stamp tool, and the image was cropped to put the game table off-center. Wouldn't that image make a great graphic for an invitation to a Halloween picnic?

Figure 7.28
A Halloween image created with the Xaos Tools' Terrazzo 2 filter.

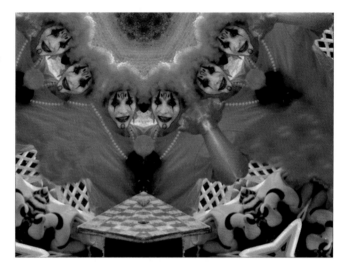

Terrazzo can also be used to make background image tiles and patterns. It is an exceptionally fun filter to use. Used creatively, it can make your work unique.

TIP

If you have one or more images that you would like to alter, but you don't want to buy a filter or you aren't near a computer with image filters, you can use the online filters that are available on the Kodak Web site. You can access Kodak Picture Playground Online from the main Web site at **www.kodak.com**.

Just as two oil painters can sit down next to each other with the same set of brushes and oil paints and not create the same work, so, too, can digital photographers use the same image editors and filters and yet not create the same digital images. It takes great talent, expertise, and passion to create good digital art. Just start and see where it leads you.

That's about all the time we have to cover the topic of image filters. This chapter signifies the end of Part II. The next chapter begins the first of three chapters that are dedicated to showing you useful and cool ways to use your images. See you there…

Part III
Useful and Cool Ways to Use Your Images

8

Displaying Digital Images Electronically

I'm glad that you found your way to this chapter. For those of you who like to view and share images, this chapter and Chapter 11, "Sharing Images Electronically," are *the* two chapters to read. In this chapter, we look at all kinds of cool things that you can do with digital photo albums, slide shows, and screen-savers, all of which are similar in terms of what they do. *Photo albums* are screen-based shows, usually with more than one image to a page. They also can include textual information about each image in database form. *Slide shows* show a series of images, one at a time in full-screen view. *Screen-savers* are special versions of slide shows that run when a computer is not being used. Screen-savers essentially are slide-show versions of computer desktop wallpaper, except that a screen-saver is active only when the computer has not been used for a user-specified number of minutes.

As my digital image collection has grown to an almost unthinkable size, these three types of applications have become my preferred way of storing, sharing, and enjoying my images. Some of my favorite shows include portfolios of digitally edited photographs, slides of our three gray cats, and various screen-savers showing action shots of my kids playing soccer, lacrosse, and hockey. I have created a CD-ROM that contains about thirty of my favorite albums and slide shows, which makes it very easy to find or share my best images.

If you have taken many film-based photographs, you'll understand how difficult and time-consuming it is to create photo albums. Sadly, soon after family photographs are taken, they often are stored in drawers, shoeboxes, plastic containers, or other kinds of boxes and left there indefinitely. We all love to take pictures and we plan to enjoy them, but contrary to our intentions, rarely do we have time to make a photo album or slide show and share it with others—which often is the very reason that we took them in the first place. Digital versions of photo albums, slide shows, and screen-savers have four distinct advantages over film-based formats:

▶ Making multiple copies doesn't cost extra

▶ They are extremely easy to share

▶ The same image can be used in multiple photo albums, slide shows, and screen-savers without the need to find a negative, order copies, and pay for them

▶ The creation process can be easier

NOTE

Eight geographically remote college friends met for a week of skiing in Colorado. It was the first time they had been together since they graduated from college eight years earlier. Five of them took photographs and had their film developed at a local photo finisher who then uploaded their digital images to the Internet. One of the friends selected the thirty best images, downloaded them, and organized them into an electronic photo album. The album was then e-mailed to the seven others, as well as to six other friends who weren't able to make the trip. The album included entertaining comments as well as an invitation to meet again in five years on Utah's ski slopes. It took under two hours to create the entire show and e-mail the copies to everyone.

Just imagine the effort it would take to identify and collect all the necessary negatives needed for the reprints—what a pain! Then, factor in the time and cost involved in creating a photo album for each of the fourteen friends. Thirty photographs for each of the fourteen friends at $.40 per photo would cost nearly $170, plus the cost of fourteen albums, envelopes, and postage! Would it be worth the time, money, and effort? Not likely. Now we have all the benefits of electronic photo albums, slide shows, screen-savers, and the Internet—enjoy them!

Using a photo album to store and view images

Photograph albums are certainly useful for holding and viewing photographs from a family vacation, a wedding, or an award-winning show-dog. However, consider some of the other, not-so-obvious reasons to create a photo album:

▶ As an inventory or asset register

▶ As an art-portfolio presentation tool

▶ As project documentation

▶ As part of a personnel or interview-candidate record

▶ As insurance records

▶ As a product catalog

▶ As a real estate inventory portfolio

▶ As a news and events library

You might use a photo album to display and maintain a record of your Lenox china set, an old book collection, or even a ten-year collection of photographs of your prized roses. You can easily inventory your woodworking tools, jewelry, or music CD-ROM collection. Use a photo album to present your artwork—sculptures, paintings, photographs, and handicrafts. You can use a photo album to store and display not only photographic images but also scanned newspaper or magazine articles, or word processing or spreadsheet documents that have been converted into bit-mapped images. You can document the work being done on a building project, such as a kitchen being remodeled or a new beach home being constructed. The list of uses for a photo album is endless.

When you combine the instant availability of digital images from a digital camera and a feature-rich photo album, you can easily keep records of things that you normally would have found to be too time-consuming and too expensive to do. If you are a parent, imagine having an electronic portfolio of all the artwork that your children have ever created, without the difficulties of keeping those large finger-paintings, the glued-glitter drawings, or the large papier-mâché sculptures that you love but just don't want to store forever. You can even have a photo album of all of those complex and weird LEGO projects. Photo albums can be created for all kinds of home and work projects.

Using an album with database capabilities

By now, you probably have many ideas as to how you would like to use an electronic photo album. Before you begin to make one, however, spend a few minutes looking at the fantastic possibilities of one of the more feature-rich photo album applications—Ulead's PhotoImpact Album. PhotoImpact Album, which is a companion product to PhotoImpact, the image-editing application, is a powerful tool for managing and viewing files. In addition to the file-management and viewing capabilities, PhotoImpact Album enables you to organize your files visually by using thumbnails to represent the contents of a file. After you create thumbnails, you can append additional information, placed in fields, for a more detailed description of the image. You can then search and sort based on these fields to help you locate thumbnails or specific record information.

How about getting some "hands-on" experience with PhotoImpact Album? Let's create a photo-album-based asset record of tools in a woodworking shop. Such an inventory would be useful as documentation for insurance purposes in case of fire or theft, as a tool asset record, and as a system to help track warranties and repair information. The first thing to do is to get images of each of the tools. The easiest way to get images is to place each tool on a white background and take pictures with a digital camera. Obviously, a film-based camera can be used if you don't have a digital camera and are willing to scan each image with a scanner.

Using PhotoImpact Album, we can create a new database by using one of the templates, as shown in Figure 8.1. Alternatively, we can customize a database template to meet our particular needs. In this case, we'll modify the Product Catalog template specifically for our tool asset register by simply renaming a few existing fields.

Figure 8.1
Selecting an album template.

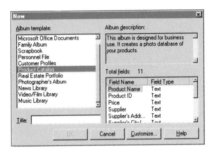

Next, we insert all the images into the database by using the Collect Files From Folder function. By selecting View Mode>Thumbnails, we can see thumbnail images that were created for each image. To further divide the database into "types of tools," we can add a "list" type field and include names for the categories of tools that we want. After the field has been created, we need to select the correct tool category for each tool record. Figure 8.2 shows how the database can be separated into power tools, hand tools, large power tools, accessories for power tools, air tools, and so on. By clicking the tab labeled Air tools, for example, the database can be reduced to show only air tool images.

Figure 8.2
Woodworking tool
database with tool
category tabs.

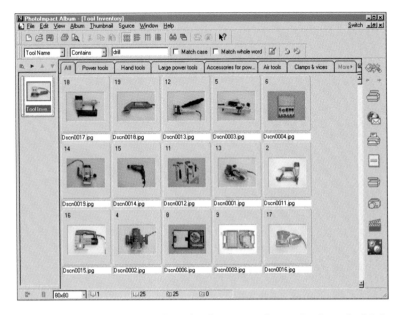

Now that we have the database built, we need to go back and add the
necessary textual information to each record. By selecting
View>Mode>Data Entry, we get to the screen shown in Figure 8.3. Using
this screen, you can enter the data for each tool that is to be recorded.

Figure 8.3
Tool database data-entry
screen.

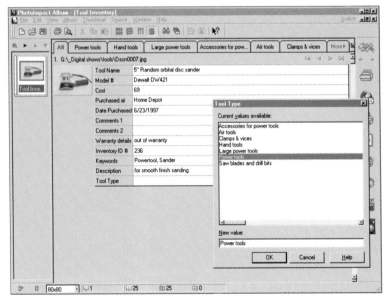

Part III Using Images

Once all the information has been entered, it can be exported to a comma-delimited file and imported into other kinds of applications, such as a spreadsheet, another database, or a word processor (see Figure 8.4). This step is as simple as checking the desired fields to export and then exporting them.

Figure 8.4
Screen for selecting database fields to be exported.

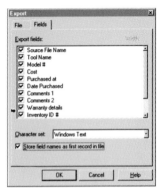

You can also search the database. For example, if you want to find all records containing the word "drill," you can use the search capabilities that are shown just below the menu in Figure 8.2. Likewise, you can perform more complex searches by using the search dialog box shown in Figure 8.4a. As the final step, if needed, you can print a color hardcopy of the entire database by using any one of several different layout styles, including images and database information. Just think of what we have accomplished. In less than two hours, we have created a database of the tools in an entire woodworking shop, complete with images, without ever touching a pencil or paper! Tell me that was not fast, easy, accurate, and fun—well, almost fun, considering the alternative ways of completing an inventory.

Figure 8.4a
PhotoImpact Album's advanced search facility.

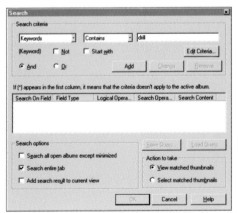

Creating a book-like picture album

We've just looked at the feature-rich PhotoImpact Album and its capability to add database information to each image. However, what if you just want a photo album—a realistic, book-like picture album with pages that turn? It also would be nice to be able to attach bookmarks to mark favorite pictures, choose images for the front and back cover, and have a table of contents and index.

TIP

FlipAlbum 3.0 is available in computer software stores, or you can download a trial version at **www.flipviewer.com/**.

Well, that is what you will find offered with FlipAlbum 3.0, plus a few more features. It not only has a contents page but also has an overview page that shows thumbnails of each photo in the album, as shown in Figure 8.5.

Figure 8.5
FlipAlbum 3.0's image overview page.

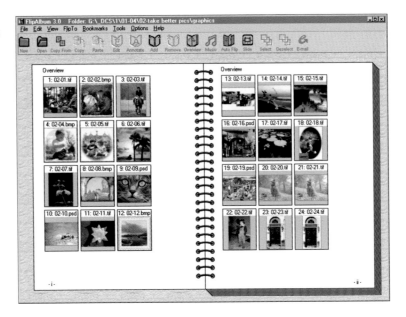

Part III Using Images

Each album page shows one picture (see Figure 8.6). Clicking the picture causes the picture to be displayed in full-screen view. If you click any page next to the image, the pages turn in a surprisingly realistic manner— it even sounds as though you are turning a real paper page. FlipAlbum 3.0 also lets you open more than one album at a time, which means that you can drag and drop images between albums. It definitely lives up to its billing as an "automatic digital album." Seems to me that if you have a digital camera, you ought to have this product—I do.

Figure 8.6
FlipAlbum 3.0's page view.

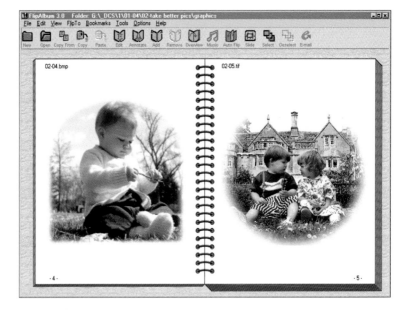

The best feature of this product is its capability to automatically generate thumbnails of your images, a table of contents, and an index—you simply select a file directory. This is a fantastic way to view folders containing images from a digital camera or any other directory. FlipAlbum 3.0 is truly a spectacular application that you will enjoy using.

Using slide shows to view images

Traditionally, one of the best ways to view photographs is as a 35mm slide show, shown against a white screen in a dark room. Unfortunately, you have to decide to make slides at the time that you buy the film. When using slide film, it is more expensive to get prints if you want them—and without prints, it is hard to see the images without using a slide projector or a light table. A 35mm slide show also requires a dark room and a smooth, bright-white background or screen—usually, neither of these is readily available. In contrast, we'll now look at what can be done with a digital slide show application.

Creating a multimedia slide show

Kai's Power SHOW is an exceptional software product—it is very easy to use and it offers outstanding text and slide transition effects, plus audio and music capabilities. Most important of all, the finished slide shows are as good as slide shows get. They can be rich multimedia shows that are highly educational, informative, persuasive, or just plain fun.

Normally, when I get ready to put together an album or a slide show, I sit down in the middle of my living room floor and spread photographs all around me. I then begin making piles—a pile of photos that I won't use, a pile of photos that I might or might not use, and several different piles of photos that I intend to use. After I have all the piles arranged, I begin to sequence them in a large area directly in front of me. When they are in order, I then begin assembling them into bound albums.

With my creation process in mind, you'll soon understand why I like Kai's Power SHOW. It is the perfect slide show for me—and possibly for you, if you are one of those "in the middle of the living room" types, like I am.

Kai's Power SHOW interface looks more like my living room floor than a typical Windows application—well almost. The IN "room" is relatively empty, with just a few menu items placed on the empty floor space (see Figure 8.7). I like this application because the software enables me to do the "pile thing." You can click and drag images around either one at a time or as a group of them—you are not constrained by rows and columns.

Figure 8.7
Using Kai's Power SHOW to select images for a slide show.

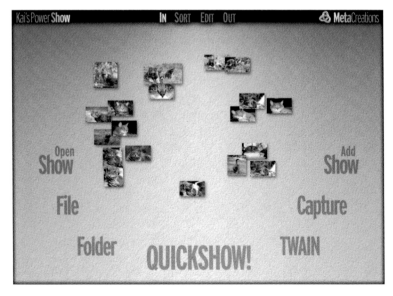

In Kai's Power SHOW, all the features and functions are logically organized into four "rooms"—the IN room, the SORT room, the EDIT room, and the OUT room. Each of these rooms represents a step in the creation process.

The IN room is the place where you bring together all of your digital photos, pictures, business slides, and video clips that you might want to use. If you have all the materials that you want in a single directory, you can use the Folder feature, which automatically loads all items from the selected directory. Alternatively, you can pick and choose by file, across multiple directories, as well as import from a scanner or download from a digital camera. After you make selections, they appear on the desktop as thumbnails. Pictures, photos, and business slides appear as small thumbnail previews, whereas video clips and existing shows appear as small pieces of filmstrip.

Once everything that you want to use in the show is on your desktop, you move to the SORT room (see Figure 8.8). The SORT room is the equivalent of my living room floor with sorted piles—the room where you arrange and organize all of your content. Besides the manual sorting and selection process, Kai's Power SHOW also offers automatic sorting capabilities that include options to sort by Name, Date, Size, Type, Width, and Height—which are extremely useful sorts when you need them.

Figure 8.8
Sorting and selecting images in Kai's Power SHOW.

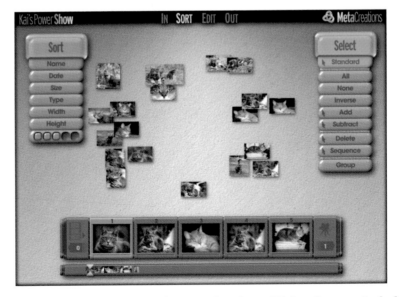

The SORT room also provides a good variety of Select features, including All, None, Inverse, Add, Subtract, Delete, Sequence, and Group. Using these features, you can sequence your show and make it ready for the EDIT room. The Sequencer and the Nano Sequencer (the slider) filmstrips at the bottom of the desktop display your show as you have created it.

Any time you want to view the show, click the projector icon, which causes the frames currently selected in the Sequencer to be shown as a slide show.

Now we can move into the EDIT room, where you can control the slide-transition techniques, add animated text, and add sound. About seventy different slide-transition styles are available, ranging from the common yet elegant Dissolve transition to very unique and exciting techniques such as the Light Burst, Fire, Color Fade, and F-stop options. Kai's Power SHOW enables you to choose not only the technique but also the speed of the transition effect.

Placing text is easy with the wide variety of preset text templates (see Figure 8.9). Various text attributes can also be changed, including color, line spacing, and shadow. After you place the text, you can choose from more than twenty cool animation features for placing the text onscreen at run time, with aptly named animations such as Parade, Perspective, Sphere, Swagger, and Wave.

Figure 8.9
Adding and formatting text for a slide in Kai's Power SHOW.

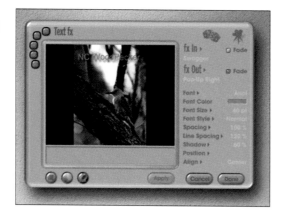

You also have the option of adding sound to your slide show (see Figure 8.10). Sound options include sound clips such as WAV or MID files. Alternatively, you can even play selected audio tracks from a CD-ROM.

Figure 8.10
Selecting sound effects for a slide in Kai's Power SHOW.

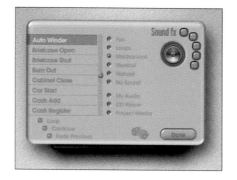

Now that your show is complete, what can you do with it? Kai's Power SHOW enables you to run slide shows on your computer screen (or projected with a digital projector onto a screen), print the shows on paper, and save the show as a self-running or manually controlled slide show. You can also upload it to the Internet for viewing by anyone with a browser. You can view several Internet versions of shows created with Kai's Power SHOW at **www.reallyusefulpage.com/dcs/08-01.htm.**

Now you know what can be done with a feature-rich slide show application like Kai's Power SHOW—try creating one, and you'll share your photos that way often.

NOTE

An artist who works with glass and steel and specializes in creating unusual gazing globes for gardens created a slide show that presented a dozen globes that she created. Significantly, the images showed the globes in each of the owners' gardens, instead of just the globes themselves. The last slide ends with the question: "Doesn't your garden need a gazing globe?" After mailing one hundred inexpensive floppy disks containing the show to a preferred customer list, she received enough commissions for new globes to keep her busy for four months. She also uses the same show in both slide show and screen-saver form on her computer in her studio.

Displaying images with a screen-saver

Does your computer screen show pictures or animations after the computer has been idle for a while? If so, that is a screen-saver at work. Screen-savers are essentially slide shows that are turned on automatically by your computer after it has been idle for a specified number of minutes. By right-clicking your computer desktop and selecting the Properties menu, a Display Properties window opens. Click the Screen Saver tab to see all the options for screen-savers (see Figure 8.11). Screen-savers can be used just for fun, as a corporate billboard, or even as a sales tool.

Figure 8.11
Selecting a screen-saver
with the Windows 98
Display Properties
dialog box.

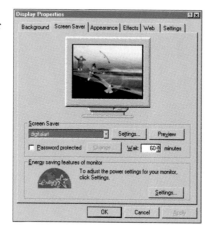

NOTE

A kitchen designer uses a screen-saver to show twenty "before and after"
photographs taken of kitchens she has designed and helped to remodel. When
clients visit her office, they see this screen-saver instead of an open software
application that she might have left on her desktop. It makes a great sales tool!

Creating a screen-saver

Many image editors, image management tools, and software packages
bundled with scanners, digital cameras, and even printers include a
screen-saver creation tool. If you are interested in just creating screen-
savers, but you don't have an application that enables you to create them,
then I recommend Screen Saver Toolbox 2.0 from Midnight Blue Software.

TIP

Screen Saver Toolbox 2.0, from Midnight Blue Software, is a good tool to use
to create your own screen-savers. You can get a trial version of this shareware
application at **www.midnightblue.com**.

Screen Saver Toolbox (SST) 2.0 enables you to easily select images, add
music, and generate screen-savers. It is a two-step process—select the
images that you want and then generate the screen-saver (see Figure 8.12).

Part III Using Images

Figure 8.12
Generating a screen-saver with Screen Saver Toolbox 2.0.

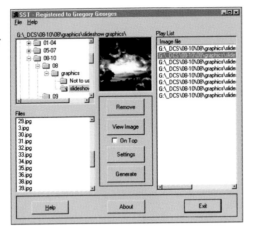

SST provides a few selectable options, which can be changed by clicking the Settings button. From there, you can change things such as image quality and size, transition mode, background color, and image position, as shown in Figure 8.13.

Figure 8.13
Screen Saver Toolbox 2.0's screen-saver configuration dialog box.

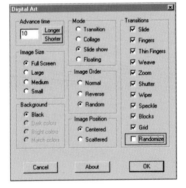

One of the most useful capabilities of SST is that it lets you generate a single file that contains an installation program and all of the show's images. This single file can be put on a disk or e-mailed, and it can be installed on any PC without requiring the recipient to have any additional software.

Now that you see how easy it is to create your own screen-saver, what will you create? On your home PC, you could display photos from a recent overseas vacation or a family gathering or display photos of your pets or children. Alternatively, you might want to display the twenty best photos you have taken or images of a new boat or antique automobile, for example. At your office, you can use a screen-saver to help promote a project or a new product design that you are currently working on. You might simply want to make a screen-saver containing ten funny images of your face! A little humor every now and then is surely worthwhile.

Incidentally, using the Display Properties dialog box shown in Figure 8.11, you can select the Background tab and then select any image to be displayed as wallpaper for your desktop. You probably have many images that would make a great replacement for the background image that shows up when you install Microsoft Windows 98.

Guidelines for choosing the best application for your needs

The first part of this chapter gave you some firsthand experience with four excellent tools. However, these are just four out of literally hundreds of such tools that are available on the market to create photo albums, slide shows, and screen-savers. Capabilities vary greatly between these applications. Without a doubt, you can inadvertently buy a product that *won't* meet your needs. For example, you can buy an application to create slide shows so that you can send a portfolio of all of your new artwork to prospective buyers, but if the application creates a slide show that requires the viewer to have the software, too, then you have the wrong application for your needs. This is just one example of the many ways you can get the wrong product.

TIP

The capability to create digital photo albums, slide shows, and screen-savers can often be found in applications that you already own. Before you buy, first look carefully at any software that you have already purchased, especially applications that are bundled with printers, scanners, digital cameras, or even rewriteable CD drives. Finally, look carefully at any media-management applications that you might have, such as those that enable you to create thumbnails of each image in a directory. If you have Microsoft Office and it includes PowerPoint, then you already have an excellent slide show creation tool under the guise of a business presentation tool.

The goal of this section is to help you understand more about what can be done—or not be done—based on a few key features. It will help you to decide which products are the "best" for you, based on how you intend to share your images.

Sharing your images with others

If your intent is to share your photo albums, slide shows, or screen-savers with others, make sure that you select an application that does not require each of your recipients to purchase that application. Some slide show products create small, run-time programs that allow the show to be shown without any additional software. Others require each viewer to have the application that it was created with.

Part III Using Images

Output options

Will you want to have printed copies of your albums and shows? If so, make sure that you have the options that you need. Do you want to show your work on the Internet? To post albums or slide shows on a Web site, you need an application that can create the necessary HTML code.

File and program size

File and program size might or might not be important to you. If you create small albums and slide shows, then the file size is likely to be small. If your shows contain rich multimedia effects and numerous large images, then your show will be large. Many e-mail providers have limits on the size of files that you can send. If you want to send e-mail and attach albums, slide shows, or even screen-savers, the files and necessary viewers or programs must be compact. Some programs are excellent at creating tiny files, whereas others aren't.

Getting images from many sources

Many ways exist to get digital images. They can come directly from a digital camera, a scanner, a digital image storage card, another PC, the Internet, an online gallery, e-mail, and a CD-ROM, as well as many other places. Obviously, it would really simplify the creation process if you could access all of these sources from within your application. If you don't make many albums, slide shows, or screen-savers, having limited access might not be a problem.

Sorting, searching, and ordering images

The capability to sort, search, and order your images might or might not be important to you. When creating an album that can be used as an asset record, as discussed earlier in this chapter, searching capabilities are likely to be needed. Likewise, if you are creating a slide show with more than fifty images to choose from, you will find that a variety of sorting and ordering features can be exceedingly valuable. In other cases, these features become essential. Imagine having to create a slide show from a CD-ROM full of sequentially numbered images taken with a digital camera. Without powerful sorting, searching, and ordering capabilities, you could go crazy!

Adding nonphoto "things"

In most cases, you will simply add digital images to photo albums, slide shows, and screen-savers. However, every now and then you might want to create something much fancier. You might want to add sound or animated text or a few elegant slide-transition effects. You might also need to be able to add textual information to each of the images. Now that you know what is possible, you can decide what you want to do and then choose a product that will meet your needs.

Adding multimedia effects

You can create a very effective photo album with just static images—and you can create an even more impressive photo album with multimedia effects. Besides image and graphics files, many photo album applications allow video and animation files, audio files, and even music from a CD-ROM. Adding these effects often is as easy as adding another image. If you want to do these things, look for an application that offers these features.

NOTE

A friend of a husband-to-be wanted to create a photo album of his friend's wedding as a wedding gift. He used one of the new digital recorders to record the wedding vows and a few conversations throughout the wedding. Using a digital camera, he took pictures of all the special moments—both of the wedding couple and of the guests. Within a few hours, he created a multimedia photo album complete with wedding music from a CD-ROM, wedding vows, and many amusing comments. Using a writable CD drive, he was able to create a priceless sixty-image multimedia gift for under $1. The bad news: He had more than thirty requests for copies within two weeks of the wedding! To learn more about digital recorders, visit **www.creativelabs.com/**.

Adding text effects

Depending on how you intend to use your photo album, you might or might not want to add text. Some images would be entirely ruined with text placed over them. On other images, text makes the image much more understandable, informative, or entertaining. Another option for placing text is to create a separate slide for the text. The text can be placed on an image or a background, or even a graphic especially designed or picked for the purpose. It is much easier to add these kinds of effects in your album or slide show application than it is to keep jumping out of one application into another.

Adding a database to your image collection

As your image database grows and you find yourself using photo albums or slide shows in more innovative ways, you likely will want a way to add textual information (or a database record) to each of your images. A good example of the use of a database with an image photo album is the asset-record application, discussed earlier in the chapter.

Applications to consider

Many high-quality, easy-to-use, feature-rich photo album, slide show, and screen-saver applications are available on the market. The following list includes a few applications that you might want to consider:

▶ **Broderbund's The Print Shop Photo Organizer**—A standalone product that also comes with The Print Shop Deluxe and The Print Shop Pro Publisher. It is an unusually simple, feature-rich product that enables you to create photo albums, slide shows, and screen-savers (see Figure 8.14).

Figure 8.14
Using The Print Shop Photo Organizer to create a slide show.

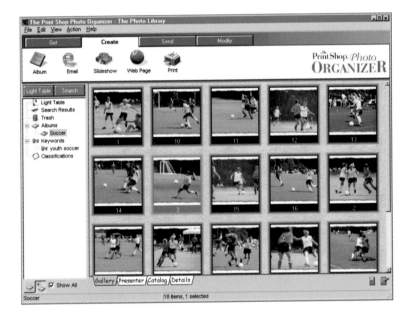

▶ **Cerious Software's ThumbsPlus 3.3 and 4.0**—A great product that, as Cerious claims, is "...the most effective, elegant, and inexpensive way to locate, view, edit, print, and organize your image, metafile, font, and multimedia files." ThumbsPlus (see Figure 8.15) is a shareware product that compares favorably against most of the commercial media-management applications.

Figure 8.15
Selecting images for a
slide show in
ThumbsPlus 4.0.

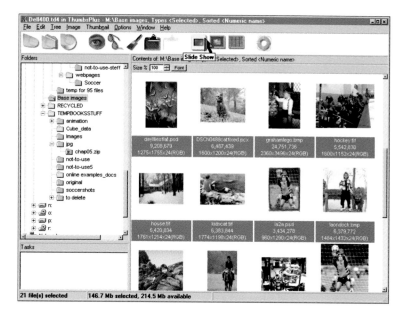

▶ **MGI's PhotoSuite III**—Not only is PhotoSuite III one of the easiest
applications to use, but it offers a wide range of ways to save and
share digital images, as shown in Figure 8.16. You can save a
collection of images as an album to a disk or as an attachment to an
e-mail, upload them to Kodak's PhotoNet Online Web site, post the
images to GatherRound.com, save them as a Web page, set one image
as wallpaper, and create a slide show.

Figure 8.16
Using MGI's PhotoSuite
III to share images.

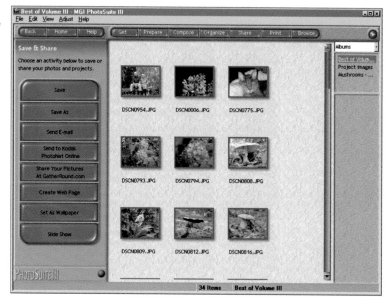

Part III Using Images

▶ **MetaCreation's Kai's Power SHOW**—One of my all-time favorite software products, it can create terrific slide shows with outstanding slide transitions and text effects. It creates HTML-based slide shows that are optimized for the Internet, or small, self-contained shows that are excellent for sending to others via e-mail. All of this can be done with one of the most unusually simple user interfaces to be found. This is a got-to-have application if you are serious about slide shows for your computer or for posting to the Internet. Power SHOW does not create screen-savers or photo albums—it is a slide show tool, and a very good one.

▶ **Microsoft's PowerPoint**—A highly capable slide show tool that, as part of the Microsoft Office suite, is readily available on many PCs. Even though PowerPoint has been designed as a business presentation tool, it can be used to create excellent image slide shows. Additionally, it allows your slide shows to be uploaded to the Internet.

▶ **Ulead's PhotoImpact Album 5.0**—A companion product to PhotoImpact 5.0, which is an unusually powerful image-editing tool that has some of the very best features for creating Web images. PhotoImpact 5.0 is unquestionably one of the best values in the graphics tool market.

WinFiles.com is part of the incredibly useful CNET Web site (**www.cnet.com**), which is billed as "The source for computers and technology." **WinFiles.com** not only provides a short description of each application and the cost for each product, but it also has hot-links to each publisher's Web site. It also allows you to purchase and register the products online and tells you the file size and estimated download time. This is an excellent place to find some very capable products for very little money—try it. You likely will find more than one application that suits your purposes, whatever they might be.

If, by some chance, you don't find what you want, or you'd like help deciding which application to choose, try **www.zdnet.com** The ZDNet site is different from the WinFiles.com site in that it offers a rating system of one to five stars, and you can see the number of times that each application has been downloaded, which might indicate the product's quality.

There it is—the chapter on photo albums, slide shows, and screen-savers. Anyone who enjoys photography and owns a PC will enjoy viewing and sharing their digital images with these tools. Now, on to the next chapter, where we'll look at other useful and fun things that you can do with your images.

9

Other Useful and Fun Things You Can Do with Images

Having the capability to take pictures and turn them into extraordinary digital images is good, but actually getting some practical value from your efforts by using your images is an entirely different challenge. This chapter is the second of three chapters that will help you learn more about what you can do with your digital images after you create them. This is a project-oriented chapter that provides you with plenty of good ideas about how you might use your images for work, home, or just for fun in a printed form.

In addition to giving you some ideas on how to use your images, this chapter introduces you to several software products that will help you complete your projects easily and professionally. Because the majority of PC users use Microsoft Office, we'll also look at ways to use your images with applications such as Word, Excel, PowerPoint, and Access.

Before we get started, though, let me make one suggestion: Don't underestimate your skills or your ability to successfully complete projects that you can be proud of. You might not think you are particularly talented, and you might have little graphic or artistic background, but fear not—with a little work and the right software products, almost anyone can complete projects that they are pleased with. With the combination of new and better computer hardware, software, supplies, and service companies, creating useful digital images yourself has never been easier. Moreover, you can produce digital images when you want to and the way you want to, and sometimes even for less money. Therefore, have confidence and try a few of these projects—you'll see how talented you really are!

All the projects in this chapter have been created with consumer-level software products that cost well under $100, with a majority of them costing under $40. As you will soon see, wizards and templates enable you to create all of these projects by following a series of simple steps.

Part III Using Images

This means that you do not have to be a design or layout expert. It's almost like painting by numbers!

Image projects for business

No matter what kind of business you are in, you can improve your business's profile by using digital images. Dozens of software products are available that can help you create everything from business cards, letterhead, newsletters, and display signs to customized invoices, product catalogs, pamphlets, and brochures. Figure 9.1 shows a wide variety of projects that you can create with The Print Shop Pro 10.0.

Figure 9.1
Business projects that you can do with The Print Shop Pro 10.0.

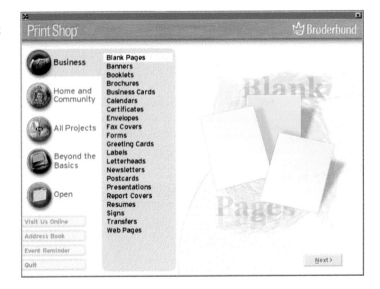

In this first section, we look at projects for creating business cards and letterhead, a project quote sheet prepared for a prospective customer, a product catalog, two postcards announcing a new chair design and a new studio gallery, and certificates for readers of this book.

Business cards and letterhead

Professional-looking business cards are essential for almost anyone in any kind of business—large or small. If you are not artistically talented, you might be asking yourself whether you are capable of creating a good-looking business card. With a good digital image or two, a few ideas about the design you want, and one of the better software products, you can! Let me show you how easy it can be.

First, you must decide what information you want to include on your card. Then, you need some idea about what you want the card to look like. If you are planning to use one or more images, you must also decide which ones to use. Often, the image that you want to use isn't as good as you would like it to be. For that situation, the three chapters in Part II, "Transforming Ordinary Images into Extraordinary Ones," offer lots of advice on how to improve your images.

For this first example project, we'll create business cards for two companies—The Mushroom Company, Inc. and Specialty Mushrooms, Inc.—both fictitious companies that produce specialty mushrooms. We'll start with four images and use The Print Shop Pro 10.0 for the first card, shown in Figure 9.2. Although this card might look relatively complex to create, it isn't.

First, we load one mushroom picture to use as the background for the card. Using The Print Shop Photo Pro photo editing tool, we will make the image look like a duotone image by using two filters. First, we'll apply the Antique Color Touch Up tool. Then, using the Lens Fog tool, we lighten the image so that it can be used as a background image, as shown in Figure 9.2. To learn more about filters, see Chapter 7, "Filtering for Special Effects."

Figure 9.2
Business card being created in The Print Shop Pro 10.0.

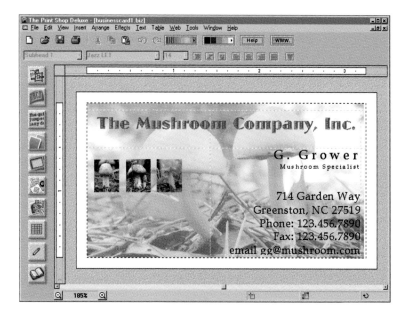

With the background complete, two steps remain. First, the name, title, and address information needs to be edited. Then, three additional small images of other mushrooms, selected from the other three images, need to be appropriately placed. The results look great! Select Print, and The Print Shop Pro 10.0 automatically formats the page so that you can print ten cards on a full sheet of business card paper.

Part III Using Images

Another good application to use to create business cards is MGI's PhotoSuite III. Figure 9.3 shows a business card being created for Specialty Mushrooms, Inc. In this case, a template was again used, but this card features only a single image. After you change the text and contact information, the card is done. The whole process takes under ten minutes.

Figure 9.3
Business card being created in MGI's PhotoSuite III.

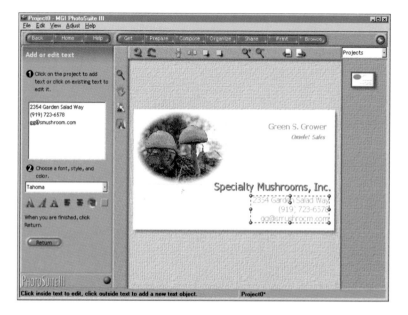

After you create a business card that you are happy with, you will need to print it. If you have a photo-quality inkjet printer, you can purchase business card paper especially created for inkjet printers. You can learn more about these business cards in Chapter 13, "Obtaining the Best Possible Printed Images." With specially formulated inkjet paper that features laser-perforated cards that tear as if they were cut, you can easily have professional-looking business cards printed, as you need them, directly from your computer on your own printer.

What if you don't have a good color printer or want to have your design printed professionally? You have several choices. First, you can save your design to a removable disk in a standard file format and take it to a local printer. With the file on your disk, they can use your design to print your cards professionally. The cost of getting a printer to print your cards obviously is more expensive than if you do them yourself. You also will find that most of the cost associated with printing is in the printer setup, and, thus, printing 500 or even 1,000 cards is nearly as cheap as printing just a few hundred.

Another option for getting professionally printed business cards is to use the printing services of one of the many online Internet service companies. The number of such companies is growing and you have many choices, but I suggest iPrint.com (**www.iprint.com**), one of the early leaders in this market. It does a fantastic job on business cards and letterhead. If you use iPrint.com, you need to supply your own image, if you want to include one. However, you don't need any software other than your Internet browser. Simply visit iPrint's Web site and follow the steps. You can select from a wide variety of templates and then make changes to text, graphics, color, fonts, card size, and layout, as shown in Figure 9.4.

Figure 9.4
iPrint Web page for ordering customized business cards.

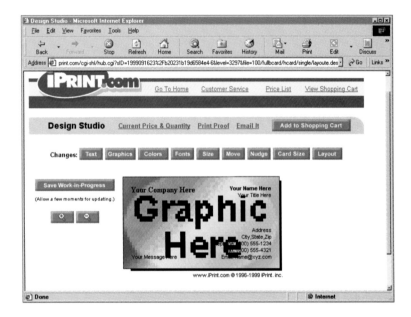

After you complete the design of your card, you can even print a "proof" on your own printer. When you are satisfied with the results, save your work and add it to the shopping cart. A few minutes later, your work is completed. Your cards will be ready to be printed and shipped directly to you within a couple of days. It doesn't get much easier than that. In addition to business cards, iPrint.com prints greeting cards, letterhead, business checks, envelopes, invitations, labels, and many other things.

Part III Using Images

TIP

If your company has branch offices in several different cities, and you want to provide a supply of letterhead, envelopes, business brochures, and business cards with the correct local addresses to each of these offices, consider using Kinko's online service at **www.kinkos.com**. You can submit orders to any Kinko's store in the world right from your home or office by using your computer. KinkoNET online ordering makes ordering over the Web easy and convenient. Your staff in each location can then pick up their supplies from a local Kinko's store without the added expense of shipping and handling. In addition, they get local onsite service. Figure 9.5 shows the Web page used for creating your own business letterhead. This page looks similar to iPrint.com's page, because they work in a partnership to serve their customers better—one (Kinko's) is a "bricks and mortar" business and the other (iPrint.com) is a pure Internet business.

Figure 9.5
KinkoNET Web page for ordering customized letterhead.

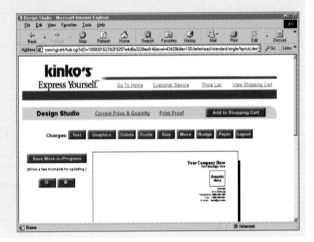

Project quote sheet

Are you good with a spreadsheet? If it is your tool of choice for calculating quotes for projects, then consider using it as the application to make project quote sheets for that new business that you are pursing. One way to increase new business is to improve the presentation of product and service offerings during the sales cycle, including the initial quote to prospective buyers. Figure 9.6 shows how the fictitious company, Garden Furniture Company, Inc., displays digital images of each proposed piece of furniture in its quotes. The images were taken with a digital camera and show each piece of furniture in a natural garden setting.

Figure 9.6
Project Quote created in Excel spreadsheet.

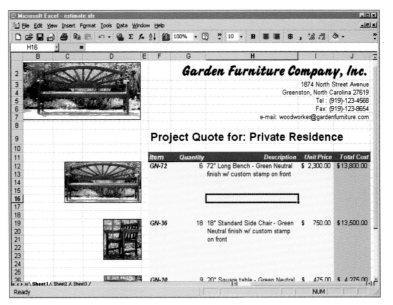

This Project Quote sheet was very easy to create. Once the spreadsheet was set up, the images were cut and pasted directly from a digital image editing application. Excel enables you to resize the images and move them around the page for precise placement. Each time a new product is created, an image is saved in a directory. This spreadsheet makes it easy to create new project quotes, which is just a matter of making sure the correct items are entered along with the order quantity. The spreadsheet then computes the total cost, including tax, shipping, and handling.

Part III Using Images

Product catalog pages

The Garden Furniture Company builds low-volume, high-priced, and—frequently—customized outdoor furniture, so having a catalog printed doesn't make sense, because the products that it offers constantly change. However, the company still needs to be able to show its products on catalog pages. Using Microsoft Word, the company can easily create catalogs showing the exact pieces that it wants to show for any given purpose. Within a few minutes, employees can add and delete new or old products and quickly update the catalog, as shown in Figure 9.7.

Figure 9.7
Using digital images and Microsoft Word to create a product catalog.

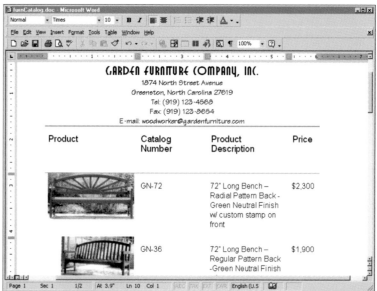

If Garden Furniture Company's product catalog needed to include more than just a handful of products, the company could use Microsoft Access to create its catalog pages. Access, the Microsoft database application, enables images to be stored as part of the database. Once stored, they can then be formatted and printed as needed. The Microsoft Office applications are powerful tools and can be used to do many things. If you use Microsoft Office applications, it is worthwhile to learn more about how digital images can be used in each of the applications. You can find many additional ideas and application tips for Office products on Microsoft's Web page at **www.microsoft.com/office**.

Postcards

Sending a postcard is a good way to announce a sale or a new product line to prospective customers. Postcards also can be used to announce a new business offering, a new partner, a change of address or just to let others know that your company is doing well and has recently won new business. Streetwise Software's Professor Franklin's Photo Print Gold was used to create the postcard shown in Figure 9.8, announcing a new bench design produced by The Garden Furniture Company. The actual card design was created with a watercolor filter in Ulead's Photo Express digital image editor. Hand-painted lettering was added to maintain the natural media design.

Figure 9.8
Using a postcard to announce a new garden bench design.

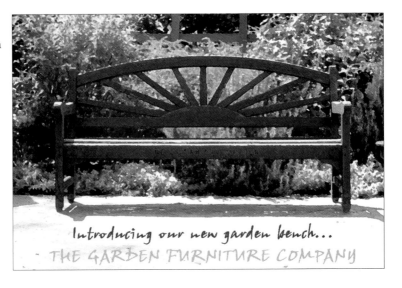

Introducing our new garden bench...
THE GARDEN FURNITURE COMPANY

Part III Using Images

Figure 9.9 shows another example of a postcard, but this one was designed with a template. The postcard announces the opening of a new studio gallery. Once you have a postcard design that you like, it is easy and inexpensive to have several thousand of them printed for very little money. Online companies such as NoNEG PRESS (**www.business-card.com**) print high-quality postcards for under $.11 each in quantities of 2,500 or more.

Figure 9.9
Postcards announcing the opening of a new studio and art gallery.

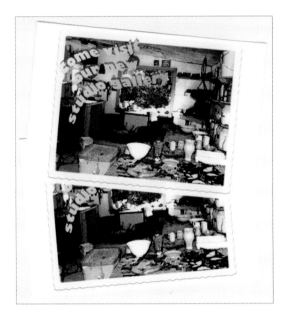

Certificates

A positive pat on the back is good—but a written certificate is even better! Using Ulead's Photo Express Platinum 2000, you can choose from a dozen templates for making certificates. Deciding that most readers of this book will be close to being digital image professionals when they complete it, I created the Digital Imaging Professional certificate that certifies each reader as being a digital imaging professional (see Figure 9.10).

Figure 9.10
A specially created
certificate for readers
of this book.

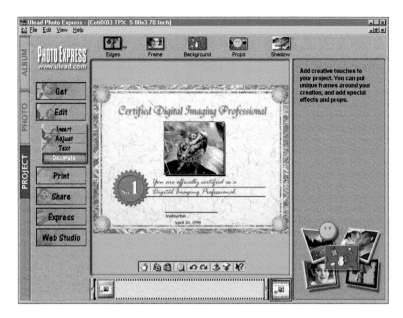

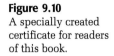

So far, we have looked at designs for only five different kinds of business
projects out of many, many possible projects. You also can create signs,
information cards and tags, pamphlets or brochures, banners, newsletters,
and a million other kinds of projects.

To obtain other ideas for additional projects for your business, just think
about your current business issues. Are you just about to roll out a new
product or complete a large project? Do you need to improve the
teamwork in a group of new employees? Maybe you need an entirely new
business image or are in need of a regular employee newsletter. The use
of appropriate digital images in your business documents can help you be
more successful in accomplishing your business objectives. If you are still
not sure how you can use images for your business, purchase one of the
consumer image editing products that offer many large "content"
collections (images, clip art, project templates, and so forth). The Print
Shop Pro 10.0, Photo Express Platinum 2000, and MGI's PhotoSuite III
are three excellent products for doing useful projects for both business
and personal use, and they all have huge content collections.

Part III Using Images

Image projects for home

The prior section gave you a few ideas of how you might use digital images for projects for your business or work. Now we'll look at a few sample home projects. More specifically, we are going to look at ways to improve the ordinary look of personal letters and how you can create a collage, greeting cards, a wine bottle label, a calendar, photo album pages, a family tree picture, and a flyer. The Print Shop Pro screen shown in Figure 9.11 shows a variety of other home and community projects that you might like to do.

Figure 9.11
The Print Shop Pro 10.0 project list for home and community.

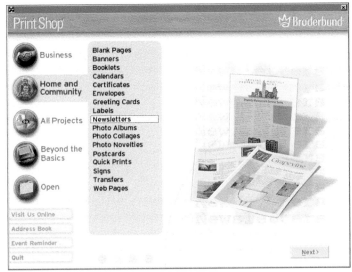

Personal letters

If you are like me, you enjoy receiving a letter every now and then. It is nice to get an envelope in the mail with a return address indicating it is from someone you are excited to hear from. The more e-mail I get, the more I seem to value getting a letter. If someone has included photographs or digital images—that is even better. With the hope of starting a resurgence in sending real letters in the mail, let's look at how we can easily create letters that people will love to receive.

Chances are good that you have Microsoft Word (or Works), so let's use it to create a letter. To add a little tradition to our letter, how about selecting a font, such as Courier, that resembles the output of an old typewriter? Now how about adding an image? For the sake of this example, assume that both the sender and recipient enjoy cooking. If you have a digital camera, you could arrange a variety of things on your kitchen counter—

maybe a few different kinds of fruit, vegetables, pasta, or even cooking oil bottles. Just take a few pictures—don't fret too much about the quality of the pictures, because quality won't matter much. Download the pictures from the camera to the computer and pick one that you like. That is exactly what I did for this example—I chose cooking oil bottles!

Using a masking technique from Chapter 6, "Performing Digital Imaging Magic," you can select the part of the image that you want to use and allow it to blend into the white background. Just before saving it, you will need to lighten it by about 50 percent. From a new document in Word, select Insert>Picture>From File, and then select the picture that you saved. After the picture loads, right-click it and select Format Picture from the pop-up menu. In the Format Picture dialog box that appears, select the Layout tab, select Behind Text, and then select Center as the choice for horizontal alignment. Click the OK button, and you are ready to type your letter, as shown in Figure 9.12.

Figure 9.12
Using Microsoft Word to create a background image.

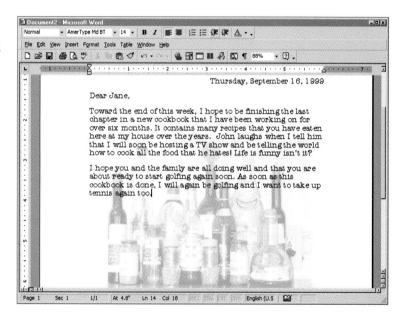

This process enables you to use any image as a "watermark" for writing paper. When you begin typing, you type right over the top of the image as if it were already printed onto the paper. When you print it on a color desk-jet printer, you will be very pleased with the results. After you do this a time or two, you'll find that you can shoot a picture, adjust and place the image, and begin to type in under ten minutes! This means that you can create great-looking letters to suit your taste any time that you need them.

Part III Using Images

You can make a background with any image you'd like to use. It can be the face of a family member, an image of your new home, an old pet, or even a picture of one of your favorite roses from the garden. After you complete one successfully with full color, check whether your digital image editor will create duotones. If so, try using a duotone (a two-color image) These make great images. If you can't create duotones, then just desaturate your image (remove all the color) and then tint it with one or two colors—you'll get the same results. To learn more about these techniques see Chapter 7, "Filtering for Special Effects."

Microsoft Word has several other features that enable you to vastly improve the look of personal letters through the display of digital images. In the same dialog box that you used to set the background image, you are given a choice of aligning text square against an image, wrapping text around an image, or picking one of a few other text-formatting options. Learn about these features and create images with your digital image editor so that you can make text wrap around your image. Using the wrap-around feature, you can, for example, have text run right up to the sloping edge of a Christmas tree on both sides. You can keep typing until the Christmas tree is surrounded by text.

While we are on the letter-writing topic, let's see what we can do with holiday letters. Over the last several years, it seems that more and more people are getting into the tradition of writing and sending family holiday letters around Christmastime. These letters usually tell what each family member has done during the year and end with best wishes for the new year. Unless these letters (or sometimes poems) are well-written and interesting, they often just sit in the Christmas card pile, unread. Using appropriate digital images and a few less words, you can say more and in a more interesting way. Consider sending a Christmas letter this year with a few digital images to differentiate your letters from the others in the pile.

I have always liked the idea of a Christmas letter but have never been able to get them out by Christmas! Therefore, each year, I plan to send a Christmas letter, and when it's not done until well into January, I send it as a New Year's letter—appropriately ending the old year and wishing the best to all for the new year. This past January, I combined a variety of pictures into one letterhead image for our New Year's letter, as shown in Figure 9.13.

Figure 9.13
A digital image used on a New Year's letter combining duotones and color images.

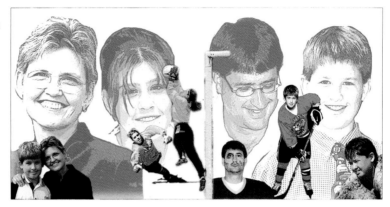

Although this image was not difficult to create, it did take time, because it was made from ten images carefully selected and cut from ten different photographs. After copying and pasting the four larger faces into a file, it was converted into a duotone. Then, each of the other six images was scaled and placed on top of the duotone in full color. The combined image was then placed at the top of a sepia-colored 8½x11-inch paper on which the New Year's letter was written.

Creating a photomontage

Sometimes you'll want to combine more than one image into a single image to get the results that you desire. Combining photographs is a very old technique that has been used for years. Until now, however, you had to cut and paste without all the benefits of the new digital cut-and-paste techniques! With any digital image editor, you can quickly create an image such as the one shown in Figure 9.14 without fuss.

Figure 9.14
A photomontage created with MGI's PhotoSuite III.

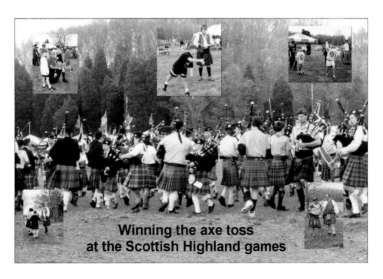

Winning the axe toss
at the Scottish Highland games

With a little more effort and a lot more time, you can even create an image such as the one shown in Figure 9.15. After carefully selecting six images from six separate photographs and inserting them into a single image, the picture looks like five goalies are in the game. Once all the images were placed, a watercolor filter was applied to give it an artsy look. It sure looks like it's hard to score a goal against the team with the goalie wearing the yellow jersey, even if you use more than one ball!

Figure 9.15
Combining soccer goalies from a variety of images into a single image.

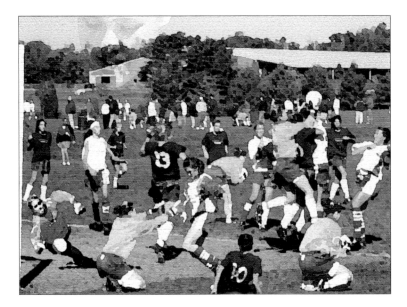

Another technique that has become very popular in recent years is creating an image composed of hundreds or even thousands of other images. When I first saw one of these images in a shopping mall, I began to wonder who would take the time to create such an image. Many of these merchants would offer dozens of these posters! Now you can create such an image in the time that it takes you to fix and eat a sandwich— which you might want to do, because the creation process takes more than a few minutes, depending on the speed of your computer. Figure 9.16 was created by using MGI's PhotoSuite III and the PhotoTapestry effect. PhotoTapestry re-creates any photograph by using small, thumbnail photos from a large thumbnail database that comes with the product.

Figure 9.16
Creating a
PhotoTapestry with
MGI's PhotoSuite III.

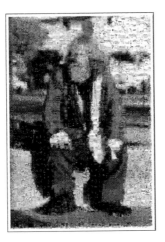

In case you were wondering, the PhotoTapestry print shown in Figure 9.16 was made with 1,500 separate images. It took twenty minutes to create, using a 400MHz Pentium computer. That's not too bad, considering how long it would have taken to do manually. The final print was 11x16 inches and was printed on photographic quality paper at 300 dpi, which required a 45MB file. It turned out quite well—well enough, in fact, to generate lots of questions asking how long it took me to pick and place all of those separate images!

Greeting cards

Greeting cards might be one of the most popular projects to create for those who have a color printer. Most greeting card creation software, unfortunately, offers far more cards with no space or little space for images than cards with space for images. This means that you have to get creative and make your own cards by extensively modifying one of the predesigned templates included with the software. When a friend fell off her horse and broke a few ribs, we decided to add a little humor to the very painful event. I found an old photograph of her horse that I had taken a year or so earlier, and I used a few filters on it to make it look more like an image for a humorous greeting card. The result of this work is the card shown in Figure 9.17. (Figure 11.11 shows an electronic version of a greeting card made for the same occasion. I liked the printed one better and so that is the one that was used.)

Part III Using Images

Figure 9.17
A get-well card
featuring the recipient's
horse.

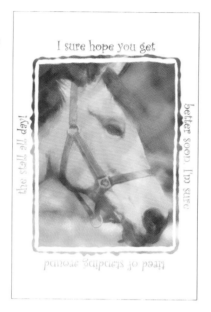

If you have a favorite image or two, you might want to make your own
note cards, like the one shown in Figure 9.18. That particular cat image
was printed on an embossed greeting card stock, which made it look
wonderful. For someone who likes cats, this card would be hard to throw
away, because the eyes are bright and magical—they appear to be looking
straight at you. It's almost a work of art.

Figure 9.18
An embossed note card
featuring a cat image
taken with a digital
camera.

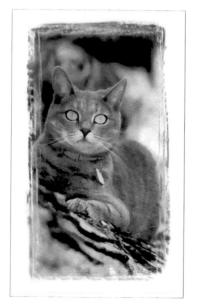

Wine bottle labels

Not too long ago, I attended a wedding at which a very impressive touch was added to the occasion—they served wine and a sparkling beverage in wine bottles that had custom labels made especially for the wedding. With a little creativity, you too can add such a special touch to a wedding, a birthday party, or other special event. Using MGI's PhotoSuite III, you can pick from a good selection of wine bottle templates or create your own from scratch. Add an image and some appropriate text, and you have created a unique label for a bottle that someone is likely to want to keep forever. Figure 9.19 shows a wedding label that was created especially for Jack and Jill. If you have an anniversary coming up, consider making a special label for the occasion. My wife is considering making one for me when this book is finished!

Figure 9.19
Creating a wine bottle label with MGI's PhotoSuite III.

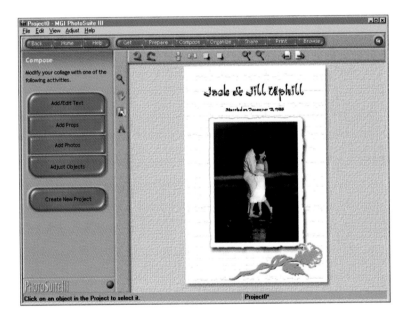

Calendars

If you have time, the inclination, and twelve good images, then you really ought to make a calendar for someone or even for yourself. Of all the things that I have seen created with various software products and services that help you do projects, I like twelve-month calendars the most. They make excellent gifts for grandparents, family members, friends, and business colleagues. They are great for showing off your best digital images, your pets, or your twelve largest fish! Remember the tricks you learned in Chapter 6, "Performing Digital Imaging Magic." To make some very believable images, you simply cut out and enlarge by a foot or so each of the twelve largest fish that you have caught. You'll have documented proof that you are the greatest fisherman in the world.

Part III Using Images

TIP

You might want to save money and especially time by getting your twelve-month calendars printed at a local photo finisher, such as Wolf Camera or Ritz Camera. Both of these national chain photo retail stores offer relatively inexpensive calendars (less than $36, or $3.00 per month) that can be made with twelve of your images. If you have taken the time to create twelve images for a calendar, you ought to order several of them, because additional copies are cheaper than the first one. Using these services will save you the time and aggravation of having to print twelve or more pages per calendar on your printer and then assemble them in the proper order.

Most of the applications that have been mentioned in this chapter can be used to create calendars, including Microsoft Word. However, Broderbund's Calendar Creator 6 takes calendar creation a few steps further by giving you all kinds of options that aren't possible with the other applications. You can select from dozens of layout options and easily add events, such as birthdays, anniversaries, and meetings. You can even choose lists of holidays for many different countries or select from a list of other special days, such as birthdays of actors or sports figures, feast days of Italian saints, or any one of approximately forty-five other categories of fun and special days. If it is your job to create calendars for youth practice schedules or for church events, this is an excellent product to use. With the Repeating Events option, you can easily create a new calendar for each month, with all the important information that you want to include on it (see Figure 9.20).

Figure 9.20
Adding a calendar event with Calendar Creator 6.

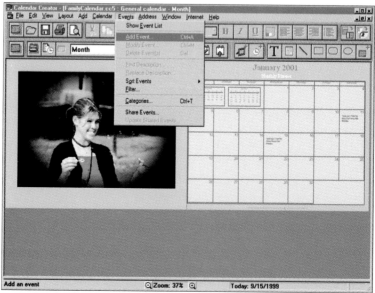

If you decide to print a calendar yourself, you ought to consider using one of the specialty papers discussed in Chapter 13, "Obtaining the Best Possible Printed Images." Specifically, consider purchasing International Paper's Invent-It! Photo Calendar Kit or a high-quality, heavy card stock.

Photo album pages

In Chapter 8, "Displaying Digital Images Electronically," we created digital photo albums to be displayed on a computer screen. However, just because you shoot pictures with a digital camera or like to manipulate your images digitally doesn't mean that you can't create a traditional photo album—one in which photos are mounted on paper and placed in a binder. In fact, you'll find that creating such an album has many benefits over using traditional photos. After you place digital images, you can print multiple copies for far less money than it would cost to have multiple photographs printed and placed on a photo album page (see Figure 9.21). In addition, you save lots of time by not having to find negatives, fill out reprint forms, drop off the negatives, and then pick up the reprints from a photo finisher.

Figure 9.21
Photo album page being created in MGI's PhotoSuite III.

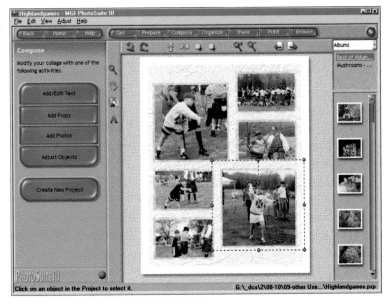

Part III Using Images

A very creative solution to making printed photo album pages is offered by Kodak. Kodak offers Kodak Picture Pages software, special high-quality durable Kodak Picture Page album pages and an online service through the Kodak PhotoNet Online Service. Using the software, you can select digital images from your PC or get them online from Kodak PhotoNet Online. You then have the option of letting a wizard organize all your images on each page for you, or you can manually place them yourself. Once your images are placed where you want them, you can add text to them and they are ready to be printed. Figure 9.22 shows the Picture Pages software and a Print Preview window.

Figure 9.22
Creating photo album pages with Kodak Picture Pages software.

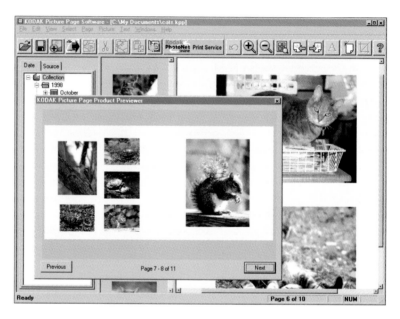

To learn more about Picture Pages software, products, and services visit **www.kodak.com/go/picturepages**. If you consider that you could have ten to twelve images (five or six images on front and back) on each page, printing albums in this manner is much less than it would be if you were to buy an album and pay $.40 per print. If you want several copies of each album, this is a great way to get them.

Additional applications that enable you to create photo albums include most project software applications, such as Kai's Soap2 (see Figure 9.23), MGI's PhotoSuite III, and Ulead's Photo Express.

Figure 9.23
An album page created
in Kai's Soap2.

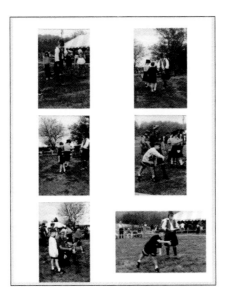

Part III Using Images

Adding images to a family tree

Another especially fun and valuable project that you can create is a family tree made up of images of each family member. Obviously, you don't have to limit yourself to making family trees of people—you can even make them of a cat family, as shown in Figure 9.24. I happen to have a family tree of all my relatives who came over from Italy through Ellis Island to work in the coal mines in Wyoming. It truly is one of my most valued prints. The best part about it is that it was easy to copy and give as gifts to other relatives. If your family is important to you, make a family tree and give it to others at your next family get-together—everyone will enjoy it.

Figure 9.24
A cat family tree created in MGI's PhotoSuite III.

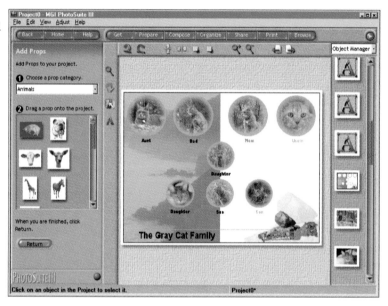

Flyers

Each year, most families have the need to create one or more flyers. Flyers are good for selling used sports equipment, finding a babysitter, selling a car, or even finding a lost turtle (see Figure 9.25). Kids can use flyers to get jobs mowing lawns or raking leaves. Flyers are easy to create with any word processor or desktop publishing package. If you use a product such as Ulead's Photo Express, MGI's PhotoSuite III, or The Print Shop Pro 10.0, they can be even easier to make, and the results might be better. The templates in these packages make creating a flyer exceptionally easy.

Figure 9.25
A lost turtle flyer being created in Ulead's Photo Express.

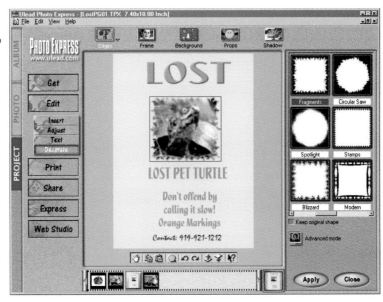

Part III Using Images

Image projects for kids

If you have children, you will probably have more ideas about how to use your images on projects for the kids than you have time to complete them. To make sure this chapter is complete, however, I will list a few useful and fun projects you might like to do.

Birthday party invitations

First, how about creating a birthday party invitation? You'll be a hero to your child as well as his or her guests if you use a little imagination and create a personalized birthday party invitation. Maybe your child is into cars, gymnastics, or baseball. Use these or other topics to create cards specifically for them, or just use a standard template and create one similar to Figure 9.26.

Figure 9.26
Birthday invitation being created in Ulead's Photo Express.

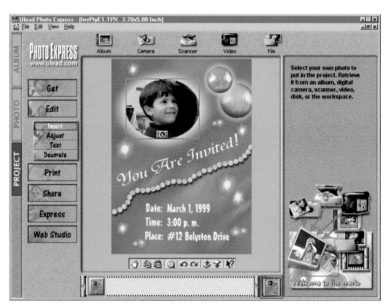

Creating fun pictures

One of the advantages of living in a neighborhood is that children often get to be very close friends as they grow up together. They can be very proud of these friendships. Think about creating an image of your children's friends that they can put on a T-shirt or use on their notebook covers. The image in Figure 9.27 was created for a greeting card that invited the neighborhood gang to a birthday party and a movie. It was a big hit—both the evening and the card!

Figure 9.27
Picture of the "neighborhood gang."

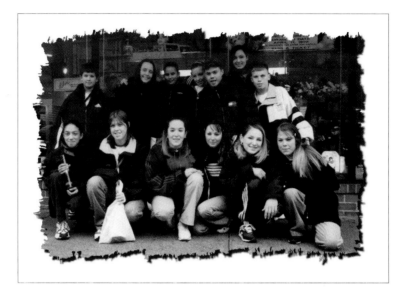

Part III Using Images

Sometimes it's fun just to create things with no real purpose in mind. The images in figures 9.28 and 9.29 were both created just for the fun of it. They were both worth a few laughs and ended up in a drawer for a few future laughs.

Figure 9.28
A newspaper created with Microsoft's Picture It!

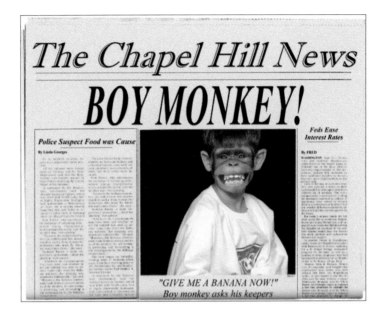

Figure 9.29
Magazine cover created in MGI's PhotoSuite III.

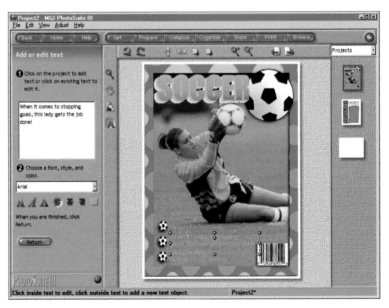

Images for coaches

Youth sport coaches donate a tremendous amount of time and effort to coach teams. Unless you have coached a team, it might appear to be much easier and more fun that it oftentimes is. Thank your child's coaches for the efforts they put into teaching your child how to play a sport by presenting them with a signed and framed image of the team. Figure 9.30 is an image that was created for a coach whose son played on the team. The coach's son was a tremendous lacrosse player and led the team in goals. If you look carefully, you can see that there are four pictures of the player wearing 21 on his jersey—that is the coach's son, and in three of those four images, he had just scored. The collage on the bottom was created by digitally cutting, pasting, sizing, and adjusting parts of four other photographs. The final image was set in a matte border and framed. Each player wrote his jersey number and signed his name on the border. This gift will be valued for a long time.

Figure 9.30
A season-end photograph created for a parent coach.

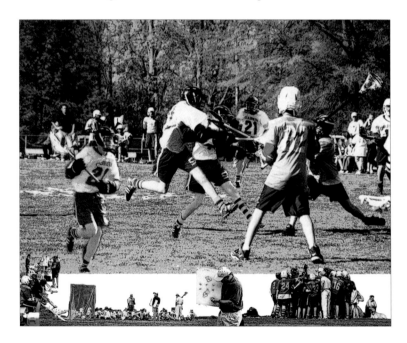

Part III Using Images

Sports cards and posters

Once you are able to create quality digital images and projects from your pictures, you might be able to use this talent to help raise funds for your child's sports teams. At the end of the lacrosse season one year, I chose the best photograph of each player and digitally edited and printed it on a high-quality fine-art paper or photographic paper, depending on the style of the work. These images then were made available to the parents for $20, with the understanding that the entire amount would be donated back to the team to purchase new jerseys for an upcoming season. Nearly all of the images were sold, and the team was able to buy new jerseys in the following year. Five of these images are shown in Figure 9.31.

Figure 9.31
Digitally edited images of lacrosse players created to raise money for the team.

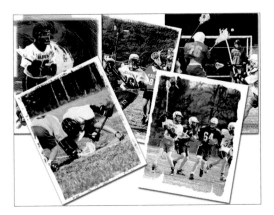

If you have limited time for creating these projects, but you need them done, consider teaching your children how to use the applications. Help them come up with a few ideas for projects that they would like to do. Suggest things such as a book or notebook cover, bookmarkers, or pages for school reports. Once they have a little success, they will continue building on it and can become your own in-house design staff. It is amazing to see how fast children can become experts on computer technologies. Who knows—maybe they can even help you do things for your own business or work, which will give you a little more time to get them to all of those soccer practices, while still keeping up with the other household chores!

Image creations just for art's sake

When you were a child, did you spend most of your free time drawing or painting? Have you always wanted to be able to create artwork that was good enough that you could frame it and put it on the walls in your own home or office? If a part of you is just dying to be creative, my advice is to begin creating art—just for art's sake.

Skip a few evenings of watching TV or aimlessly surfing the Internet and instead spend your time working with a digital image editor. Go back through your old photographs and pull out a few dozen that look interesting. Scan them and then experiment to see what you can do with them. Buy a digital camera and begin shooting pictures specifically to create digital images. Chapter 2, "Learning to Take Better Pictures," offers a "starter set" of fifteen digital imaging techniques that will help you shoot images that you can use to create work that you will be pleased with.

Artwork to be framed

About ten years ago, I stopped on a very long, desolate stretch of highway to take a few pictures of several old rusty cars. When I looked for a few photographs to use for this book, I found those pictures and immediately realized how good they might look after a few filters were applied. Twenty minutes later, one of those photographs had turned into a 6x10-inch print on fine-art paper. The highlights in the window, on the headlights, and in the open suitcase make this a spectacular print (see Figure 9.32).

Figure 9.32
Art-quality print depicting an open suitcase and old cars.

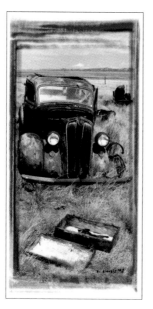

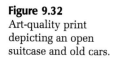

Part III Using Images

After adding a signature, a date, and a border, it looked like a real painting. Figure 9.33 shows a second image that was transformed into an art-like print. Incidently, this is the same image that we used in Chapter 6. If you recall, we added a third flower and seven butterflies. There is no reason why you can't create images like these. Try it.

Figure 9.33
Photograph turned into artwork with filters.

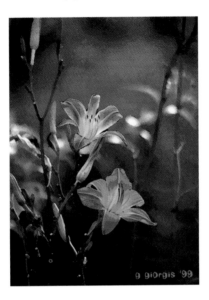

Images to accompany short stories

Do you enjoy writing, as well as taking photographs and creating digital images? If you do, here is an idea that might appeal to you. Take ten or so of your favorite digital images, transform them into similar types of images with a few filters, and add an appropriate frame to them. Use each one as the basis for a short story. You can choose to use images with a common subject and write stories for children, or for anyone for that matter. You might even want to write these stories just about the real events that surround the images that you have chosen. The transformed images can often be a strong impetus to help you write a great story with more clarity and detail than you might have written without the images (see Figure 9.34). Who knows, your stories might be so good that you can get them published.

Figure 9.34
One of several duotone images created for a series of short stories.

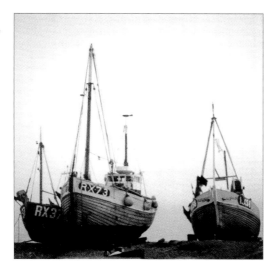

The point here is that if you enjoy being creative, then create. Buy a few software applications and a good color printer and enjoy yourself. You'll never know how good you can be until you try.

Other cool things to do with images

Most of the projects covered in this chapter so far have resulted in images that were to be printed on one kind of paper or another. Your images can be put onto many other things, such as T-shirts, mouse pads, coffee mugs, sweatshirts, puzzles, hats, ties, aprons, buttons, tote bags, and a wide range of additional items. Check with your local photoprocessor to see what items they offer. If you don't find something that you like, visit one of the Internet sites, such as **www.wolfcamera.com** or **www.ritzcamera.com**. Make sure to read Chapter 13, "Obtaining the Best Possible Printed Images," because it also covers this topic.

In the preceding few pages, we have looked at projects for home, work, kids, and you. Don't forget that you can also use digital images in projects for your church, special-cause groups, and other organizations. Tradition is the basis for many of these types of organizations. Often, these traditions can be strengthened and grown by creating some documentaries of people and events. Help make your church bulletins or newsletters become more interesting by adding some appropriate digital images. Scan photographs to document fund-raising events or work done by charity groups. People enjoy seeing themselves in pictures, if they are good ones.

Part III Using Images

The projects in this chapter are just a few of the millions that you can do. The point of this chapter is a simple one: You can do many more things with your digital images than simply using them digitally (on a Web page or as an e-mail attachment) or printing them like photographs. Be creative and invent your own projects, or use templates and modify them to suit your own needs.

At this point, if you are going to be caught in the vicious circle of digital imaging, you are in it now. This vicious circle begins when you reach the point at which you can create images that you really like, and you begin using those images to make things such as those mentioned in this chapter. The more you use your images to complete projects, the more projects you will want to do—and the more images you'll need to complete these projects! I am most certainly caught in this circle and hope that you will join me. Life is supposed to be fun, and digital imaging projects can certainly be fun—especially when you start seeing the joy that others have when receiving your work. I hope that you will experience the joy of seeing someone else truly appreciate your work— then it is all worth the time, effort, and, yes—money, too.

In the last chapter, we looked at ways to create digital things—digital photo albums, slide shows, and screen-savers. This chapter introduced you to many projects that resulted in nondigital things, such as printed calendars, greeting cards, business cards, sports cards, and bookmarkers, to name just a few. In the next chapter, we'll return to the digital world and learn how to create some truly amazing things, such as virtual panoramas, animations, and even videos.

10
Doing Extraordinary Things with Images

Wait!—don't skip this chapter just because you think you don't want to do something extraordinary with your digital images. You'll never know what you are missing. This chapter shows how you can use your images to do some awe-inspiring things. You'll also get a little comic relief when we get to the section on morphing. That might be where you can get a chuckle or two by altering a photograph of your mother-in-law or a crabby, autocratic boss. So, read on, my friends.

Seriously, as the title suggests, this chapter explores doing extraordinary things with images. Some of these extraordinary things might be absolutely invaluable to your business. They might be used to sell your home, auction your artwork, or rent more rooms in a bed-and-breakfast hotel. You might even use some of these innovative tools to create a Web page that will help you get a new job designing Web pages—or if you're already a Web page designer, they might help you to win a new project— because these are leading-edge tools.

We'll look at how you can electronically stitch together your images to create perfect panoramic views, and even how they can be linked in a full circle to produce a 360-degree movie. We're also going to look at how you can make an object spin as if it were turning in front of you. Creating animations, morphing images, and putting your images into 3D worlds are the last few topics that will be covered.

Stitching images together to create a panorama

Anyone who has taken pictures with a camera has, at one time or another, felt the frustration of not being able to get the full view of what you want in the picture. Until recently, solutions to this problem were limited. You could use an expensive wide-angle or fish-eye camera lens, which has a tendency to warp the world to make it all fit in an image. Alternatively, you could shoot multiple photos and tape them together—I have done that before! Now we have digital image stitching software—software that enables you to digitally stitch a series of digital images together in a seamless and continuous manner for perfect panoramic images or prints or even movies.

With digital image stitching software and a printer that enables you to print on paper wider than 11 inches, you can create those panoramas that you have always dreamed about. As one of those work-at-home types, I am a member of the SOHO Club—the Small Office/Home Office Club. For my Web page, I wanted to include a view of my office, which has windows on three sides. Without digital stitching software, this office is terribly difficult to photograph and even more difficult to show online. I took eight pictures in the fall with all the rich fall colors showing through the windows. After I scanned the images and put them into a folder, I was able to flawlessly stitch them together in about ten minutes, using PictureWorks Technologies Inc.'s SpinPanorama. The result is the image shown in Figure 10.1. Ah, how right you are—the image is too wide to show on a single book page. To see it in a reasonably large size, you'll have to visit **www.reallyusefulpage.com/dcs/10-01.htm**.

You can scroll the image inside your browser's window to see the entire image. Pretty cool, wouldn't you say? If you think that's cool, read on to learn how you can create a full 360-degree panoramic movie with zooming, panning, and tilting capabilities.

Figure 10.1
Panorama view of a home office made by digitally stitching multiple images together.

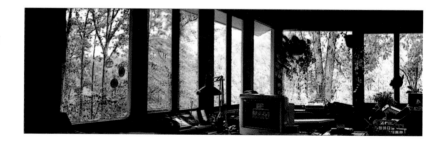

NOTE

Hoping to create a different kind of art that would sell well in galleries, an artist decided to create exceptionally wide and narrow panoramic views of famous landscapes and cityscapes. Using multiple photographs, digital image editing software, and some digital image stitching software, he was able to create some unique and outstanding prints. A commercial printer of tourist posters saw several of his images and commissioned him to complete panoramic views of twenty-five cities to be sold in stores attracting tourists.

MGI Software's Photo Suite III Platinum Edition includes a "lite" version of Enroute's Quick Stitch software, which is sufficient to stitch a few images together. It even enables you to choose from three stitching methods: wide (for horizontal panoramas), tall (for vertical scenes), or square (combination of wide and tall). If you want even more capabilities, consider Enroute's full-version Quick Stitch.

TIP

Before you spend money on a digital image stitching application just to create wide panoramic views, check all of your current software to see whether it might have the capabilities to stitch together images. Some digital cameras come bundled with a basic version of image stitching software.

Creating 360-degree panoramas

The title of this chapter suggests that we are going to do some extraordinary things with our digital images. Extraordinary is absolutely the word to use to describe 360-degree panoramas, which are also known as QuickTime Virtual Reality (QuickTime VR) movies. The best way to understand what a QuickTime VR movie is is to see one. For a quick example, I used a digital camera and PictureWorks Technologies Inc.'s SpinPanorama to create a QuickTime Virtual Reality (VR) movie of a place deep inside a hurricane-ravaged forest in North Carolina. You can view it at:

www.reallyusefulpage.com/dcs/10-01.htm

If you can't visit that page, the second best way to understand a QuickTime VR movie is to imagine that you are standing in the middle of a merry-go-round in the middle of the forest. As the merry-go-round spins to your left, you'll see more of the forest to your left—obviously, as it spins to the right, you'll see more of the forest on your right. As you continue around, you'll finally end back where you started. Now imagine that as you spin in either direction, you can also look up and see more of the treetops and as you look down you'll see more of the forest floor. Now imagine that all of that can be seen in a window on your PC screen and that you can control the movement with your mouse. You can even zoom in!

QuickTime VR movies are easy to create, and they load easily onto a Web page. They can be a very powerful tool to show places or things that are very hard to show any other way. For those of you who want to learn more about QuickTime VR, visit **www.apple.com/quicktime**. This is also the place to go to get the QuickTime VR plug-in. (A plug-in is specialized software that enables things like QuickTime VR movies to be viewed inside a Web browser.) If you want even more information, I highly recommend *The QuickTime VR Book,* by Susan A. Kitchens, (PeachPit Press, ISBN: 0-201-69684-3).

In a moment, I will walk you through the process of creating the forest movie, but first let's look at what the final creation looks like. Figure 10.2 shows the QuickTime VR movie window. I chose to create a window that is 640 pixels wide and 400 pixels deep. The movie was created by digitally stitching together ten digital images that were taken with a digital camera mounted on a tripod. Shooting the pictures is very simple—shoot one picture and rotate the camera until you get to where you need to shoot the next picture; leaving a small overlap between the two pictures, shoot the next picture and then continue in this manner until you are back to where you started (plus a small overlap). To minimize warp, you should use a lens that enables you to shoot between ten and twenty-four images. Once again, don't take my word about how cool these movies can be—go see a few at:

www.reallyusefulpage.com/dcs/10-01.htm

You'll find the forest movie there, as well as several other movies that I have created, plus links to a few other sites that have QuickTime VR movies. Go on—set the book down, go to your browser, and type in the URL. It will be worth the time it takes you to visit. If you don't have the Apple QuickTime VR plug-in that is required, instructions are provided for getting it free of charge and downloading it. When viewing any of the movies, make sure you zoom in and out as well as move left, right, up, and down. You do all of this by placing your cursor in the middle of the movie window and moving it in the direction that you want to move. The farther you move your cursor from where you initially clicked the image, the faster the movie will move. Don't go too fast, though, because you'll truly get dizzy!

Figure 10.2
A 360-degree QuickTime VR movie of a hurricane-damaged forest.

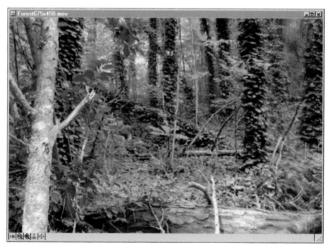

Once you have all the images that you want to use in a single directory, launch SpinPanorama and follow the four steps suggested by the four tabs shown in Figure 10.3. The first tab is Get Photos—and that is what you do—simply use the browser to find the directory where your images are stored. Click the Insert All button, and all the images are loaded. The next step is to stitch together the images. You can use either the SmartStitch feature and allow the software to intelligently match all the images—which worked perfectly in this case—or the match-up-points feature, shown by the green lines and circles in Figure 10.3. Notice that you have a detail view below the images, showing the exact points that you are matching so that your alignment is perfect.

Figure 10.3
Stitching images together with SpinPanorama.

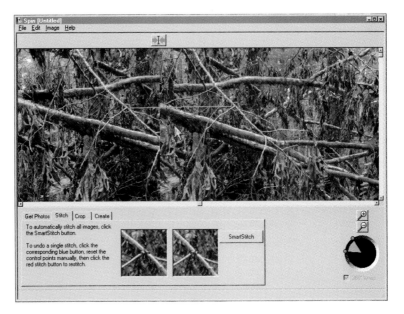

The next step is to crop your panorama. If you used a tripod, took some care in shooting the pictures, and your camera was level, you will lose very little of the image. If not, just set the crop lines to a place where every frame shows a complete image. Then, on to the final stage—the create step. You can set the viewing window size in pixels, and you have control over the level of file compression and image quality. Optionally, you can save all the images as a panorama, similar to the office in the first section of this chapter, or you can complete the circle and turn the set of images into a full 360-degree panorama. That's it—you are ready to view your panorama as soon as it has been written to a file! Using a digital camera, it is very possible to shoot eighteen pictures, create a movie, and upload it to the Internet for viewing on a Web page in under one hour.

Other software applications besides SpinPanorama enable you to create hot-links in the movie, too. Thus, for example, you can create a movie of a home that enables the viewer to take a 360-degree tour of one room, click a hotspot on another room's doorway to be transported to that room for another 360-degree tour, and so on. A few more clicks, and the viewer can tour an entire house, plus any other place that's included in the movie, such as the back yard and pool area. Just think of the possibilities—virtual tours of your home, your building, or design projects on the Internet!

NOTE

An interior designer needed a new Web page to help sell her services. Digital images provide reasonable views of the rooms that she has decorated, but they don't show her work as well as she would like. One week, she visited five of her best projects and shot a series of pictures with her digital camera to use for movies. In less than four hours, she was able to create five QuickTime VR movies of those five projects and put them on her Web page. Now, when she talks on the telephone with prospective clients, she suggests that they visit her Web page and look at some of her projects, where they can even zoom in and out for more detail when needed.

There is a sculpture garden near Charleston, South Carolina, called Brookgreen Gardens. It is home to one of the most amazing collections of outdoor sculptures in the world. It is also an unusually beautiful garden. To record my visit there, I set up a camera on a tripod in the center of the garden and shot a series of pictures to be used for a panoramic movie. I wanted it to be different and entertaining, so I used several of the magical techniques that you learned about in Chapter 6, "Performing Digital Imaging Magic."

I placed a variety of objects in the garden, including a cat, an old bicycle, a horse with a rider, a turtle, a monkey, and a few other things just for fun. Many of these objects are totally out of scale—the cat is sitting behind a five-foot hedge and is looking over the top. The soccer ball is as large as one of those huge beach balls. There is a turtle large enough for a grown person to ride. The entire garden looks like a place created for a movie of *Alice in Wonderland*. One segment of this movie is shown in Figure 10.4. With a little creativity, just imagine the worlds you might be able to create! If you are interested, you can view this movie at **www.reallyusefulpage.com/dcs/10-01.htm**.

Figure 10.4
One segment of the
Brookgreen Gardens
movie with added
elements.

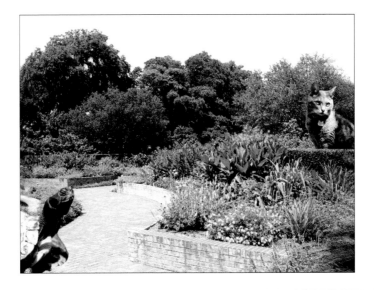

NOTE

An owner of a bed-and-breakfast hotel situated in an idyllic setting near a
waterfall wanted prospective guests to be able to see the beauty of the site.
With an ordinary 35mm camera and a tripod, he shot a series of pictures of
the hotel and surrounding area. Using services from his regular, local photo
finisher, he had the images scanned and returned to him on a CD-ROM. With
these images, he created a panoramic movie and put it on his Web site.
Within a few weeks, he noticed a significant increase in the number of
telephone calls and reservations.

Now that you understand more about QuickTime VR movies, you might
want to see a few more and learn more about how they can be used.
Three additional Web sites worth visiting are:

www.vrview.com/
www.pbs.org/wgbh/nova/everest/climb/
www.harrods.com/qtvr/front/index.htm

Displaying rotating objects

Imagine that you have just completed a new statue for a garden, and you
have a potential buyer on the other side of the country. You might not
want to send photographs, because the sculpture is much more
magnificent when it is viewed in three dimensions. Perhaps you are a
woodworker, and you want to be able to show a new piece of furniture
from all angles on your Web page. The need to display all kinds of objects
so that they can be viewed from any angle is common for anyone wanting
to display objects electronically—either on a Web page, on a computer
screen, as an e-mail attachment, or in an electronic presentation.

Guess what? There is a terrific solution to this requirement. PictureWorks Technologies Inc.'s Spin PhotoObject enables you to easily turn still images into 360-degree panoramic movies. When you first see one of these videos, you'll wonder if you can believe what you see. The results make you think you are somehow magically able to control the speed, direction, and angle of a video camera while you watch it! How can that be possible? Believe it or not, creating one of these videos is an easy five-step process based upon a series of still pictures taken with an ordinary film-based or digital camera.

Spin PhotoObject is very similar to SpinPanorama, except that instead of standing still and having the scene spin around you, you stand still and watch as an object is rotated in front of you. As I suggested when I introduced the panorama QuickTime VR movies, you also really ought to watch an object movie before you continue reading. They are quite cool. You can view several movies created with Spin PhotoObject at **www.reallyusefulpage.com/dcs/10-02.htm**.

If you don't have a browser handy, Figure 10.5 shows a QuickTime VR movie window displaying a clay water pitcher. You can see the icons located below the movie. They let you control the video—you can zoom in and out and drag the image as you choose.

Figure 10.5
QuickTime VR movie window of a rotating water pitcher.

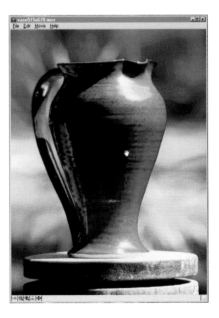

NOTE

A potter who opened a new gallery next to her studio also launched a new online gallery to help build sales outside her home market. Using clay, she sculpts wonderful vases, flower bowls, and water fountains. To show these 3D artworks on a Web page, she took digital pictures of her work as she rotated them a few degrees at a time on her potter's wheel. After taking eighteen images, she used software to turn those images into a QuickTime VR movie that could be placed on her Web page. The video enables prospective buyers to see each object from any angle—it even enables them to zoom in and out. Sales from her new Web site were far better than she expected, and she had to hire a potter's assistant to help meet the demand. Additionally, she decided to provide an inside look at her studio with a second movie that enabled her Web site guests to see her in action.

Spin PhotoObject enables users of all skill levels to create, view, and share high-impact object movies. All the work is done in a simple application screen with four tabs, as shown in Figure 10.6. Creating a QuickTime VR movie with Spin PhotoObject is a five-step process:

Figure 10.6
Spin PhotoObject application showing the creation of a movie of a pitcher.

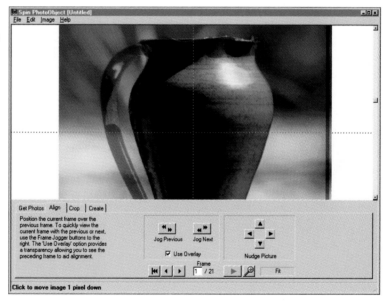

Part III Using Images

1. Shoot pictures of the object as it is rotated around its center point. That is 30 degrees per picture, or eighteen shots in total. You can shoot a different number of pictures, but it is easy to measure 30 degrees per turn.

2. Digital versions of the pictures need to be placed in a single file folder on a PC. They should be numbered sequentially so that they can load in order automatically. If you used a digital camera, they are probably all sequentially numbered; otherwise you'll have to rename each file manually.

3. Starting with the first picture, each successive picture can be nudged to match up with the preceding picture. This step helps create a smooth video.

4. All images can then be cropped in one step by adjusting a box around the portion of the image that you want to show in the video.

5. As a final step, set the output size in pixels and select a folder and file name for the video. Click the Create button, and the video will be ready to be viewed within a few seconds.

This book is not a how-to book, so you are probably wondering why a list of how-to steps is included. The reason, basically, is to show you how easy it is to create one of these useful movies. Try one!

Animating things for special effects

If you have spent any time surfing the Internet, you have a good idea of what animation is all about. Unfortunately, not all Internet animation is good, and most of it takes too much time to download, which becomes a nuisance when you visit the same site more than once. However, that doesn't mean that animation can't be useful and fun. Besides putting animation on Web pages, you can include it in presentations, slide shows, some kinds of electronic documents, and multimedia projects.

One of the more capable animators is Animation Shop 2 from Jasc Software, the makers of Paint Shop Pro 6. Just for fun, I took twenty photographs of an awesome kid. Having taken the shots with a digital camera, it was easy to choose the twelve best (see Figure 10.7) and then crop and animate them for a small animation that makes you feel almost like you are sitting in front of the awesome kid as the animation begins.

Figure 10.7
Images to be used in animation.

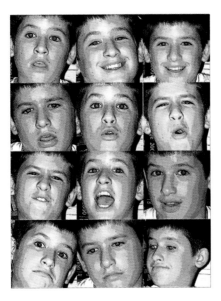

The animation is very easy to create when using Animation Shop 2, as shown in Figure 10.8. Once the animation is complete, it will run any time the file is opened for viewing, or it can be dropped into a Web page. You can see this animation at:

www.reallyusefulpage.com/dcs/10-02.htm

Figure 10.8
Using Animation Shop 2 to create an animation.

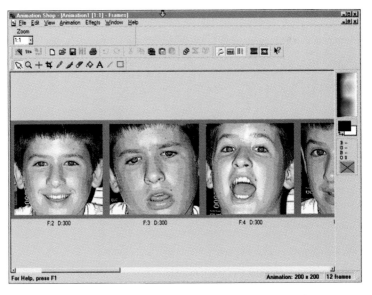

Used appropriately, animations can be very effective elements to make your documents, Web pages, or presentations more enjoyable. The addition of simulated movement in an animation can also be useful to explain concepts that are difficult to explain with static images.

Part III Using Images

Morphing things for fun and entertainment

For those of you who think this book has been too serious, with nothing but practical and useful stuff on each page, here is something that you might enjoy. We'll look at ways to morph one image into another image. While there are serious applications for morphing technology, it can also be used for pure entertainment.

Morphing is the act of transforming one thing into another. This transformation process generally happens over time. Many of the tools that enable you to transform one image into another image also enable you to animate the transformation process. One of the most capable morphing applications is MetaCreations' SuperGoo, which is billed as "real-time liquid imaging funware."

SuperGoo enables you to stretch, warp, and distort your images in just about any imaginable way. After you complete your work, you can save the distortion as a series of images, showing your effects from the initial view to the final distorted image. You can also save these images as a movie to be used on a Web page, included in a multimedia presentation, or even e-mailed to a friend. Figure 10.9 shows an image of an awesome kid that is about to undergo full facial morphing.

Figure 10.9
The awesome kid before morphing.

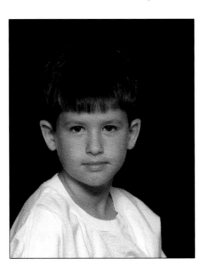

Figure 10.10 shows the results of some careful and fun morphing. Using ordinary filters from a digital image editing application like Paint Shop Pro 6 or Photoshop, you can then turn a morphed image into a more cartoon-like image like the one shown in Figure 10.11. This resulting image might make it more appropriate for use on a greeting card, on a screen-saver, or in a family newsletter.

Figure 10.10
The even more awesome kid after morphing.

Figure 10.11
The morphed kid with a "poster edges" filter applied.

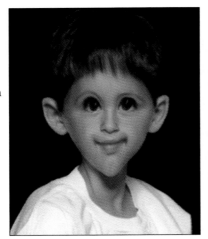
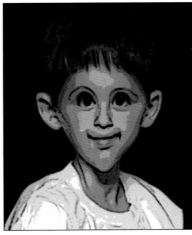

NOTE

A parent creating a CD-ROM-based family history record wanted to show how similar facial features seemed to be passed down through several generations. Using a few old photos of prior generations, he took new photographs of living family members and morphed them through several generations. The final movie showed a great-great-grandfather morph into a great-grandfather and then into a father and then into a teenage child. Just for fun, the newest member of the family—a two-month-old baby—was morphed back into the great-great-grandfather! The morphs were one of the most enjoyable parts of the family history, and all family members can enjoy them for generations in the future.

Mapping your images into 3D worlds

Three-dimensional software is almost beyond the scope of this book, but the results of using digital images with some of the new consumer-level 3D products can be terrific. MetaCreations offers three products that fit this topic: Bryce 3D, Painter 3D, and Ray Dream Studio. Just to give you an idea of what can be done with these products and a few of your images, I have inserted several of the images from Chapter 2 into figures 10.12 and 10.13. The first image was created with Painter 3D and the second with Bryce. I am considering using Painter 3D to create a series of Christmas tree ornaments, not unlike the one in Figure 10.12, and placing them in a digital image of a Christmas tree. That might become a family Christmas card one of these years. If you want to learn more about these products, visit the MetaCreations Web site at:

www.metacreations.com

Part III Using Images

Figure 10.12
Image applied to
a sphere, using
Painter 3D.

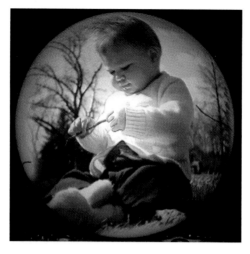

Figure 10.13
Image created by
applying images to 3D
objects in Bryce 4.

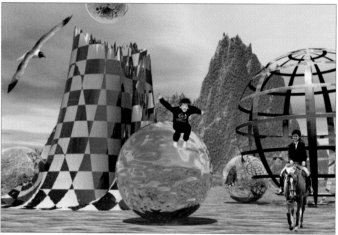

TIP

All of the applications discussed in this chapter are full commercial software products. There are, however, many highly capable shareware products that compare quite well with their more expensive commercial competitors. A great place to find what you need is at **www.zdnet.com** or **www.shareware.com**.

That concludes this chapter and Part III. In Part IV, "Sharing and Enjoying Your Images," you will learn many, many ways to share and enjoy the images that you learned to create in the first part of this book. As you make your way to the next chapter, make sure to take a few completed images that you would like to share with others—or, for that matter, take a whole bunch, because you'll learn how to create and share many images in a slide show or an electronic photo album.

Part IV
Sharing & Enjoying Your Images

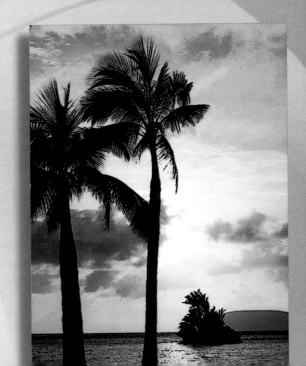

11

Sharing Images Electronically

As you learn to create quality digital images and your digital image portfolio grows in size, you probably will want to share your work. In this chapter, you will learn how to use e-mail, e-postcards, and e-greeting cards to share digital images. Additionally, you will see some exciting new possibilities for sharing images in real time by using chat applications or one of the new instant messengers (IMs). The use of IMs is growing incredibly fast, and one of the reasons is related to the interactive capabilities that IMs offer. Such interactive capabilities are wonderful for sharing digital images.

Several of the more significant benefits of working with digital images are gained only when you take advantage of the capability to share them electronically. Using the Internet makes sharing images incredibly easy, with virtually no cost involved. You can send a digital image to one hundred friends almost as easily as you can send it to one friend, and for very little cost—which surely isn't the case for traditional, film-based photographs!

Not too long ago, I completely gutted my kitchen down to the wall studs and floor beams. I enjoy woodworking and building projects, so I opted to do it myself. Many business colleagues, family, and friends knew I had undertaken the project and were always interested in how it was going. I posted images to a Web site and frequently sent e-mail telling them where on the Internet I had posted images of newly completed electrical, plumbing, or sheetrock work. Occasionally, I had questions and was able to e-mail images to friends who are contractors and, thus, could help. With the benefit of the images, they could offer good advice. Likewise, twice I got advice from builders on home-building or kitchen-design forums. It was a great building experience that I was able to share with others who cared—and that made it even more enjoyable. Now two of our friends have decided to redo their kitchens, and they say that they have enough experience to tackle the project based upon watching ours being done! By the way, you can see a 360-degree panorama view of my kitchen at **www.reallyusefulpage.com/dcs/11-01.htm**.

Expertise in using these new communication technologies can be very rewarding. At the very least, it enables you to communicate more effectively, share images without cost, renew old friendships, communicate more frequently with geographically remote contacts, and more fully enjoy your images through the interactive sharing capabilities of IMs. This is a valuable chapter that I know you will find useful.

Sharing Images

To share images, everyone involved must have the right stuff. What is the right stuff? First, some examples of what it means to *not* have the right stuff might be helpful. Have you ever:

▶ Received e-mail that you could not read?

▶ Had someone send e-mail to you at the right address, but it never arrived?

▶ Received e-mail with an attachment and, upon opening it, got an incredibly long file full of strange characters?

▶ Received an electronic document, such as one created in a word processor, but didn't have the software or the correct version and, thus, couldn't open it?

▶ Had someone send e-mail to your office while you were home, but because you have a different e-mail service at home, you could not receive it?

If any of these examples is familiar to you, then you know what can happen when you don't have "the right stuff."

So what exactly is the right stuff? The right stuff is whatever is required to make communications work as intended. That means that you need the right hardware (sometimes a PC instead of an Apple computer), the right communications link (a network or networks that can connect), the right viewer (an application that lets you view what was sent), and the capability to receive the file (not too large, because some e-mail providers limit file size). Finally, you have to be able to access your e-mail, meaning that you must be able to physically get to a machine that has the right software and communication capabilities to get the e-mail. If any one of these variables is not correct, you will experience frustration instead of successful communication.

Accessibility is everything

Taking a simplistic view, there are two types of e-mail applications:

▶ Desktop-based e-mail applications, such as Microsoft Outlook or Eudora, currently offer more features than browser-based e-mail applications and integrate well with other desktop applications. However, these and other desktop-based e-mail applications all must reside as application code on a PC's hard drive.

▶ Internet browser-based e-mail applications, such as Hotmail, Excite Mail, and some office e-mail systems, enable you to send and receive e-mail anywhere in the world that has Internet access.

Note that neither application type is necessarily superior—they are just different. The point here is to recognize what you can and can't do with your e-mail and your intended recipient's e-mail configurations.

If you have a desktop-based e-mail service, you can add flexibility to your e-mail capabilities by also signing up for a free, Internet-based e-mail service. The downside with free e-mail services is that they typically allow a maximum of 2MB of storage, so if you receive many images, you'll have to clean out old e-mail frequently.

> **TIP**
>
> If you want to sign up for a free e-mail service, visit **www.hotmail.com**. Hotmail has more than 40 million happy users, including me. If you would like to find other such services, visit **www.cnet.com** and search for "e-mail." CNET provides a recommended list of free e-mail services.

In conclusion, if you want global accessibility, then sign up for an Internet-based e-mail service—you'll be able to access your e-mail from anywhere that you can get access to the Internet and on any kind of computer.

> **NOTE**
>
> A professional photographer who travels frequently uses an Internet-based e-mail application so that he can easily send and receive e-mail, often with digital images. This enables him to read or send e-mail or view images from any hotel, library, or office in the world that has a connection to the Internet.

It takes the right kind of viewer to view

If something goes wrong with an e-mail message, odds are that it is an attached image file. Many e-mail servers either mutilate image files or reject them because they exceed a predefined maximum file size. If the image file is successfully sent and received, then the next step is for the recipient to view it.

To view an attached image, an appropriate viewer is needed—either the application that was used to create the image or a viewer application that can read a variety of image file types. If you send the image in one of the more standard formats, such as BMP, TIFF, or JPEG, your recipient is likely to be able to view it with a standard viewer that comes with the operating system. These standard viewers are very limited in their capabilities. If you send large images, using one of these viewers makes viewing them difficult. If an image is turned sideways (which is common when you shoot a picture in portrait mode), the recipients might have to turn their heads sideways to view it.

TIP

To maximize enjoyment when sending or receiving images, try Ulead's PhotoImpact Viewer. It is freeware (not shareware), available at Ulead's Web site: **www.webutilities.com/pv/pv_downf.htm**.

PhotoImpact Viewer requires very little memory, and it loads fast. It also offers the capabilities to zoom in and out, rotate images, print images, and even calibrate your monitor for optimal color (see Figure 11.1). If you have any question about your recipients' capabilities to receive your images, just send them a link to Ulead's Web site so that they can download and install this viewer once and enjoy it forever, free of charge!

Figure 11.1
Rotating and viewing an image with PhotoImpact Viewer. PhotoImpact Viewer also enables you to view images directly from Windows Explorer by right-clicking a file.

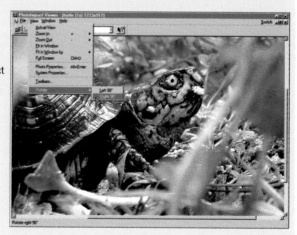

File size matters more than you think

When sending e-mail, it is considered rude to send large image files—unless the recipient has requested that you do so or has agreed in advance that you send them. You'll understand this the first time that you are in a hurry to get your e-mail and it takes ten minutes or more to download a single e-mail loaded with images!

To avoid annoying others with excessively large e-mail attachments, consider one or more of the following:

▶ Reduce the size of an image (e.g., from 1280x1024 pixels to 640x480)

▶ Reduce the file size by using one of the compressed image file types, such as JPEG. See Chapter 5, "Getting Images into Shape," for a complete discussion of this topic.

▶ Combine and compress your images by using a compression utility, such as WinZip, a compression and archiving tool that you can download at **www.winzip.com** as a free evaluation version. Be aware that when files are compressed and zipped on one end, they need to be unzipped on the other end. Thus, both the sender and the recipient need WinZip or an equivalent application.

▶ Don't e-mail the image or images. Instead, post them to a Web site and then send an e-mail with a pointer to the URL. This approach is covered later in this chapter.

Incidentally, many e-mail services have limits placed on the file size that can be sent or received. If you exceed this limit, your e-mail simply is returned to you. Because many of the free e-mail services limit e-mail storage space to under 2MB, having e-mail with image attachments returned due to insufficient storage space is a common experience.

Using e-mail to send images

E-mail is often referred to as a "killer application," because it is useful and enough fun to prompt many people to buy a computer just to have e-mail capabilities. The easiest way to share images is with e-mail. Using e-mail, you can share images in any one of the following ways:

▶ Send an image as an attachment to e-mail

▶ Send an e-mail with a URL pointer, pointing to the Web site where the image is posted

▶ Embed an image into the e-mail, providing the sender and the recipient have HTML-based e-mail applications

Most e-mail applications support the first two methods, but HTML-based e-mail is usually only possible on the newer e-mail applications, such as Microsoft Outlook 2000. The following section looks at some of the advantages and disadvantages to each of these approaches.

Part IV Sharing & Enjoying Images

NOTE

An interior designer making an out-of-town shopping trip for several clients thinks that she has found the perfect desk for one of her client's home office. The question is whether the client will also think it's perfect. Using a digital camera, she shoots several pictures, making sure to show the beautiful wood grain and detailed carvings. She knows that she has captured the images that she wants because she can view them in the LCD. Using her notebook computer, she sends an e-mail to her client with the images attached. Within a few minutes, she gets an e-mail back from her client saying, "It looks terrific. Buy it!"

Sending images as an e-mail attachment

The easiest way to send images is simply to send them as an e-mail attachment. This is as painless as selecting Insert>File from your e-mail application and then selecting the image file by using a file browser. The e-mail application then attaches the file when you send the e-mail message and indicates in the message that it has an attached file, as shown in Figure 11.2.

Alternatively, many applications such as image portfolio, greeting card, and digital camera software make it equally easy to send images. With an image, images, or document of some type selected, you simply select Send To>Mail Recipient. Your e-mail application is then automatically launched and the appropriate file (or files) is included as an attachment. Once you complete your e-mail message, you can send it—it's that easy, really! This is one technique that you must learn how to do if you intend to share your images.

Figure 11.2
Sending an image as an attachment to an e-mail message.

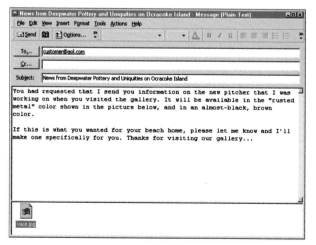

Part IV Sharing & Enjoying Images

The advantage to sending an image as an attachment to an e-mail message is that it is very easy to do. The disadvantages are that the recipient has to have the right kind of viewer application, and sending the image requires the recipient to download the image to get the e-mail. These disadvantages might make more sense after you read about the next two ways to send images.

When the recipients receive the e-mail, they see the image represented as a file icon embedded in the message. To view the image, they simply need to double-click the icon, and the image will be displayed in their default image viewer. The key here is that they must have an appropriate image viewer for the file type that you send.

Sending e-mail with a URL pointer

The best way to avoid sending a large image (or lots of images) to someone who might not want to take the time to download and view it is to post the image to a Web site and then send an e-mail with a URL pointer, telling the recipient where the image can be viewed (see Figure 11.3). The "hot-link" pointer makes it very easy for them to jump from their e-mail to the images on your site by using an Internet browser. This approach also eliminates the problems that occur when the recipient does not have sufficient storage capacity or the appropriate software to view the images.

Figure 11.3
Using a URL pointer to share a digital image.

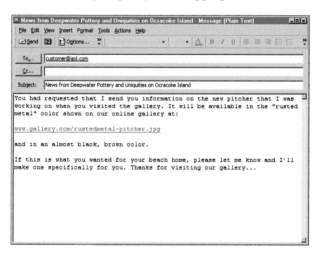

An advantage of this approach is that the e-mail will not contain the images, so it will be small and quick to download. It also enables your recipients to decide when (and if) they want to view the images. Another advantage is that if they have access to the Internet, then it is highly likely that they will be able to view your images with their browser. They will not need a viewer application and can view the page by using any kind of computer, including an Apple, IBM PC, or Unix.

One final advantage to this approach is that as long as you leave the images on your Web site, they can be viewed from anywhere with a browser and an Internet connection. This is in sharp contrast to having them attached to an e-mail that is located on a PC that might not be accessible.

On the other hand, sending a pointer to a Web site has several potential disadvantages:

► Not everyone has access to the Internet and, thus, might not be able to view your Web page with a browser.

► You must have a Web page where you can post the images, and you must know how to post them. (This topic is covered next in Chapter 12, "Using the Internet to Share Images.")

TIP

PhotoLoft.com claims to be the #1 online photo-sharing community. You can create portfolios up to 20MB free of charge. Visit its site at **www.photoloft.com/**.

Two other quality, free Web-hosting sites you might want to consider are **www.homestead.com/** and **www.folksites.com/**.

Using HTML-based e-mail to send images

If you have ever received e-mail that looks just like a Web page, you have received HTML-based e-mail. HTML-based e-mail is becoming an increasingly popular way to send e-mail. It allows e-mail to include anything that can be included on a Web page, such as formatted text, graphics, background colors, hotlinks, and textures.

For instance, using Microsoft Word 2000, you can create a Web page directly in Word. You create this page just like any other Word document. Then, instead of saving it as a DOC file, you save it as a Web page file with the .htm extension. After you save it as a Web page, you can select Send To>Mail Recipient and send it as a Web page. When you choose to do this, Word 2000 changes into a hybrid Word and Outlook package, as shown in Figure 11.4.

Figure 11.4
Using Microsoft Word
2000 to create an
HTML-based e-mail.

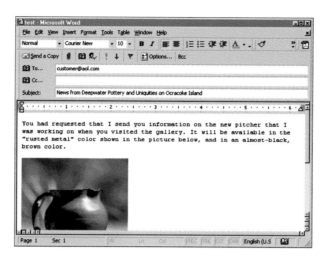

If the recipient does not have an HTML-capable e-mail application, it can viewed in a browser, as shown in Figure 11.5.

Figure 11.5
Viewing an HTML-
based e-mail in a
browser.

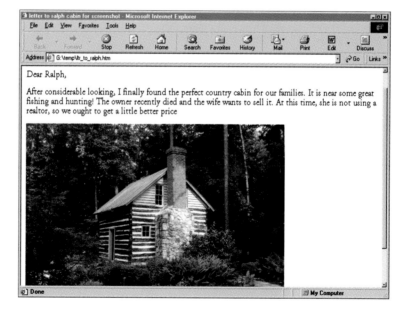

Like the other two approaches, HTML-based e-mail also has advantages and disadvantages. The advantage is that you can lay out a page containing your images by using an application that you might be used to using (such as Microsoft Word) and then use it to convert the document into a Web page. Your recipients can then see the entire layout exactly as you created it.

The disadvantage is that the recipient must have a browser or an e-mail application that can display HTML Web pages. The recipient also must download all the images on the page. The fact that the images are displayed on a Web page, however, is a good indication that they are small, compressed files. You are likely to see more e-mail being sent in this format in the future.

Now that you know about three possible ways to let your e-mail recipients view your images, you should be able to share your images more effectively. Next, we'll look at some exciting variations of desktop e-mail.

Sharing images with electronic postcards

I have always liked postcards—one side shows an image or graphic, and the other side has a small amount of room for a short, to-the-point message. Postcards are fun to send and fun to receive. Now you can send the digital equivalent of a postcard using your own images—which in my opinion is even better!

On the 1-to-10 "cool" scale, with 10 being the coolest, PictureWorks' NetCard is a 12.5! This is truly one of my favorite applications. It is an exceedingly simple application that creates electronic postcards. When you launch the NetCard application, a postcard is created on your desktop, ready to go except for the photo (or video and audio if you choose to add them), your message, and the "send to" address. You can either click the Import button to place a picture (or even a video) on the front of the card, or drag and drop a file from Windows Explorer onto the front of the card. Either way, you instantly have a postcard with your image on it.

In addition to placing an image on the front, you can attach an audio file, which can contain sound, music files, or your own voice message! To add a voice message, you simply click the microphone icon and record the message by using a microphone attached to your PC. To finish the postcard, you click an icon on the bottom-right corner, and the card turns over. This is where you type your message and add the address. The postcard even comes complete with a postage stamp with the current date already stamped—so it is ready to go—no trip to the post office or mailbox! Finally, you click the Send button, and the e-postcard is sent to your e-mail application to be sent and logged as any other regular e-mail.

A NetCard can be created with the Windows Player program attached, which means that the Windows application is included in the NetCard and will run when double-clicked. Alternatively, you can send it as a JPEG image, which can be viewed from any JPEG viewer or browser. After you select an image and fill in the text, you click the "wings" icon, and the NetCard zooms away with a swooshing sound to your e-mail application, where it is sent either immediately or the next time you decide to send e-mail. After attending the "Daddy of 'em All" rodeo in Cheyenne, Wyoming, I created and sent the NetCard shown in Figure 11.6.

Figure 11.6
The front of an e-postcard created in PictureWorks' NetCard.

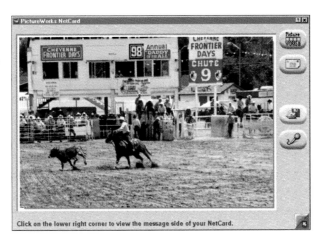

The recipient of your e-postcard gets a regular e-mail message. NetCard automatically adds instructions and shows the NetCard as an attachment, as shown in Figure 11.7. Double-click the attachment icon, and the e-postcard flies onto the desktop with the same cool swooshing sound. To read the back of the postcard, you simply click the corner and it turns over so that the message can be seen (see Figure 11.8).

Figure 11.7
Instructions for viewing PictureWorks' NetCard.

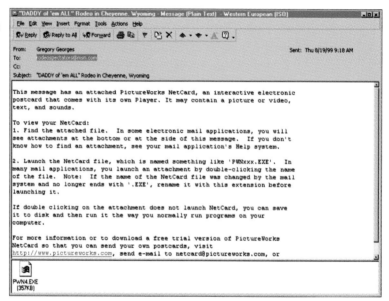

Figure 11.8
The back of an e-postcard created in PictureWorks' NetCard.

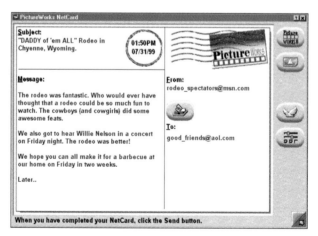

If you like sending postcards, and you'd like to send one with one of your digital images on the front, then this the way to do it.

Sharing images with electronic greeting cards

If you can send e-postcards, then you ought to be able to send e-greeting cards, as well, right? Yes, you can. The two biggest greeting card companies—Hallmark and American Greetings—both have products on the market that enable you to create e-greeting cards.

If you think a standard greeting card can say it best, then wait until you see what you can do with a greeting-card creation tool. Not only do you get to use all the artistic and creative talent that companies like Hallmark and American Greetings have, but you also get to take their cards one step further and personalize them for the occasion. When a friend fell off her horse while jumping a fence and broke her arm and a few ribs, it seemed appropriate to add a little humor to the event. Digging back through some photographs, I was able to find a picture of her horse. In about ten minutes, I was able to scan the photograph, pick a card, insert the photograph, modify the text, and send it electronically. Figure 11.9 shows the American Greetings' CreataCard Gold screen where you modify the card step by step. After you complete the card, you click the E-Mail button, fill in the e-mail address, and add any message that you choose. Then, you can send it from your regular e-mail application.

Figure 11.9
The front of an e-greeting card created with American Greetings' CreataCard Gold.

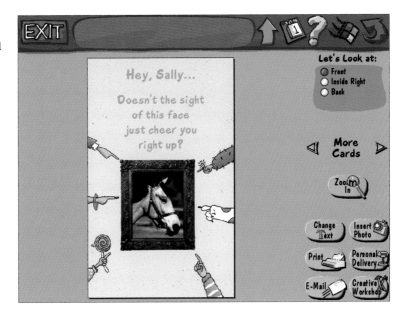

The recipient of the e-greeting card receives a normal e-mail with some instructions and an attachment. Double-clicking the attachment causes a background screen to be shown with the greeting card placed in the middle, as shown in Figure 11.10.

Figure 11.10
An e-greeting card with a background screen, created with American Greetings' CreataCard Gold.

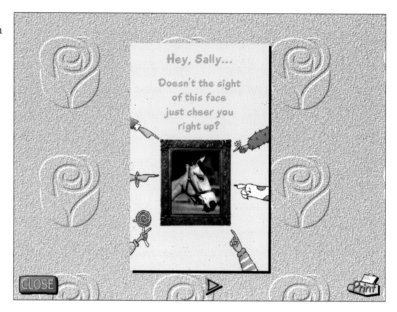

Clicking the arrow opens the card (see Figure 11.11). One more click and you can see the back of the card. With American Greetings' CreataCard, your recipient can also print the card on a color printer simply by clicking the printer icon. For those of you who procrastinate and wait until the very last minute to send a card, this is a great way to procrastinate and still look good!

Figure 11.11
The inside of an
e-greeting card created
with American
Greetings' CreataCard
Gold.

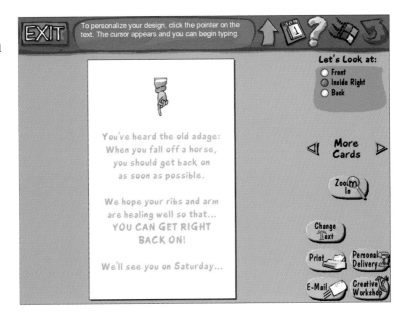

Part IV Sharing & Enjoying Images

Sharing images with instant messenger and chat applications

Chat and IM applications quickly are becoming two of the most popular ways of communicating electronically. Toward the end of 1999, AOL claimed that there were more than 750 million messages sent per day via ICQ and the AOL IM—in comparison, there are only 500 million letters mailed each day via the US Postal Service. Initially created as a means of enabling people to chat online for entertainment purposes, IMs and chat applications are now rapidly being implemented as business tools, and many more people are using them as a serious personal communication tool. During this next year, when visiting an online store, it will be increasingly common to have a sales assistant offer to help you via an IM or chat box.

IMs enable you to send and receive messages to any computer connected to the Internet, enabling you to chat from work, home, school, a friend's house, or anywhere you can get on a computer with an Internet connection. IMs also enable messages to be stored on a server, so they are always accessible. An IM might be likened to a real-time e-mail application with a simulated telephone ring announcing that you are calling—there is no waiting for e-mail to be received. As you type, those that you are chatting with can see the letters being typed. When you pause or misspell a word and go back to correct it, they see it all!

One of the more interesting aspects of the IMs is that they enable you to create *buddy lists*—lists of people with whom you occasionally like to chat. Unless your buddies set themselves up to be invisible or hidden specifically to you, their names are listed whenever they are online. You can even assign special audio sounds for them, which will play when they either sign on or sign off. Most IMs enable you to categorize your buddies into family, friends, business contacts, or any other category that you'd like to create.

Instant messaging, by some accounts, is growing faster than any communications medium in history. AOL says that its three instant-messaging services have nearly 80 million users, and they crossed the 50 million mark in less than two-and-a-half years—compared with five years for the Internet and thirteen years for television.

Many of the online service vendors are including chat applications in their basic packages. America Online offers AOL Instant Messenger, which is based on Mirabilis' ICQ product. AT&T offers I M Here in its WorldNet service package, based on the Tribal Voice PowWow client, which is one of my favorites, because it is very feature-rich. Microsoft's MSN offers MSN Messenger.

You might ask why IMs are covered in a book on digital cameras and digital imaging. The reason is that using IMs is a wonderful way to share images and interact in real time. You send or post to a Web page only the images that the recipient asks for—and then you can talk about that image. For example, after taking a trip to England to shoot pictures of castles, you could have a chat with one or more friends and share your digital images of the castles with them, as in Figure 11.12.

Figure 11.12

Sharing and chatting about an image of a castle.

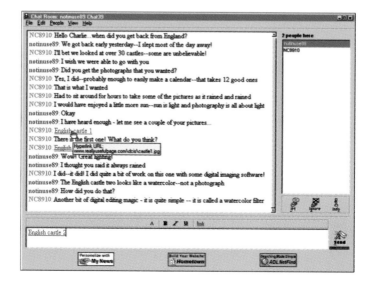

After a request to send an image, a URL was inserted into the chat box by using a pop-up box, as shown in Figure 11.13.

Figure 11.13
Sending a URL with
AOL's Instant
Messenger.

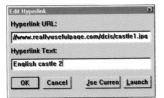

Everyone else in the chat room can then click the URL and see the image in their browsers.

Sharing electronic documents containing images

You might want to insert your images into many different kinds of electronic documents, such as those created by word processors, desktop publishing applications, spreadsheets, or graphics and illustration tools. After you complete your work, you might need to share these documents with others. Generally, three ways exist to share these documents:

▶ If the intended recipient has the same application, you can simply send e-mail with the file as an attachment. The recipient can then click the attachment, which will launch the native application. This works well with software such as Visio, Adobe Illustrator, or other products that have proprietary files that generally can't be shown in standard viewers.

▶ If the intended recipient does not have the native application, you need to either find a viewer for that type of file or identify a file type that is common between that application and any software that your intended recipient has. Again, using Visio as an example, you can export the chart as a TIFF or JPEG file, which should make it easy to view. After you export the file, you can send it as an attachment.

Part IV Sharing & Enjoying Images

Working with Microsoft Office documents

Because the Microsoft Office products have become omnipresent, it is worthwhile to know how you can use them to share documents with images. The most commonly used product in the suite is Microsoft Word. It is a wonderful tool to use to combine text with images. However, files from various versions are not always compatible. To overcome this problem, you must save the file as a Word 97 file and then either make sure your recipient has Word 97 or later or make them aware of Microsoft Word Viewer 97, which can be downloaded free of charge at **www.officeupdate.microsoft.com/downloadDetails/wd97vwr32.htm**.

With Word Viewer 97, Microsoft Word users can share documents with those who do not have Word, and users without Word can open and view Word documents. This product also enables users who wish to post rich-formatted Word documents on the Internet to expand their online audience to people who might not have Word. Word Viewer 97 also enables users to view and print documents created in the Word native file format even if they do not have Word. Users are able to zoom, outline, or view the page layout, headers/footers, footnotes, and annotations.

Microsoft's PowerPoint presentation tool enables you to share images in PowerPoint presentations by posting them to a Web site or by creating run-time versions of the slide shows. These slide shows can be viewed without any additional software.

That concludes this chapter. By now, you should have a good understanding of the many possible ways of communicating electronically. My hope is that you'll enjoy these new technologies and share your digital images with friends, family, and business colleagues. The next chapter continues to look at ways to share your images, including ways to use the Internet.

12

Using the Internet to Share Images

As e-mail has dramatically changed the way that we communicate with one other, digital images and the Internet will dramatically change the way in which we share photographs. Companies of all sizes have launched major business initiatives to make it easy to use the Internet to share images.

Within a year's time, press releases have announced: "Kodak and Intel have entered an agreement to bridge traditional photography with digital imaging in ways that are easy, fast, and affordable." "Hewlett-Packard creates a Web site utilizing its imaging expertise to allow users to share photos over the Internet." "Kodak and AOL team together to create AOL's "You've Got Pictures" service." "Adobe Systems' ActiveShare.com site is the result of applying its market-leading graphics software expertise to the needs of the growing photo-sharing market." "One of the 'five facets' of Bill Gates's new technology vision for the upcoming Microsoft Windows 2000 operating system is digital photography."

The underlying message in all of those press releases is this: Using the Internet is rapidly becoming *the* way to share photos. The purpose of this chapter is to help you learn about the photo-sharing opportunities available and how to take advantage of them. More specifically, we will look at the following:

▶ Using photofinishing labs to upload your pictures to the Internet so that they can be shared

▶ Using photo-sharing communities to share images

▶ Getting your own Web space for sharing images

▶ Using software that automatically creates image-based Web pages

▶ Using tools that help you author your own Web pages

Using photo labs to share digital images

One of the easiest and least expensive ways to share your photographs with others is to use one of the digital services provided by an increasing number of photo labs. Using the digital services offered by a photo lab has advantages. When you shoot pictures with a film camera and have your film scanned at a photo lab, you can have the photo lab create digital images and upload them to the Internet at the same time that they develop and print your prints.

Even if you use a digital camera, online services will still be useful to you. You just won't have to worry about a trip to a local photo lab, and you'll save a few dollars, because you won't have to pay for the developing, printing, and scanning. However, you will have to pay for a roll of online "spaces" (online digital storage for digital images) so that you have room to upload your image files.

Obviously, the first step to being able to share digital images on the Internet is to get your image files uploaded. The three basic ways to do this are as follows:

▶ Drop your film off at a local photo lab and have them scan and upload digital image files to the Internet

▶ Use a mail-in envelope and send your film to a mail-order photo lab that can process your film, scan it, and upload digital images to the Internet

▶ Create an account with an online service and upload your images to one of the online labs from your own PC

We'll now look at two online photo-sharing services in detail. First, we'll look at the Kodak PhotoNet Online service. Then, we'll look at the Seattle FilmWorks online service, which is a similar service to Kodak PhotoNet Online, but with a slightly different business model and some innovative features.

Using Kodak PhotoNet Online Services

Using PhotoNet Online to share your photographs with others is easy, quick, and inexpensive—especially when you compare it to the costs of sharing ordinary printed photographs. This section explains how you get your images onto PhotoNet Online and what you can do with them after they are there.

The first step to getting your pictures online is to have them converted into digital image files. You can drop off your film at a local photo lab (or use the services of a mail-order photo lab) and have it both scan the film and upload the digital files to PhotoNet Online.

Alternatively, you can have the photo lab scan your film and put the digital images directly onto a CD-ROM or floppy disk. After you have the image files, you can then upload them yourself to Kodak PhotoNet Online directly from your PC. Either way, your images will be ready to be shared.

Using a photo lab to get your pictures uploaded to Kodak PhotoNet Online

To get your participating Kodak PhotoNet Online photo lab to upload your pictures to the Internet, you need to check the appropriate box on the photo-processing envelope. Depending on the photo lab, the envelopes have a check box for Via AOL or Via Kodak PhotoNet Online, or for both. Make sure you fill in your e-mail address. If you don't provide your e-mail address, you will not receive an e-mail notifying you that your roll has been posted. Instead, you'll have to wait to pick up your film and get the Roll ID and Owner Key from the processed film package. That's all—you are done and ready to share your pictures.

Uploading images to Kodak PhotoNet Online from your PC

In Chapter 3, "Turning Photographs into Digital Images," you learned how you can use a photo lab to put your pictures onto a CD-ROM or floppy disk. You also learned how you can scan photographs yourself. If you used either of these approaches or took pictures with a digital camera, you need to upload your digital image files yourself. Again, it is quite easy to do.

First, you must log on to the Kodak PhotoNet Online site and make sure that you have room for the photos that you want to upload. If you don't have "spaces" available, you need to buy a few spaces on an existing roll or buy a new roll. Then, click the Upload Photos to a Roll button to see the page shown in Figure 12.1. With the Browse feature, you can find the file that you want to upload on your PC's drives. Select it and click Upload Now. Then, repeat those two steps for each picture that you want to make available online.

Figure 12.1
Uploading images
from a PC to Kodak
PhotoNet Online.

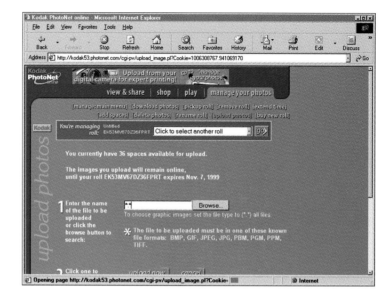

Using Kodak PhotoNet Online to share your images

After you upload your images to Kodak PhotoNet Online, they are
available to be shared with others. To share them, select the roll that you
want to share and then click view & share. After you fill out the four
boxes shown in Figure 12.2, click the share roll button, which sends e-
mail to the recipients, inviting them to view your roll of pictures.

Figure 12.2
Using Kodak PhotoNet
Online to send e-mail to
invite others to view the
online pictures.

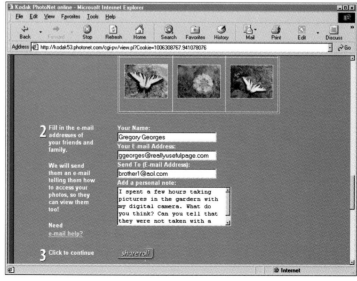

When your recipients receive the e-mail inviting them to view your roll of pictures, they need to log in to Kodak PhotoNet Online to view them. If they are not already registered, they have to create a free account. After they are logged in, they can select your roll to view—once selected, the roll is displayed in thumbnail form, as shown in Figure 12.3. They then have the choice to either view the thumbnails in one of three sizes or click each image to display it at 348×248 pixels. If they want larger images, they can download them in any of the three different sizes that are shown in Table 12.1.

Figure 12.3
Using Kodak PhotoNet Online to view a roll of film that someone shared with you.

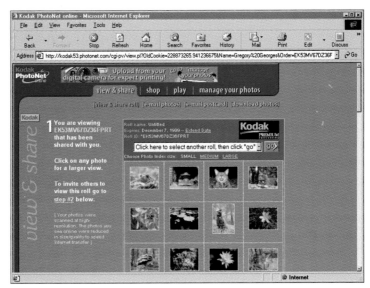

Table 12.1
Kodak PhotoNet Online Image Sizes

Image Resolution	Pixel Size	Download Time Based on 28.8Kbps Connection
Minimum	384×256 pixels	7 seconds per photo
Medium	768×512 pixels	20 seconds per photo
High	1536×1024 pixels	3.5 minutes per photo

The two lower-resolution image sizes can be downloaded free, but there is an additional charge for downloading high-resolution image files. SmoothMove Screensaver and medium-resolution photo options also are available, which enable visitors to download screen-savers for their PCs that use the medium-resolution images.

In addition to downloading digital images of varying sizes, your recipients also can order reprints, photo gifts, e-mail photos, and e-mail postcards. The obvious advantage to sharing photographs in this manner is that you can share your photographs with anyone and with as many people as you want—free of charge, after you have paid to have your film processed and uploaded to the Internet. If someone views your roll of film and wants an image, *they*—not you—can order and pay for it directly over the Internet. This saves you all the hassles and costs of getting reprints done and having the prints delivered to whomever you want to share your photos with.

Incidentally, Adobe PhotoDeluxe, Microsoft Picture It!, and MGI's PhotoSuite are all Kodak PhotoNet Online-enabled software products. Using these products makes it much easier to manage your photographs and share them on Kodak PhotoNet Online.

Using Seattle FilmWorks' online services

When I first used this service, I was really impressed. It was so cool! I used it to share some images of a furniture auction that I had attended. When I sent an e-mail with a voice message to several friends, they were quick to respond—both as a reply to my e-mail and later on the telephone. I can't promise these results for you, but you surely ought to give Seattle FilmWorks one or more rolls of your film and try its services—they are truly unique.

Seattle FilmWorks, founded in 1978, is one of the early pioneers in the online photo-sharing business, and it continues to innovate and offer a service that is an excellent value. Unlike many of the online photo-sharing services, Seattle FilmWorks is a mail-order-only service—that is, unless you live in Washington or Oregon and can visit one of the local stores. But that is okay, because using a mail service sometimes can be easier than driving to a packed mall or shopping center to drop off and pick up your film—in this case, you just put your film in a FilmWorks mailer and walk to your mailbox. You even get to see your pictures online before your printed film is mailed back to you. By the way, as soon as your film is scanned and uploaded to the Internet, you get an e-mail message notifying you that your pictures are available for viewing. The e-mail also provides a hot link to get you there quickly and with no fuss.

To get started using FilmWorks, visit its Web site at **www.filmworks.com/gettingstarted/kit.htm**. This takes you directly to a brief form that you must fill out to get two free rolls of 35mm color-print film, order forms, and postage-paid envelopes. Can you believe that? Two rolls of free film and postage-paid mailing envelopes—that's value! But, wait—you also get a free roll of film for every roll of film that you send to FilmWorks for processing. That's still not all. You also receive free lifetime archiving of your images online as long as you continue to use the service to process at least two rolls of film per year, as well as free Internet delivery of your paid processing order. All of this is backed with a 100 percent satisfaction guarantee. That bargain isn't matched anywhere else! You are also likely to find FilmWorks' prices to be competitive.

By now, you probably are convinced that I used to sell knives or vegetable choppers on late-night TV. Actually, I haven't—I just think that FilmWorks offers good value for the money and has some unique features that will help to foster further industry innovation that all of us can enjoy. After all, taking photos, working with digital images, and sharing our work is supposed to be fun, right?

A few paragraphs back, I mentioned that I sent a voice message with an e-mail, notifying the recipients that I had made some online photos available to them. How is this possible? Actually, FilmWorks and Vstream teamed up to enable you to use your computer and telephone to enhance the presentation of the images that you want to share with others.

To send an unbelievably clear message with your photos, you don't need any special hardware or software (except a browser plug-in that you likely already have or can get free) to either create the message or listen to it. After you select the images that you want to share by clicking them, as shown in Figure 12.4, you then click the Email Selections button. When the page shown in Figure 12.5 appears, fill out the boxes, as required, by entering your recipients' e-mail addresses, your e-mail address and name, and a text message (if you want to send one). Then, to attach a voice message, click the box in step 5.

Figure 12.4
Selecting images to share at Seattle FilmWorks.com.

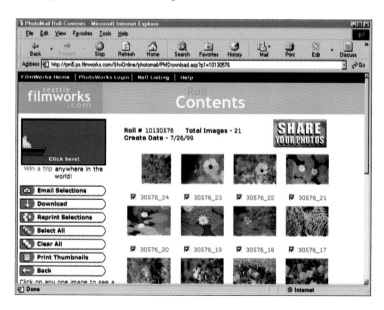

Figure 12.5
Sharing a roll of film via
Seattle FilmWorks.

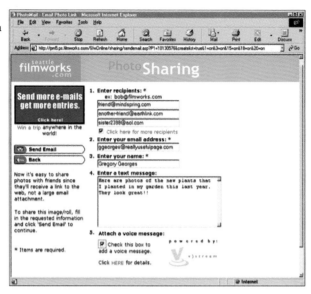

After you click the Send Email button, you will be given a Message ID
number, and you will have five minutes to call a long-distance number
and leave a one-minute message. To match your voice message with your
images, you must enter the Message ID number by pressing the numbers
on your telephone, followed by the # sign.

Those to whom you sent the e-mail receive an ordinary e-mail message,
as shown in Figure 12.6, with a small attachment icon shown at the
bottom of the e-mail. After they click this icon, their browser will launch,
and they will see a page similar to the one that is shown in Figure 12.7.
At the top, you can see the thumbnails of the images that you sent. If
your recipients click one of the thumbnails, they can see a full-sized
version of the image. Just below the thumbnails, notice a red Play
Message button. When they click that button, they will hear your
recorded voice message. If, by chance, they don't have the RealPlayer G2
browser plug-in that is required, they can click a Download RealPlayer
G2 button to download it. If they want reprints of your images or want to
download the high-resolution versions, they can click the appropriate
buttons to get what they want.

Figure 12.6
An e-mail message
notifying the recipient
that online photos are
available to be viewed.

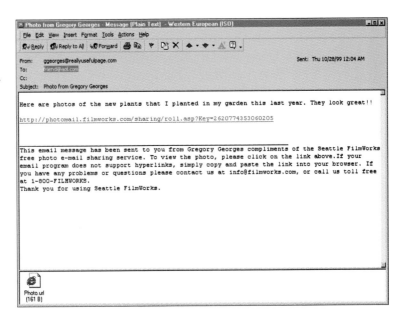

Figure 12.7
Receiving images to
view.

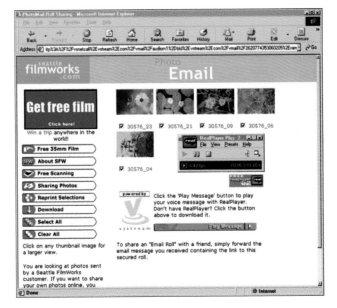

FilmWorks recently announced another exciting innovation that should be available by the time you read this. This new feature enables users to create and share streaming slide shows composed with their own images. Unlike most other slide show applications, you don't need additional software, and the process is fully automated. The cool part here is that you can publish these slide shows in public or private Web sites without consuming the bandwidth to ship the image and sound files between sites.

NOTE

A part-time breeder of show dogs who travels a lot for his regular job uses FilmWorks.com to store more than fifty images of dogs that he has bred. Frequently, when he travels, he meets people who are interested in purchasing his dogs. When he is near a PC with a connection to the Internet, he can show the prospective customer the images. On several occasions, he has sold a dog to an out-of-state customer based solely on the images, which the buyers could look at and share with their families when they got home.

Other services to consider

Although there are many different photo labs, a vast majority of them are using the increasingly popular digital services offered by Kodak, known as Kodak PhotoNet Online. To avoid confusion—both now and later as you are shopping for online services—a little corporate background about Kodak should be helpful.

PhotoNet Online is a name that you'll see often. It is a service that was created by PictureVision. Kodak PhotoNet Online is based on PictureVision's PhotoNet Online services. PictureVision itself is a majority-owned subsidiary of the Eastman Kodak company. PictureVision has successfully partnered with many companies, including Wolf Camera, the national chain of camera stores and one-hour photo labs (that service is known as Kodak PhotoNet by Wolf Camera). Kodak has also partnered with AOL, and these two have jointly offered AOL's "You've Got Pictures" service, which is covered in detail in Chapter 14. AOL in turn has partnered with two mail-order photo labs—Mystic Color Labs and York Photo. As many of these companies continue to become partners, you'll see more "PhotoNet Online" services being offered.

So why did I take your time to tell you all of this? Because, over time, many of these services will become increasingly integrated—meaning that you can share your images with more people in more places more often! From what I can tell, once a roll of film gets onto any PhotoNet

Online service, it can be viewed and shared on all the other services as well. In the future, you will be able to get prints from online digital images at your favorite local photo lab no matter where the images came from. You just have more choices—you can use a mail-order service, use a local photo lab, or upload your images yourself. Then, you can pick up the roll on your AOL service or any other PhotoNet Online service.

Using photo-sharing communities

Photo-sharing communities are Web sites that enable you to post digital images to be shared with others. Besides enabling you to post images, photo-sharing communities typically offer many other community features, such as chat, discussion forums, community event calendars, and image comment features. With the tremendous growth in the sales of digital cameras, scanners, and image digitization services, getting photos turned into digital images is easy and commonplace. Joining a photo-sharing community is one of the ways that you can easily share your images. Surprisingly, most of these sites are even free!

Because so many photo-sharing communities exist, we will look at only two of them to give you an idea of the wide range of features that are available. At the end of this section, you'll find a list of other photo-sharing sites you might want to visit, in case you want to do something other than what these two communities offer.

Using Adobe's eCircles.com

Adobe's eCircles Web site is more than just a photo-sharing site—it is a complete community, with features that enable members to post announcements, hold discussions, keep track of group events with a community calendar, use text and voice chat, make lists, play games, share music, and even register in a gift registry! eCircles are completely private—only those who have been invited can access an eCircle. Only an existing member of an eCircle may invite others to join. This is a slightly different approach from other photo-sharing communities, in which your site typically is open to anyone unless you choose to make it private.

When you create a new eCircle, you are given 15MB of storage, which is the equivalent of more than 300 50K images! With this much storage space, you shouldn't run out of image space, but if you do, just start another eCircle. To upload images, you have two choices—either upload each image one by one or use Adobe's ActiveShare or PhotoDeluxe Home Edition software to acquire, organize, enhance, and upload a group of images simultaneously.

The process of uploading an image to the site from a browser is simple. Just click the Upload button and then click the Browse button to select the image from a directory. You also have an option to enter a caption and a description for the image. Then, click the Upload File button one more time, and your image is uploaded and displayed in the album that you selected.

If you want to upload more than one image, using ActiveShare or PhotoDeluxe, which are both PC software applications (as opposed to Web applications), makes it much quicker and easier. Figure 12.8 shows the Adobe ActiveShare window that is used for uploading images. From this window, you can collect images from various devices, such as scanners, digital cameras, and disk drives, and from Kodak Picture CDs. You can then select the images that you want and combine them into an album. ActiveShare also offers some basic image-enhancement features. After you select and enhance the images that you want to use, you can e-mail them, print them to a printer, or click the Share on Web button and upload them in a batch to an album on the eCircles Web site.

Figure 12.8
Using Adobe's
ActiveShare to upload
images to eCircles.

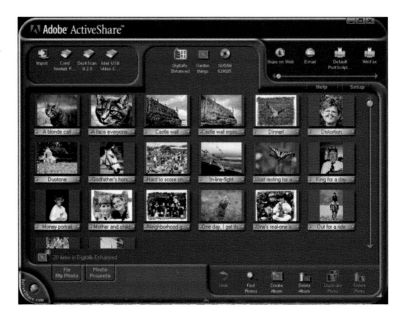

TIP

When Adobe launched the eCircles.com site, it offered a free downloadable version of ActiveShare. To find out whether you can still get a free copy of ActiveShare, visit **www.activeshare.com**.

To view the images in an album, click the Photo Albums button and select the album that you want to view. This selection displays a thumbnail page, similar to the one shown in Figure 12.9. To see a full-size view of one of the images, just click it, and it will be displayed, as shown in Figure 12.10. Directly under the image is space for an image caption. Below that, you'll find space for a list of comments. Each viewer of the album can add his or her own comments, which are then added in list fashion. This is a particularly nice feature if you want to get feedback on your images or if members of your community want to offer interactive comments on each image.

Figure 12.9
Viewing thumbnail images in an eCircles album.

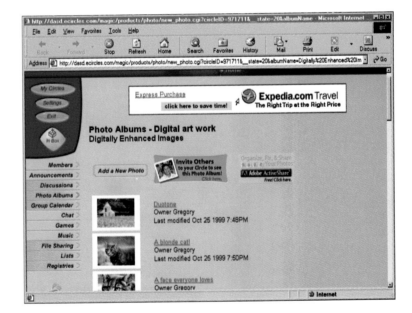

Figure 12.10
Viewing a full-size image in an eCircles album.

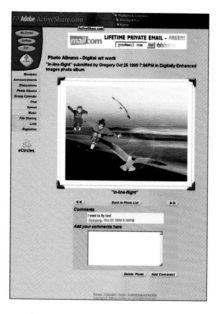

At this point, we have selected and uploaded images and created albums—now we are ready to share the result. How do we invite others to our eCircle? Once again, you have several options. You can invite members individually, invite a group of members simultaneously, or invite members from another eCircle. Figure 12.11 shows the screen used to invite a group to view an eCircle photo album.

Figure 12.11
Inviting a group to view an eCircles image album.

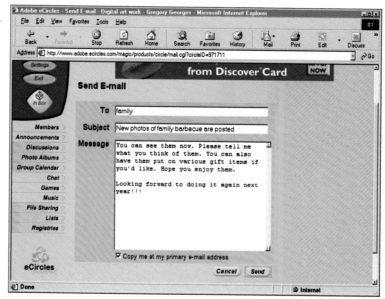

If you need personal space for family, friends, teams, or clubs, or just need a place to store a few images that you'd like to be able to access from anywhere you can get on the Internet, Adobe's eCircles.com is the place for you.

> **NOTE**
>
> A group of neighbors set up an eCircle on the Adobe eCircles Web site to post messages and pictures of people and events in their neighborhood. One of the most-viewed albums was the "project album," in which neighbors could find the names of both good and bad contractors. Often, digital images were posted of completed projects, such as decks, new additions, landscaping, and sunrooms. The use of this eCircle community actually gave some leverage to homeowners when they told contractors about the site, because the contractors did not want a negative posting, which could affect their ability to get any more work in the neighborhood. Likewise, if they did a good job, they were more than likely to be invited to bid on many other jobs.

Using PhotoLoft.com

The tagline for PhotoLoft.com is "The #1 Online Photo Sharing Community." Once you spend some time on this site, you'll understand why PhotoLoft.com makes that claim. The site offers many features that make it one of the best photo-sharing sites around for both amateur and professional photographers.

PhotoLoft.com offers several unique features. The Web-based software enables members to zoom in and focus on minute details of an image. You can also download free proprietary software that enables you to print exceptionally high-quality prints on your own color printer. Additionally, anyone posting images at PhotoLoft.com can earn money from the sales of their images. By simply choosing several "enable" buttons, your images become available for sale either as prints, greeting cards, or photo-personalized gifts.

After you sign up for a "loft," you are given 20MB of free space. You can also pay for a supercharged account that enables you to increase your storage by 25MBs for $20, and PhotoLoft.com offers guaranteed storage of those images.

The PhotoLoft.com site enables you to create multiple albums in your loft. Each album can be locked with a password or made available to anyone who wants to visit. You also can list your albums in one of ninety categories, such as Animals, Friends & Family, Travel, Seasonal, and many more. You can see the main category listing on the home page screen shown in Figure 12.12.

Figure 12.12
PhotoLoft.com's
home page.

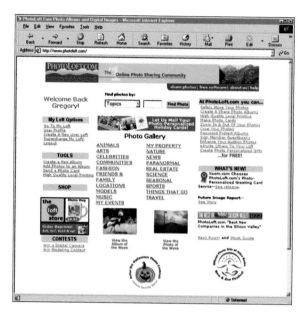

To get your images uploaded to the appropriate photo album, you can either enter them one at a time in the "upload photo" page or use the eMail Upload feature. When you click the eMail Upload button, your e-mail application is launched with a special "to" address inserted. Then, you simply drag and drop all the images that you want from the Windows Explorer to the e-mail window and send it. A few minutes later your album is viewable worldwide!

I created the two albums shown in Figure 12.13. The first album, which contains 21 cat images, is named "Cats, cats & more cats." I assigned the album to the Cat subcategory under the Animals category. If you want to view this album, you can easily find it by using the Find Photo function. Just enter my last name, the album title, the topic Cats, or the city I live in. Likewise, you can look it up by selecting the Animals category and then the Cats subcategory. Go ahead and try it—it is there for your viewing. You can even print an image if you'd like.

Figure 12.13
Two albums in the author's photo loft at PhotoLoft.com.

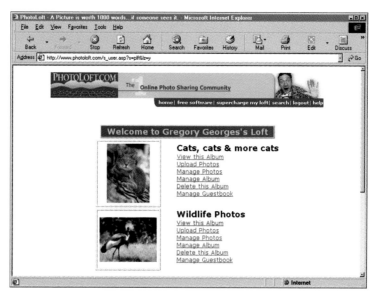

The second album that I created included the wildlife images that are shown in Album View in Figure 12.14. From this Album View, you can enlarge any thumbnails just by clicking them. When you do, they are presented, as shown in Figure 12.15. From this screen, you can select from the many options that are shown on the left side. You can change the viewing options and the viewer size; opt to have your photos turned into gifts or greeting cards; invite others to view the photos by sending e-mail to them; make or read a comment in a guestbook; and use the photo-quality printing feature.

Figure 12.14
PhotoLoft.com's album view.

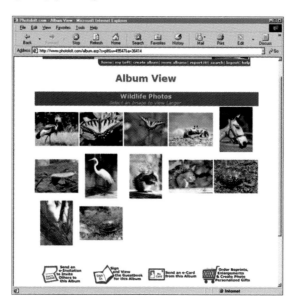

Figure 12.15
Enlarged view of
an image posted at
PhotoLoft.com.

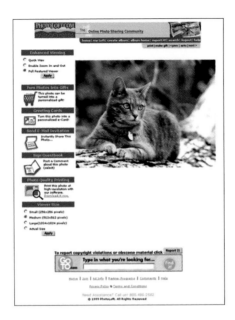

One of my favorite features is the guestbook. If you are serious about
photography, you will want to share your images, and when you share
them, you might be curious about what others think about them—I am.
An optional guestbook feature enables you to get e-mail notification of
guestbook comments. This is a great way to get feedback on your images.
You might think that you have taken some incredibly good pictures—but
what do others think? To find out, post some images and see what kind of
comments you get. The guestbook enables those who view your site to
post comments about each image on the site. If you have selected e-mail
notification, then you will get e-mail with the comments each time one is
posted.

A month after I posted the images previously shown in Figure 12.14,
I began to get daily e-mail providing me with comments about my images.
Then, one week, I got many more than I had seen in the prior weeks.
When I visited PhotoLoft.com's home page, I learned why—my album
was featured as album of the week. The best part of being selected was
that I was able to learn which of my photos were most liked and why. The
comments were wonderful, and on a few occasions, I responded to them.
Consequently, I now have online friends with whom I frequently share
images.

After you upload your images, you can easily invite others to your site by entering their e-mail addresses into one field and your message into another, as shown in Figure 12.16.

Figure 12.16
Inviting others to a PhotoLoft.com photo loft.

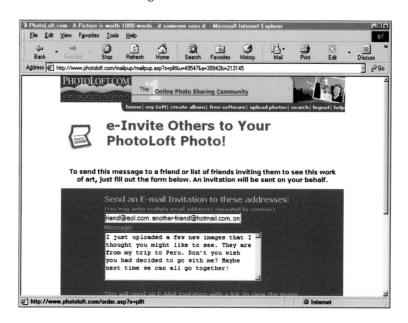

NOTE

A frequent seller of goods on several Internet-based auction sites posted images of the goods that he sold on PhotoLoft.com. By doing this, he provided very high-quality images of the merchandise he was offering for sale. Those interested in bidding used PhotoLoft.com's superior viewing features to zoom in on details, such as the face of a watch. Offering this capability to his prospective customers was as easy as uploading an image on the PhotoLoft.com site and putting the appropriate URL on the auction site. An unexpected benefit was that viewers of some of his images at PhotoLoft.com found other items that they wanted and were then able to go to the auction site to bid on them. He hadn't expected this added benefit.

The amazing bit of magic performed at PhotoLoft.com is that the site enables you to upload an image and then allow someone to download and print it as a high-quality image on photographic paper. That's assuming that the image you uploaded is of reasonable quality; obviously, they won't get a good printed image if your image was lousy to begin with.

When printing from PhotoLoft.com, you can choose your print size as 8×10, 5×7, 4×6, or wallet size. You first have to download a file to work with your browser, after which you can print whenever you'd like, just as if you were working from an image file on your own PC's hard drive.

Other photo-sharing communities

Photo-sharing community sites are fun! I could easily tour you through many other sites, but we have other things to do. Therefore, if you'd like to learn more about some other sites, I suggest that you visit the following:

► Club Photo: **www.clubphoto.com**

► eGroups: **www.egroups.com**

► Excite communities: **www.excite.com/comm/new**

► Familypoint: **www.familypoint.com**

► Folksites: **www.folksites.com**

► GatherRound: **www.gatherround.com**

► Photo Island: **www.photoisland.com**

► Zing: **www.zing.com**

NOTE

A youth soccer team wanted to have an online community to share photos, chat, and post messages, maps, travel information, player contact information, and other team information. The team wanted all of these features, but no one wanted the responsibility of creating a Web site with these capabilities or even becoming a Webmaster. Using a free Excite community, they were able to have what they wanted without much work.

Getting your own Web space

If you want to share your images on the Internet, but you don't want to use an online service offered by a photo lab or one of the photo-sharing communities, you need to get your own Web space. Digital images can consume considerable storage space and command lots of bandwidth when they are downloaded, so it is important to find an appropriate site to meet your needs. The good news on getting Web space is that there are many options—including many free ones.

Before looking for Web space, you need to decide whether the address or URL for your site needs to be short and simple to remember and whether it needs to look professional (as opposed to looking like it is located on a free, personal-use type of site). If you own a business that sells gazing globes to customers on a worldwide basis, for example, you don't want to have an address such as **www.somefreeservice.com/member2395340xb/ttsdke32450.htm**. Odds are that you'll be much happier with **www.gazing-globe.com**.

On the other hand, if you are just sharing personal pictures with friends and family members, the actual address might not matter, because it will usually be sent in e-mail as a hot-link. In this case, you have many more choices than if you want to have a "good-looking" URL.

So, where should you begin your search for Web space? First, you should check to see what your current online service or Internet service provider (ISP) offers as part of the service you already have or as an upgrade. Most ISPs offer between 5MB and 20MB or more of Web space with their basic service package. In addition, they usually offer home page templates, wizards, or even a proprietary or "lite" version of a commercial Web page creation tool to help you get your Web page up and going.

If your ISP offers space and you decide to use it, you need to be aware of any restrictions that might apply to the usage of this space, such as bandwidth limits. If you are just sharing images with a few friends, then you aren't likely to consume much bandwidth. However, if you post images that are going to be looked at by thousands of visitors, you might find yourself being charged additional money for the excess bandwidth that is above your limit.

If you don't have Web space available with any of your existing services or don't want to use it, then you need to look elsewhere.

Part IV Sharing & Enjoying Images

Getting free Web space

If you want free Web space, you simply have to sign up for it! I know that sounds unbelievable, but many Internet companies have come up with all kinds of innovative business models that enable them to provide free services—such as photo-sharing communities and Web space.

The following sites are a few of the more popular free Web hosting sites that provide good service and a wide variety of tools and site services. Most of them offer between 5MB and 10MB of space:

▶ Lycos Angelfire **www.angelfire.lycos.com**
▶ Yahoo! GeoCities **www.geocities.com**
▶ Homestead **www.homestead.com**
▶ iVilliage.com **www.ivillage.com**
▶ Familypoint **www.myfamily.com**
▶ Tripod **www.tripod.com**

Buying Web space

If you are serious enough about your Web space that you are willing to register and pay for a domain name and pay the monthly fees, then you probably ought to consider many other issues that I won't take the time to cover in this book. However, I can make a few suggestions. One, buy Peter Kent's *Poor Richard's Web Site (Top Floor Publishing, ISBN: 0966103289)*. It covers all that you need to know. If you don't want to buy it but want the links and a lot of the advice, just visit **www.poorrichard.com**.

To learn more about finding and choosing a Web host, I also suggest that you visit another excellent CNET site that is loaded with useful information and a searchable Web hosting company list: **www.webhostlist.com**.

Using software that automatically creates image-based Web pages

So far in this chapter, we have looked at how you can share images online by using services that are offered by photo labs. We also have seen how fun and easy it is to share your images in a photo-sharing community. Then, we covered the topic of how to get your own Web space. In this section, we look at software that makes it extremely easy to create image-based Web pages that you can post to your own Web site. More specifically, we will look at ways to do the following:

▶ Create an online image portfolio

▶ Create an online slide show

▶ Create an online rotating picture cube

Creating an online portfolio

Creating an online portfolio is a feature that is available in many image management software applications. To give you a good idea of the kinds of things that you can do with such software, we will look at creating image portfolios with Cerious Software's ThumbsPlus 4.0 and MGI's PhotoSuite III.

Using ThumbsPlus 4.0

Cerious Software, Inc.'s ThumbsPlus 4.0, one of the more feature-rich image-management tools (discussed in Chapter 4, "Managing and Storing Images"), offers a wide range of options for creating an online image portfolio. Creating a portfolio with ThumbsPlus 4.0 is as easy as answering a few questions posed to you by the Web Page Style wizard shown in Figure 12.17. This wizard enables you to choose from, modify, and save templates, which determine how your Web portfolio will look. Selecting the number of columns and rows per page, table border size, thumbnail size, file format, and thumbnail JPEG quality are just a few of the many other options available to you.

Figure 12.17
Using ThumbsPlus 4.0's Web Page Style wizard to create a Web page image portfolio.

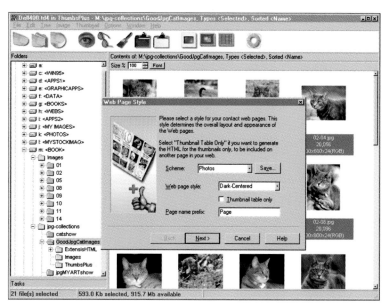

The portfolio may contain one or more pages. You also have an option to have thumbnails only or thumbnails and full-size images, as shown in Figure 12.18. If you use both, as shown in Figure 12.18, click the thumbnail image or hot link below each image to cause a full-size image to display. To return to the thumbnail page, just click your browser's Back button.

Figure 12.18
Web-based portfolio created with ThumbsPlus 4.0.

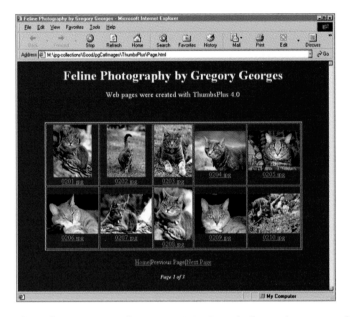

If you have ever tried to write HTML code for an image portfolio, such as the ones that are created by ThumbsPlus 4.0 in a few seconds, you'll love this feature—it really saves a tremendous amount of tedious coding, which is highly prone to errors.

Once ThumbsPlus 4.0 has created the necessary HTML code and thumbnail images, it stores them in file directories that you specify. From there, you must copy these file directories to the Web site on which you want them to be displayed. A good software utility to use to do this is WS_FTP, which will be covered toward the end of this chapter.

NOTE

A woodworker created multiple digital images of each project that he had built over the years. He manages these images with ThumbsPlus 4.0. Every December, he adds the work from the prior year to the work from all earlier years. File directories are named after the kinds of furniture that are contained in them. Images of desks, for example, are saved in a file directory named "desks," and images of chairs are in the "chairs" directory. When he has a prospective customer who wants to see his work, he loans them one of the CD-ROMs containing his work. To make the images easy to view without requiring any additional software, he uses ThumbsPlus 4.0 to create an HTML-based portfolio that can be viewed quickly with a standard browser.

He also uploaded the portfolio to a Web site so that he can show others his work from anywhere he has access to the Internet. On many occasions, when he visits clients' homes or businesses, he gets an order for a new piece of furniture simply by showing them the work that he has done by going to his Web page on their computer. This saves him from having to create a photo album and carry it around all the time. Plus, he can talk to a prospective customer on the telephone while they look at his work on a Web page.

Using PhotoSuite III

MGI calls PhotoSuite III "The PC & Internet Photography Power Pack." As expected, it is one of the more Internet-enabled PC photography software applications on the market. One of the unique aspects of this program is its embedded browser that enables Web viewing from within the program. This feature enables users to save photos from the Web directly into the application simply by dragging them off the Web page into the photo library that is part of PhotoSuite III. Then, the images can be directly edited or used in a photo project. The browser feature also offers seamless connections to online photo services, as well as to the MGI Web site, where additional content and templates can be downloaded. MGI's site also enables users to send customized postcards and greeting cards over the Web.

PhotoSuite III offers three different ways to share digital images on the Internet:

▶ Create Web pages for your own Web site and upload them

▶ Post images to the GatherRound.com online photo community

▶ Upload images to Kodak PhotoNet Online

To create your own Web pages, you simply need to collect and organize the images that you want to use in the album feature, located by clicking the Organize tab. Then, in one step, the software automatically converts your album into a Web page (or pages) ready to be posted to your Web site.

Figure 12.19 shows the Create Web Page button that you click to instantly create the Web page shown in Figure 12.20—it really is that easy. By the way, when you click the image file name or the image, your browser will display the full-size image. To return to the thumbnails view, click your browser's Back button. Again, after the pages have been created, you have to upload the images and Web pages to your Web site. Otherwise, there is no more work to be done.

Figure 12.19
Using MGI's PhotoSuite III to create image-based Web pages.

Create Web Page Button

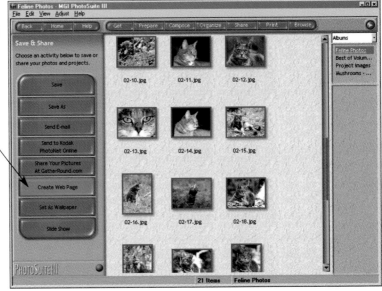

Figure 12.20
An image portfolio created with MGI's PhotoSuite III.

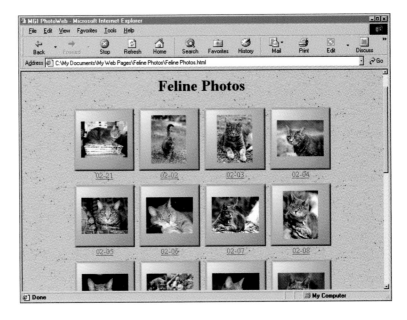

Using PhotoSuite III, posting all of your images to an online photo-sharing community is just as easy as posting them to the Web. Select the images that you want to share, and click the Share Your Pictures At GatherRound.com button. You then have the option of creating a new album or adding the selected images to an existing album. Then, click the green Upload button, and the upload process begins. After your images have been uploaded, they will be displayed in the embedded Web browser, as shown in Figure 12.21. From here, you can do any one of the tasks listed on the left side of the window. This is also the screen from which you share pictures with a guest, by sending them e-mail. You can even create an address book to make sharing images with others faster.

Figure 12.21
Sharing images with MGI's PhotoSuite III and GatherRound.com.

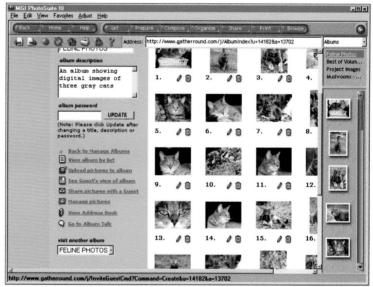

Looking once again at Figure 12.19, you can see a green button for Send to Kodak PhotoNet Online. This button enables you to connect directly to the Kodak PhotoNet Online service and upload your pictures, after which you can share them or get them printed and mailed to you.

A variation of the portfolio is the photo album. Some of the more creative browser-based photo albums are those that can be created with Kai's PhotoSoap 2, as shown in Figure 12.22. You get to choose from a wide variety of unusual-looking album covers. You can also choose from a variety of page designs and layouts. If you want to add captions to your images, a space is provided. To view the album, just turn the pages. When you want to see one of the images in more detail, click the image and it will be displayed full size. Another click and you are back to the Photo Album view.

Figure 12.22
Browser-based photo album created in Kai's PhotoSoap 2.

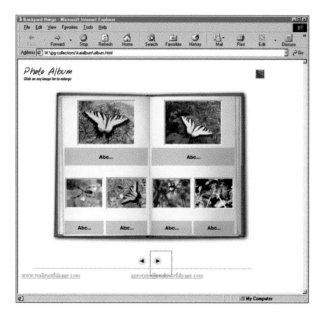

Creating an online slide show

In Chapter 8, "Displaying Digital Images Electronically," you learned how to create outstanding slide shows to share your digital images. In this section, instead of creating a slide show that runs as an application on your PC, we will create slide shows that can be viewed inside a standard Internet browser from any kind of computer anywhere with a connection to the Internet.

To create our Web-page-based slide show, we'll use Kai's Power SHOW. The steps that you must take are nearly identical to the ones that were covered in Chapter 8. The only difference is that when you are finished creating the slide show, you go to the Out room and select Web>Output to HTML. At that point, you can enter an e-mail address and an address for a "home" page and select from a few templates that change the background and button controls.

As soon as you click the OK button and select an output directory, your images are prepared for the Internet and the Web pages are created. You are then ready to post them to your Web site. Figure 12.23 shows one slide in the show.

Figure 12.23
A Web-page-based slide show created with Kai's Power SHOW.

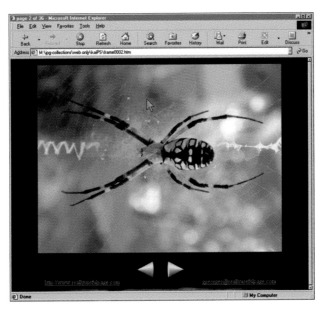

NOTE
An industrial salesperson created five different online slide shows for use when discussing the five products that he sold. On those occasions in which he has to do some selling over the telephone, he often gets the prospective buyers to look at those slide shows. He talks to the customers while they view the slides, thus enhancing his presentation. His close rate is always better when the buyers are willing to let him talk his way through the half-dozen slides in a show.

Creating an online rotating picture cube

In the purely just-for-fun category is the rotating picture cube that can be created with PhotoSoap 2. You might have a real one of these cubes on your desk. They are usually plastic, and you can put a photograph on each of the six sides and rotate it to choose a photograph.

The picture cube created by PhotoSoap 2 is just like the real thing, except that it moves inside a browser. It continually rotates about an axis, and when you want to, you can grab it with the cursor and rotate it, stop it, and send it back into motion. It is a very creative way to show six digital images. If you think that this might be too hard to create—well, you can drop that notion. You simply need to select six images, crop them so that they are square, put them into a PhotoSoap 2 album, select the menu item labeled Export to PhotoCube, and then select a directory. Your picture cube is ready to be posted to your Web site. Figure 12.24 shows the picture cube being displayed in a browser.

Figure 12.24
The picture cube shown inside a browser.

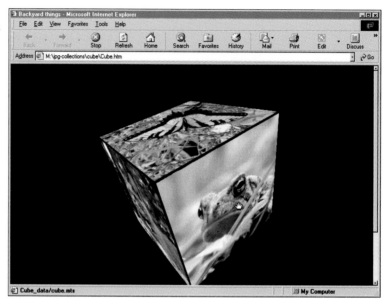

Consider putting one of these picture cubes on the front page of a family Web site or even on a business Web site if you have some good product images that you'd like to display. It is so much fun to control the rotation of the cube that visitors to your site are more than likely to see all six pictures many times.

Other applications to consider

The applications that we have covered in this section are by no means the only ones that provide the capabilities shown. They do represent a wide range of the features that are available, and they perform these tasks in a very elegant manner. Increasingly, you will find such features in many other software products.

Authoring your own Web pages

"Wait a minute," you might be thinking. "Why is a section on authoring your own Web pages included in a book on digital cameras and imaging?" The answer is a simple one. If you want to be able to do something that is more sophisticated than what we have seen so far in this chapter, then you need to know about the tools that can help you accomplish your objectives.

Sure, I could have skipped this section entirely, but I have included it for one reason—some of the tools that we will look at briefly are so useful that you can do some amazing things without having to become a programmer. Without including this section, you would not have learned an important point that I feel is invaluable—you can do more than you think you can with some of the new software products. As I previously challenged those of you who don't have a digital camera to try one, I now challenge those of you who really do want to create quality Web pages to try using a Web page authoring tool or two. My bet is that you'll be surprised at what you can do with one, if you haven't tried one lately!

A few words about HTML

Web page creation is all about writing HTML code. HTML stands for *hypertext markup language*, which is a fancy term for a text formatting language. In the early days, just about all HTML could do was format text on a page and enable hyperlinks. Now, however, its capabilities have expanded greatly.

If you haven't ever looked at HTML code, take a quick peek at some. The easiest way to do this is to launch your browser and visit any Web page that you like. If you use Internet Explorer, you can view the HTML code (source code) by selecting the menu item View>Source. You will see the HTML code that created the page that you are viewing. If you use Netscape Navigator, you can see the source code by selecting View>Page Source. The bad news is that the code on many pages can be pretty darn ugly stuff if you aren't familiar with HTML (or JavaScript, which also might be present). The good news is that you don't have to know much HTML to do some amazing things—provided that you are using the right tools.

Depending on what you are trying to accomplish on a Web page, you might not ever have to learn or even look at HTML code. During the last few years, a number of software vendors have worked hard to develop tools that enable users to create Web pages through what is know as WYSIWYG (What You See Is What You Get) editors. The idea behind these Web page creation tools is that you build your pages exactly as you want them to look in a graphical environment, and the software creates all the necessary HTML code without your even having to look at it.

Using Microsoft Office 2000 to create Web pages

Some of the best examples of software programs that enable you to create Web pages without coding are the applications included in Microsoft Office 2000. For example, you can use Microsoft Word 2000 to create a standard document and then add a few digital images, titles and various headings, graphics, and even tables. After you compete your work and are happy with the way it looks, you save it as a normal DOC file. Then, after you save the document, you can save it again, only this time you select the Save As menu and, in the dialog box that appears, select Web Page in the Save as type box. You now have a Web page that looks like the Word document that you created.

Another approach is to use Word 2000's Web page templates and start by creating a Web page instead of a Word document. To get to these templates, select File>New and then click the Web Pages tab. Notice that there is even a Web Page Wizard, which will help you select a theme, create multiple pages, and more.

After you see what you can do with Word 2000, you might assume that you can do the same kinds of things in the other Office 2000 applications. Your assumption is correct—you can. Creating a Web page that looks like a spreadsheet is as easy as creating a spreadsheet in Excel 2000. You also can use PowerPoint to create a slide show that uses your digital images and then have PowerPoint create a Web-page-based slide show. Even Microsoft Publisher 2000 enables you to create Web publications. Access 2000 can be used to manage images that then can be shown on a Web page.

The important point is that creating Web pages is quickly becoming a common and popular thing to do. Anyone with Office 2000 has the capabilities. Shouldn't you try making a Web page, either for fun or with a purpose in mind?

Using WYSIWYG editors

Adobe PageMill, Macromedia Dreamweaver, and Microsoft FrontPage are just three of the many highly capable WYSIWYG editors that are available to create Web pages. FrontPage and PageMill are two of the easier ones to use. Dreamweaver, on the other hand, which was designed for professional Web site designers, is widely recognized as the most powerful of all the editors and, consequently, is more difficult to learn how to use.

Just to give you an idea of how these WYSIWYG editors work, let's briefly look at how to use FrontPage 2000 to create a page for showing digital images. We could, if we really wanted to, start with a blank page and create each element that is needed. Another option is to use one of the templates included with the software and then make a few modifications to meet our needs.

Part IV Sharing & Enjoying Images

Figure 12.25 shows a Web page being created with one of the basic templates. Looking at the bottom of the window, you can see three tabs—one for Normal view, one for HTML view, and one for Preview. These tabs enable the designer to quickly switch between views. You might want to start in Normal view, which is the view that you use to insert text and other objects and to change their properties. When you want to see what the page looks like, click the Preview tab. If you need to add, delete, or modify HTML code, click the HTML view. After you complete your Web page, you can view it in a browser, as shown in Figure 12.26.

Figure 12.25
Creating a Web page in FrontPage 2000 in Normal view.

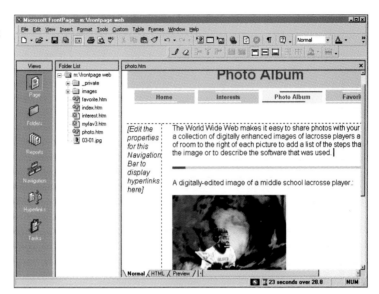

Figure 12.26
Completed Web page created with a FrontPage 2000 template.

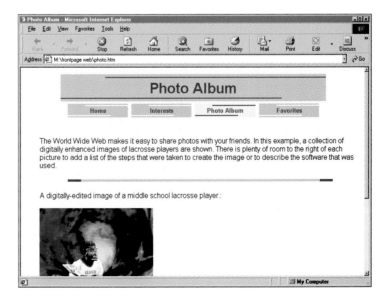

TIP

Even though FrontPage, PageMill, and Dreamweaver offer the capabilities to directly edit HTML code, there are far better tools to use if you want to work directly with HTML. One such tool is Allaire's HomeSite 4.0. It is a development tool for heavy-duty programmers. If you don't know much about HTML or don't intend to learn it, this is a tool that you won't need. For those of you who do intend to learn HTML, HomeSite 4.0 makes learning HTML easier and helps you to create it much faster and with fewer errors.

Uploading files to your Web site with WS_FTP

Before we end this chapter, one last program is worth discussing: WS_FTP. This program was designed for the novice to upload and download files between a Web site and a computer. Many of the applications covered in this chapter, such as those that created Web-based portfolios, create many image files and Web pages on your PC's hard drive. To post those images and Web pages to a Web site, you have to transfer their files to a Web site. WS_FTP is one of the tools that can be used for this purpose.

Figure 12.27 shows WS_FTP being used to upload the collection of JPEG images of cats used to create the portfolio shown earlier in Figure 12.18. WS_FTP is a simple application that works similarly to Windows Explorer. On the left side, you select the drive, directory, and files that you want to upload from your PC. On the right side, you select the directory on the Web site where you want the files to be transferred. WS_FTP is a very efficient program that makes the task of transferring files as error-free and quick as possible.

Figure 12.27
Using WS_FTP32
to upload images and
Web pages to a
Web site.

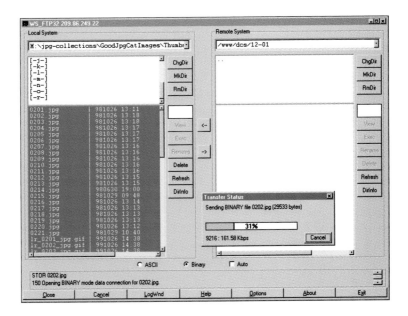

WS_FTP is available for download from **www.wsftp.com**.

Two versions of WS_FTP are available—one is free for noncommercial home users, students, and faculty, and the other is a commercial version with a few extra features for about $40.

Besides Dreamweaver, FrontPage, and PageMill, dozens of other Web page creation tools are available on the market. Many of the online services have even created their own proprietary page creation tools for creating pages on their free Web space. If you are considering buying a Web authoring tool, you might find it worthwhile to visit ZDNET at **www.zdnet.com/products/**.

If you select Web Authoring page under the Internet & Networking category, you will find a page full of valuable resources. The tips, product reviews, tutorials, and other features are likely to be useful to you. You can even download trial versions of the products. It is worth a visit.

A few good books to help you learn to create Web pages

Up until a little over a year ago, I had never even created a Web page, let alone an entire site. I am not a programmer and, even now, I have limited knowledge about HTML. However, my interest in photography and digital imaging and my desire to share my work on the Internet have motivated me to get Web-savvy. Without too much work, I've been able to create several entire Web sites, which have turned out well and have produced the results that I wanted.

The trick to rapid success in Web page creation is to use the correct tools for your needs and abilities (or lack thereof) and a few good books. I highly recommend the following books for learning about HTML and a few of the leading Web page creation tools:

▶ *Creative HTML Design—A Hands-on HTML 4.0 Web Design Tutorial,* by Lynda Weinman and William Weinman (New Riders, ISBN: 1-56205-704-9). This is the absolutely, positively best first book on HTML for those new to creating Web pages. It was written by one of the most respected authorities on Web design and training—Lynda Weinman.

▶ *Dreamweaver 2 Bible,* by Joseph W. Lowery (IDG Books Worldwide, Inc., ISBN: 0-7645-3322-3). An excellent book for an excellent product that I have yet to begin to master—but I plan to keep trying.

▶ *HTML 4 for the World Wide Web: Visual QuickStart Guide,* by Elizabeth Castro (Peachpit Press, ISBN: 0201354934). This small book has been an invaluable reference book to me. It is the perfect guide for finding out how to tweak HTML code produced by a WYSIWYG editor so that it meets your needs.

▶ *Special Edition Using Microsoft FrontPage 2000,* by Neil Randall and Dennis Jones (Que, ISBN: 0-7897-1910-x). A mammoth 1,200-page book that seems to have what I need every time I go looking for it or have a particular problem.

▶ *Web Design Templates Sourcebook,* by Lisa Schmeiser (New Riders, ISBN: 1-56205-754-5). This book offers a collection of more than 300 templates for Web pages. The best part is that it comes with a CD-ROM, so you don't even have to type the code. Select a template that is close to what you want and modify it. You can't create a Web page much faster.

▶ *Web Style Guide—Basic Design Principles for Creating Web Sites,* by Patrick J. Lynch and Sarah Horton (Yale University Press, ISBN: 0-300-07675-4). As the title suggests, this is *the* guide for basic Web page design principles. This entire book is also available online at **www.info.med.yale.edu/caim/manual**.

That concludes this chapter on using the Internet to share images. I hope it has given you several project ideas that you are keen to get started on. In the next chapter, we'll continue on the topic of ways to share and enjoy your images—only we are going to leave the digital world and return to the printed world. In Chapter 13, we'll look at how you can turn your digital images into printed images.

13

Turning Digital Images into Prints

Do you have digital images that you want to print? Maybe you've received them as e-mail attachments, downloaded them from the Internet, taken them with a digital camera, or scanned them yourself with a desktop scanner. It doesn't matter how you got the digital images—the task now is to get them printed. What options are there? What kind of printer should you use? If you don't have a printer, how can you get prints made? Can you print your own prints if you don't have a PC? What kinds of specialty papers are available? If you want the absolutely best print possible, where should you go? How can you make prints available to a friend who lives in another city? If you have these or similar questions, you are reading the right chapter!

In this chapter, you will learn how you can turn your digital images into a print by:

▶ Uploading them to an Internet-based printing service
▶ Using the digital image services of a local photo lab
▶ Using a desktop printer
▶ Using the services of a custom photo lab

Looking into the future

The number of ways that you will be able to get photo-quality prints made from digital image files is increasing rapidly. Many companies are focused on introducing new printing services that will revolutionize the way we use, share, and print pictures. This vision is being built upon three elements that will make sharing pictures almost as easy and common as sending e-mail.

The first element consists of digital mini-labs and photo kiosks. The new integrated digital mini-labs will accept virtually every input source from silver halide film to digital camera media, CD-ROMs, PC cards, floppy disks, Zip disks, and more. They also can print regular photographs as well as upload digital images to the Internet. Photo kiosks are the self-serve consumer versions of a digital image lab that enable users to scan photographs or read images from CD-ROMs, floppy disks, or digital camera media. These kiosks can be used to digitally edit images, upload them to the Internet, and produce photo-quality prints. The kiosks of the near future also will enable you to download images from the Internet so that they can be printed or written to digital storage media.

The second important element is the personal computer—which is available in an increasing number of homes and offices. A large percentage of PCs can be connected to the Internet, and they are frequently connected to an inkjet printer capable of making photo-quality prints.

The final element—as you might have guessed—is the Internet. The Internet links the PCs, the digital mini-labs or kiosks, and a digital picture network such as Kodak PhotoNet. With that background, you can probably see the same vision that is driving many companies to provide us with a way to easily share our pictures with others no matter where they are. If you live in Sioux Falls, South Dakota, and you want to share a photo with a friend in Salem, Oregon, or your grandparents in Ft. Lauderdale, Florida—it is easy. After you have a digital image, you can upload it to the Internet and send the recipient an e-mail telling how to access it. The recipient can then download it to his PC and print it on his own printer if he has one. He can download the image on a photo kiosk and have it printed while he waits. Alternatively, you can send a digital image to a specific photo lab in his neighborhood where he can pick up the prints after they have been made. Your brother in Rome, Italy, could even get a print merely by picking it up at a nearby photo-lab.

Figure 13.1
The Internet makes
it easy to share pictures
with others no matter
where they are.

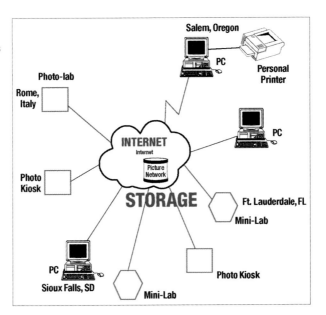

That is a quick peek at the future. Two problems are keeping this vision
from becoming reality. First, most of the large chains of one-hour labs
(mass merchants, camera stores, and drug stores) do not yet have their
mini-labs or kiosks connected to the Internet. Second, many photo labs
do not have the new integrated digital mini-labs or kiosks installed, or
existing ones have not been upgraded to enable them to accept digital
image file media such as CD-ROMs or digital camera media. Both of these
problems are rapidly being addressed.

Ordering prints through the Internet

One of the easiest ways to turn your digital images into prints is to order
them through the Internet. Prints can be ordered in many ways and
through a number of companies. As you might expect, Kodak has worked
hard to position itself as a leader in the digital photography marketplace.
Kodak services are available through Kodak directly or through many
participating Kodak photo retailers.

Kodak PhotoNet online services

Kodak, through its wholly owned subsidiary, PictureVision, Inc., offers extensive Web site services for viewing, storing, sharing, and ordering prints of your photos. This online service, which is a combination of the Kodak Picture Network and PictureVision's PhotoNet services, will soon be available at 40,000 outlets worldwide. This new total digital solution is available through every level of the photofinishing industry—mini-labs, wholesale labs, and mail-order labs.

Significantly, PhotoNet services are available on such an extensive basis that it makes it easy for you to share photos with others, no matter where they are. Chapter 14, "Using AOL and 'You've got Pictures,' " discusses in detail how PhotoNet can be used to share pictures and order prints. AOL, by the way, is just one of many retailers offering the Kodak PhotoNet service.

Kodak Quick Print service

If there is a digital image file on your PC or on the Internet somewhere that you want to have printed, you can order one in just a few steps directly over the Internet. To access Kodak's Quick Print service, visit the Kodak Web site at **www.kodak.com** and click on the Quick Print link. This will download the Web page shown in Figure 13.2. Click on the Browse button and use the browser to select the file that you want to have printed.

Figure 13.2
Uploading a digital image file to be printed with Kodak's Quick Print service.

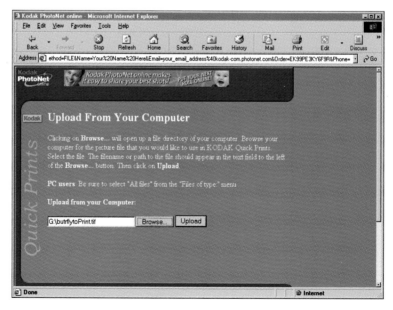

Your image must be in one of the following file formats: JPEG, BMP, TIFF, GIF, PBM, PPM, or PGM. It also must be less than 3MBs in size. After you've selected a file, you can either add additional ones or you can continue with the order process. When your image has been uploaded, you will be presented with a screen that shows the image that was uploaded, indicating that the upload was completed successfully. The remaining steps include choosing the number of copies and the size of prints that you want. Click on the Add to Order button, and you are ready for the final step of entering your name, shipping address, and credit card information. These steps take place in the Web page shown in Figure 13.3. Within a few days of placing your order, you will receive your print in the mail.

Figure 13.3
Ordering prints from a digital image file with Kodak's Quick Print service.

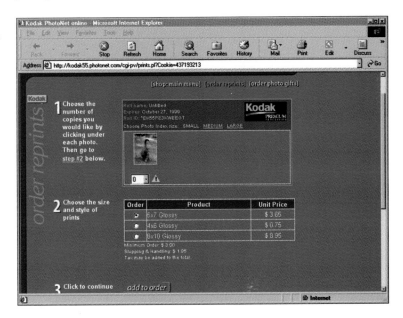

Besides printing the regular 4×6-, 5×7-, and 8×10-inch glossy print, you can also order an 8×10-inch photo jigsaw puzzle, two sizes of photo mugs, a photo mouse pad, photo T-shirt, or sweatshirt.

If you want to use Kodak digital print services, but you'd prefer to use a mail-order photofinisher, you might want to consider using Mystic Labs (**www.mysticcolorlab.com**) or York Photo (**www.yorkphoto.com**).

Other services to consider

Besides Kodak participating photofinishers, there are other Internet-based services that you might want to consider using. They are AGFANet (**www.agfanet.com**), Club Photo (**www.clubphoto.com**), EZ Prints (**www.ezprints.com**), and Seattle Film Works (**www.filmworks.com**). Seattle Film Works is one of the pioneers of Internet-based photography. You can learn more about its unique offering in Chapter 12, "Using the Internet to Share Images."

NOTE

More than 120 friends and family members got together for a wedding. One of the family members took photographs with a film-based camera. After shooting four rolls of film, he took them to a nearby, one-hour photo-processing lab (located inside a drug store) to be developed. When he dropped off the film, he indicated on the processing request envelopes that he wanted four sets of reprints. Additionally, he checked a box to have the images uploaded to the Internet and checked another box to have the images put on a CD-ROM. In one hour, he could pick up the four sets of reprints. Within two days, he could pick up the CD-ROM, and he received an e-mail notifying him that he could view and download images for all four rolls of film from the Internet. The e-mail included his user name and an access code for each roll of film. He then viewed the images, added titles to a few, and deleted others.

Next, he sent one e-mail message to everyone he knew who had e-mail (about sixty people) and had asked to see the pictures. All the recipients of that e-mail were then able to view the images simply by clicking the link embedded in the e-mail message. If they wanted prints of any image, they could order them from their PC, either to be mailed directly to them or to be picked up at a local photo-processing lab. Alternatively, if they did not have a PC, they could visit a local photo-processing lab and have them print the images within a few minutes.

Getting prints made at a local photo lab

As mentioned at the beginning of the chapter, many photo labs do not yet have equipment that can read digital files on removable media such as a CD-ROM, floppy disk, or digital camera storage media. These labs must send your digital media to an out-of-store lab to be printed—frequently a lab that is a Kodak-participating photofinisher. Until these photo labs are properly equipped, you might find it easier to order your prints by uploading them to the Internet from your own PC.

Alternatively, check around to find an outlet that has an appropriate kiosk like Kodak Picture Maker, as shown in Figure 1.14 of Chapter 1. Many photo-processing outlets either have a Kodak Picture Maker or a competitive kiosk like Fujifilm's Aladdin Digital Picture Center that enables you to get prints from your removable storage media. The Kodak Picture Maker contains a Kodak Digital Science 8650 Color Printer that uses a sophisticated dye-sublimation print technology that provides high-quality prints up to 8×10 inches. It is a 300 dpi continuous-tone print, which provides superb color and fine detail. The Kodak Picture Maker also enables you to enlarge or reduce your photos, fix red eye, zoom and crop images, adjust color balance, and add creative borders before the print is made. Most of the Picture Makers will be able to read from CD-ROMs and floppy disks in 2000. Kodak has plans to have 100,000 of these kiosks worldwide, so they will be readily available wherever you might be.

Ritz Camera and Wolf Camera are the two dominant national camera store chains in the U.S. Ritz Camera has 1,000 stores nationwide and more than 890 one-hour labs. Wolf Camera has 800 stores in thirty-four states—which makes it likely that one of them has a store near you. Both are rapidly implementing their own plans to provide a wide range of digital imaging products and services. You can learn more about their current offerings or find a store in your neighborhood by visiting their Web sites at **www.ritzcamera.com** and **www.wolfcamera.com**.

In addition to the Internet-based services, there are also thousands of mass merchants (drug stores, supermarkets, and discount stores) that provide, or will soon provide, services to process your film, scan it, and upload it to the Internet. Just about every national chain store you can think of—Kmart, Wal-Mart, Target, Walgreens, Osco Drug, Eckerd Drug, Harris Teeter, and Safeway—will offer digital services in 2000!

If you want to find the location of one of the Kodak services discussed in this section, just visit the Kodak Web site at **www.kodak.com/US/en/service/dealers.shtml**.

Just enter the city name, state, or ZIP code for the city where you are looking for a Kodak service, and you will get a list of locations.

TIP

Visit the Wolf Camera Web site at **www.wolfcamera.com** or Ritz Camera's Web site at **www.ritzcamera.com** to find and print Internet coupons to save on a variety of products and services. Savings typically range from 25 to 50 percent. They frequently have discount coupons for using digital services.

To get your first glimpse of where the vision and reality meet, check around and find a place that has one of the newer digital print stations. Have them print a few of your images. If you have good images, the prints will be spectacular. I took the close-up picture of a butterfly that I found in my garden (see Figure 13.4) with a Nikon CoolPix 950 digital camera. The camera settings resulted in a 1600×1200, 800KB file. I had it printed at a Ritz Camera store as an 8×10-inch print. The print was outstanding. It looked as though it were taken with a film camera and processed and printed as an ordinary photographic print. My suggestion—go try one yourself!

Figure 13.4
Digital print of a butterfly taken with a digital camera.

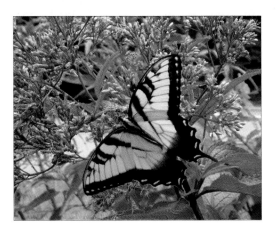

Using custom photo lab services or specialty printers

When you want the best possible print made, find a custom photo lab or a specialty printer that has the equipment and services to meet your needs. Such companies cater to a professional customer base. They are used to the high expectations of professionals and have skills and equipment that enable them to do a better job than consumer-focused, one-hour photo labs. These custom labs have built their business on quality rather than volume, and they tend to charge a premium for a better quality print.

For a particularly good photographic print, get one of your images printed with a Fuji Pictography 4000 printer. It is a 400 dpi continuous-tone device, and it offers brilliant photographic color quality. The prints are true photo-quality output, just like a conventional photograph. Images are printed on glossy photographic paper capable of being displayed in the same way as conventional photographs. The printer utilizes an innovative process in which photosensitive donor paper is exposed by laser diodes—a process which yields a print far superior to the more common dye sublimation print used in most consumer photo labs. If you want to get a Fuji Pictography print from a local photo lab, you can order it at one of the Wolf Camera stores. You can learn more about this printer at **www.wolfcamera.com/photofinishing/index.html**.

Many specialty printers have high-end digital printers that can print with archival-quality ink on museum-quality paper. Prints like these can cost several hundred dollars for a 30×40-inch print. Several high-end printers you might want to consider using are Corporate Color (**www.corpcolor.com**), EverColor (**www.evercolor.com**), Fine Print, Inc., (**www.fineprint.org**), or Imagers Digital Production Center (**www.imagers.com**).

TIP

To save time and an unnecessary trip, call before you visit a custom photo lab and ask a few questions. What will a print cost? What storage media can the lab read? What kinds of paper can it print on? What kind of digital image file format can it read and which ones does it prefer? What dpi setting should you use? Can the lab accept files over the Internet? How long will it take to complete the work?

Using a desktop printer to make prints

If you haven't seen a print made by a photo-quality printer, you will truly be amazed. Many printer manufacturers offer a range of photo-quality printers from around $100 to well over $1,500, many of which are capable of printing prints on photo-quality paper that very closely resembles an actual silver-halide print (a true photographic print that is exposed by light). If you don't have a photo-quality printer, you might want to consider purchasing one. In this section, you will learn how to pick a printer that meets your needs and, I hope, your budget as well.

Types of printers

As you might expect, there are many different types of color printer technologies—some are good for photographic images, and some are not. There are color lasers, thermal inkjet, dye sublimation, and inkjet printers to name just a few. As so many inkjet printers are available that can do an outstanding job of printing photo-quality prints and because most printers using other printer technologies cost substantially more than $1,500, we'll limit our discussions here to just inkjet printers.

Printer features that might be important to you

Once again, I will point you to one of the many wonderful ZDNet Web sites. This time I suggest you look at **www.zdnet.com/pcmag/** to find printer comparisons, printer reviews, and prices and to shop for the printer that you want—you can even bid for one at an auction. With this and other online resources available to you, I will limit the content in this section to features that I have found to be particularly important when printing digital images—either as regular 4×6-inch photo-quality prints or as large-format, fine-art images. You might not ordinarily consider some of these features. As you become more successful at editing your digital images and you begin to print more of them in larger sizes and on different print media, however, you'll be glad you considered them.

With our discussion narrowed to inkjet printers under $1,500, we will now look at several characteristics or features you should consider when hunting for the perfect photo-quality printer for you. Key differentiating features that might be important to you, depending on how you want to use your printer and how much money you are willing to spend, are:

▶ **Print quality, print quality, and print quality**—Print quality is likely to be the most important thing you will consider when choosing a photo-quality printer. If it isn't, it should be. Although print resolution has a lot to do with print quality, many other factors are involved in producing a good print. Print quality is often a subjective notion, so I suggest that you look at prints from every printer that you are considering and decide for yourself whether or not it is the quality that you want. A good inkjet printer will print even, continuous gradations, and it will not show any banding (straight lines parallel with the printer head path). The colors will be correct—not faded–and close to what your computer screen shows, providing you have calibrated your printer and screen

▶ **Print resolution**—Print resolution is specified in dots-per-inch (dpi), and the general rule (with a few exceptions, especially many of the HP printers) is that an image will be sharper and have smoother gradations, higher highlights, and darker shadows as the dpi increases. Printers with higher resolutions generally print a better image than printers with a lower dpi. Inkjet printers with 300 dpi or more are capable of printing a good photo-quality print.

▶ **Maximum print size**—When purchasing a printer, we all envision printing large photographic images. The reality, however, is that photographic images larger than 8×10 inches require huge image files, often many times larger than can be taken with a digital camera. These large files also can consume incredible amounts of RAM to process and considerable hard disk space as well. For example, an uncompressed 8×10-inch print printed at 300 dpi and 24-bit color depth would require a file size of 21.6MBs. A 11×14-inch print at 300 dpi would be 41.6MBs. The point is that you shouldn't plan to buy a printer capable of printing large images unless you also have the necessary processing power, RAM, and drive space. The one exception is that if you want to print panoramas, then a printer such as the Epson 1200, which can print a 13×44-inch print, is an excellent choice. I create quite a few panoramas with about a 4:1 width-to-height ratio, which matches the way our eyes enable us to see. Figure 13.5 was printed as a 4×24-inch image at 300 dpi. The uncompressed file size is nearly 26MBs. A good panoramic print, properly framed, can be outstanding—but without a large-format printer, you simply can't print it.

Figure 13.5
A 4×24-inch panoramic print on watercolor paper.

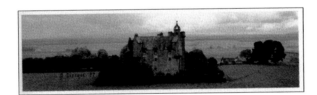

▶ **Adjustable printer head height**—If you are serious about printing and plan to use some of the thicker fine-art papers, such as watercolor paper or artist canvas, then look for a printer that enables the printer head to be raised. Some of the more expensive Epson printers offer this feature. Without it, you will be limited to the lighter-weight media.

▶ **Paper-feed path**—This might not seem like an important feature until you see what happens when a thick piece of paper is fed into a printer that makes it turn around a narrow-diameter roller! Printers that enable thick paper to be fed straight into the printer enable you to use thicker paper with better results. If you want to use heavy watercolor paper or other thick media, don't consider a printer that won't enable the paper to be fed straight in.

▶ **I/O interface**—As you get into PC photography, you will find that you need to hook up a scanner, your digital camera, and perhaps a digital tablet (in addition to other devices). The more devices that you connect to your PC, the more likely you are to run out of interrupt requests (IRQs)—those nasty Windows things that make your system not function properly if they conflict. If you have an available USB port on your PC, I suggest that you look for a printer that offers USB capabilities, which will not only help to avoid the IRQ problem but also will provide a faster connection than parallel or serial ports.

▶ **Print speed**—Print speed may be an issue to you if you plan on printing many prints. Generally, photo-quality printers are not particularly high-speed printers, because they are optimized for quality, not speed. One compelling reason for getting a high-speed printer is that printing large image files to an inkjet printer can slow down your PC so much that you will want to wait until the printing is complete to continue working.

▶ **Ink cartridges and print heads**—Inkjet printers are not cheap to use. The print cartridges are expensive—anywhere from $25 to nearly $40, depending on the brand and model. Full-page color prints consume lots of ink. When you are looking at inkjet printers, be aware that you can get printers that offer three colors in one cartridge, plus a black cartridge. Alternatively, you can get printers that have a separate cartridge for each color. If you print lots of landscapes with blue skies, and you have a single cartridge for red, green, and blue ink, you might end up throwing out a fairly unused cartridge simply because it no longer contains blue ink. Some of the newer printers offer six-color ink systems, which include cyan, magenta, yellow, light cyan, light magenta, and black to create an extremely wide color gamut. In this case, you simply replace one color cartridge when it runs out. Be aware that at least one printer vendor sells a multiple cartridge printer, but it only sells the cartridges in a package of four—meaning that you can never buy just one color!

▶ **Full-page print costs**—Here is a question no printer vendor seems to be keen to answer. How much does it cost to print one page with 100 percent ink coverage on an 8×10-inch space? It should be an easy question to answer, but I've never seen it answered. My experience suggests that a full page costs from $.75 to $1.25 or more to print one page. That is expensive on a per-page basis, but when you consider that an 8×10-inch photograph usually costs around $9—it seems like a bargain.

TIP

With inkjet printers costing as little as $100, it is easy to spend many times more than the initial cost of the printer on ink cartridges. While printer vendors often claim that you save money by having a printer with separate cartridges for each color, plus black, it might not be true for you. If you are an infrequent user of your inkjet printer, you will find that your cartridges can dry out, for they do expire. If you have four ink cartridges that cost $30 each that dry out, you will have to spend $120 to replace them all. Instead, if you purchase a single cartridge printer, you only have to replace a single cartridge at about $30.

When purchasing new inkjet cartridges, especially for older models of inkjet printers, carefully check the packaging for the expiration date to make sure that you are purchasing a new cartridge rather than one that has expired or is about to expire.

Printers for the PC-less environment

Yes, there are printers that enable you to store, edit, and print photo-quality prints without having a PC! As the digital camera market continues to grow, you'll see many more of these printers. Two manufacturers making a PC-less printer are Lexmark and HP. Kodak offers the Lexmark printer under the name of the Kodak Personal Picture Maker by Lexmark.

If you have a digital camera and you don't have a PC, but you want to be able to print your own photo-quality prints and store digital files, one of these printers will be perfect for you.

Printers you might want to consider

What printer should you buy? That depends on how you intend to use your printer and how much you are willing to spend. When you get serious about purchasing a color printer, spend an hour on the ZDNet site mentioned earlier. It is full of valuable information about how to purchase a printer. It offers product reviews, buyer's guides, expert picks, and how-to-buy articles, plus directories that enable you to shop and compare both by manufacturer and by price—and these directories have links directly to merchants who sell the products.

The great news is that you don't have to spend much money to get a printer that can print photographic images that you will be very pleased with—some can be found for as low as $100! This is especially true when you use high-quality paper, which leads to the next section—selecting paper for your prints.

Choosing print media

The media you choose for printing makes a very significant difference in the overall quality of your print—this is especially true for inkjet printers. Because you invest your time and energy shooting a picture and working on it with digital editing tools, you want to get the best possible print of that image. To do that, you must choose the right paper.

Types of paper

For simplicity, this section divides printer media products into five categories: low-cost inkjet paper, high-quality nonglossy papers, photographic papers, fine-art papers, and specialty papers.

▶ **Low-cost inkjet paper**—Nearly all paper vendors provide one or more grades of inexpensive paper manufactured especially for inkjet printers. These papers cost as little as $3 for a 250-sheet package. Although these papers have their uses, they don't have the weight or sufficient surface quality to use for printing photographic images. Use them for test strips and for design work and then print on a higher-quality material for your final prints.

▶ **High-quality nonglossy papers**—Often, you will want the best possible print quality without having to print on glossy photo-like paper. Numerous products are suitable for this purpose:

—**HP Premium Inkjet Heavyweight Paper**—A 36-pound paper that is sufficiently heavy and is coated on two sides to enable successful two-sided printing. It is ideal for brochures, calendars, report covers, and certificates. This is an excellent paper to use when you don't want to print on glossy paper or another high-cost specialty paper. It is a heavy-weight paper that accepts ink well.

—**HP Premium Inkjet Paper**—A bright-white, smooth, coated, normal-weight paper that produces crisp, bright images. This and similar papers are the kind to use for good-quality prints if you don't want a glossy or other specialty paper.

▶ **Photographic papers**—Quite a few good-quality photo-grade papers are available for inkjet printers. I use—and have been happy with the results from—Kodak and HP papers, including:

—**Kodak Inkjet Photographic Quality Paper–Photo Weight**—A bright-white paper for vivid color pictures. It looks and feels like photographic paper and has a Kodak watermark on the back, like most of Kodak's photographic papers.

—**HP Premium Photo Paper**—This paper is nearly indistinguishable from the Kodak paper just noted—except, of course, that it has an HP watermark on the back.

—**Hammermill's JetPrint Photo Paper**—This paper is a 4×6-inch heavyweight photo paper with a photo-gloss finish. It comes in 24-sheet packs and is an excellent paper to use when you want only one 4×6-inch print. It saves using a full sheet of photographic paper for a 4×6-inch print.

▶ **Fine-art papers**—Unless you have experimented with digital image editors—particularly software products such as MetaCreations Painter, Dabbler, or Photoshop—and have seen what can be created by using watercolor, auto-Van Gogh, or Conté Crayon filters, you might not yet appreciate the value of using fine-art papers. My bet is that you'll be hooked the first time that you change one of your favorite photographic images into a watercolor and print it on a high-quality watercolor paper. It will be a work of art that you'll want to frame! You'll soon be deciding what to do next, at which point you should look at some of the oil-brush filters, create an oil painting, and print it on real canvas that is created especially for inkjet printers. Be careful, though—don't get caught forging the Mona Lisa!

If you are an artist or photographer just getting into digital imaging, you might already have a keen interest in different paper types. If so, you might want to experiment with many of the same papers that you have been using. Although I don't advise against trying these papers, because you might get the desired result, you will find that coated papers produced especially for inkjet printers will give you a better print more often than not. Most art papers are not coated, which enables the ink spray to soak in and spread. This turns your fine lines into fuzzy lines and, in some cases, enables bordering colors to merge and create a third color, which isn't what you want to happen. Another problem with uncoated papers is that they soak up more ink than they should, which will transform your sharp, brilliant-colored work into a muted image.

Finding fine-art paper created especially for inkjet printers is getting easier as the demand for it has grown. I suggest that you visit one of the large office-supply stores or your favorite art supply shop. The art supply shops have lost so much business due to all the digital art tools that they usually are eager to carry products for artists who use computers for their artwork.

For those of you who are serious about your printed artwork, you ought to consider the paper products offered by Digital Art Supplies. It offers more than a dozen outstanding papers, ranging from glossy photographic papers to unusually good fine-art papers. My favorites include Watercolor Soft 285, Brilliant White Canvas Paper 180, and Heavy Textured Artist Canvas. If you want to try a few of these papers, Digital Art Supplies sells ten-sheet sample packs. You can learn more about these papers and the company by visiting its Web site at **www.digitalartsupplies.com**.

If you want the very best fine-art paper for your digital prints, use those offered by Digital Art Supplies or ones similar to them. Figure 13.6 shows a portion of a watercolor print on DAS Watercolor Soft 285. Figure 13.7 shows an oil painting-like print on DAS Heavy Textured Canvas 180.

Figure 13.6
Watercolor-like print on watercolor paper.

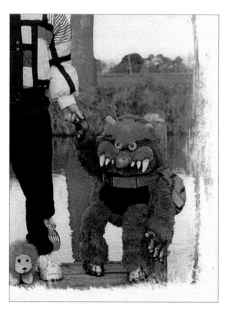

Figure 13.7
Oil paint-like print on heavy textured canvas.

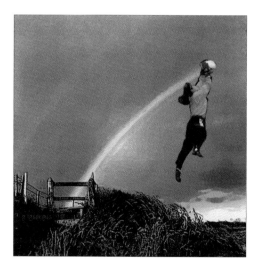

Specialty papers

Besides premium inkjet paper, glossy photographic paper, and fine-art papers, several other products are available on which to print. You can use these specialty products to print everything from greeting cards to business cards, stickers, labels, and transparencies. You can even use transfer sheets to print directly on cotton fabric! Some of the more fun and useful products are listed in the following sections.

Greeting cards

Companies are making more greeting card papers than probably any other kind of paper on this list. International Paper produces embossed greeting cards on smooth white card stock with white vellum envelopes. These are very classy cards for "fine-art" works and for formal invitations with images (see Figure 13.8).

Figure 13.8
Embossed greeting card featuring a cat image.

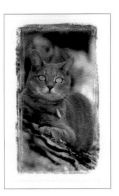

Avery offers a white card variety pack that has been created in conjunction with American Greetings. The pack includes twenty-four assorted cards, which are high-quality, heavyweight stock with two-sided coating for brilliant color—some are half-fold, some are quarter-fold, and the balance are full-sheet. The package also includes sixteen envelopes. This is a great starter kit if you want to create your own greeting cards.

Another especially nice half-fold card offered by Avery is called the print-to-the-edge greeting card. These cards are specially designed so that images can be printed right to the edge of the card. To do this, each card has a microperforated edge that can be neatly torn off after the card has been printed.

Calendars

If you have a dozen or more images and the time to make a twelve-month calendar, you should get International Paper's Invent-It! brand Photo Calendar Kit. The kit includes 15 sheets of 8.5×11-inch heavyweight photo paper with gloss and matte sides, two sheets of Print & Stick Project paper, two heavyweight paper covers, two clear-plastic covers, and an easy-to-use spiral binder. Using The Print Shop or another product offering calendar-creating formats, you can create an outstanding twelve months' worth of images (see Figure 13.9).

Figure 13.9
Calendar page featuring an image of a butterfly.

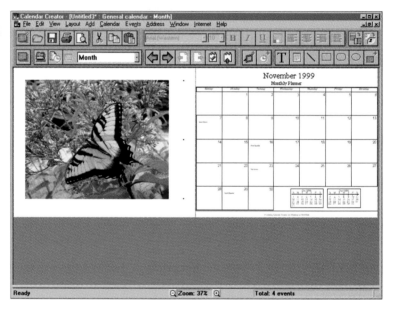

Postcards

One of my favorite specialty papers is the Avery glossy photo quality postcard. These cards are glossy heavyweight stock with a full-bleed format that enables you to print right to the edge. After tearing off the microperforated edges, the postcards are 4×6 inches (see Figure 13.10).

Figure 13.10
Avery Glossy Photo Quality Postcards with micro-perforated edges.

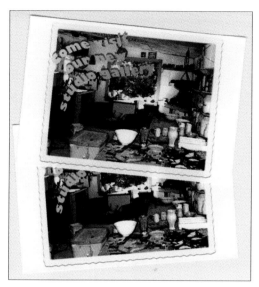

Iron-on transfers

Believe it or not, you can transfer your digital images onto any white or light-colored cotton or cotton-blend fabric with iron-on transfer sheets. These transfers can be used on T-shirts, tote bags, placemats, aprons, sweatshirts, jerseys, and more. Using an ordinary household iron, you simply iron the transfer sheet onto the fabric and then peel off the backing sheet. Designs stay bright and clear through repeated washings if the laundry directions are followed.

I created the "Soccer Mom & Soccer Kid" T-shirt image shown in Figure 13.11 for a friend to wear when she attends her daughter's soccer games. You'll notice the image is mirrored so that when it is ironed on to the fabric it will show correctly.

Figure 13.11
Soccer Mom image for use on a iron-on transfer sheet.

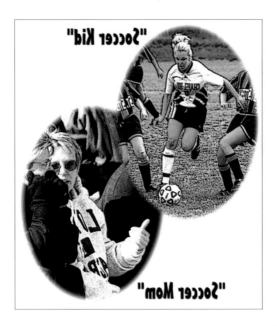

TIP

Hanes' T-ShirtMaker Iron-on Transfer Paper comes in packs of twenty 8.5×11-inch sheets. The bargain here is the Hanes Oops Proof Guarantee. If you goof up decorating a first-quality, heavyweight Hanes garment, Hanes will take it back and give you a new one—up to six "oops" per household per year!

You can order white Hanes Beefy-T T-shirts for $4 each directly from Hanes. Hanes also offers another thirty or so products made especially for use with transfer papers, such as sweatshirts, sweatpants, mouse pads, coasters aprons, fabric calendars, and even a director's chair. You can order these and other items by calling 1-800-HANES-2-U or by visiting the Web site at **www.hanes2u.com**.

Posters and banners

If you want to print a large poster or banner and are willing to use the quantity of ink necessary to print these large formats, you can buy paper that is fan-folded and use it with printers that enable continuous page printing. If you want to print banners, make sure your printer has this feature before buying the paper—most printers don't have it.

Stickers

Stickers come in all sizes and shapes and in both matte and glossy versions. If you are into brewing your own beer or creating your own wine, you can make very elegant bottle labels with sticker materials.

Business cards

You can create wonderful business cards by using photographic images. Various paper manufacturers offer both glossy and matte versions of business cards. Most of the better business cards are available with the microperforated edges that enable you to print to the edge and tear off the edges, leaving an almost perfect cut.

CD labels

Have you just recorded your first music CD and are now ready for the big time? If so, use CD labels to create custom labels that include photographic images on the disk and on the jewel-case insert. You also can get removable labels for DVDs, Zip disks, audiocassette labels, videocassette inserts, and more from NEATO Corporation, at **www.neato.com**.

Jigsaw puzzles

This is a great one for grandparents. After printing an image of the grandkids, you can break up the puzzle and send it to them to put back together. Make several of them for their next visit—that'll keep them busy.

Decals

One of the more unusual things to print on is a see-through, repositionable film for creating stickers and decals for windows, mirrors, and other nonporous surfaces.

TIP

The Kodak Inkjet Photo Variety Pack includes the Kodak Picture Easy Software for easy printing of multiple images on the same sheet. The real value here is that it enables you to print the same picture multiple times or print selected, different pictures on the same page. This can be a real paper- and time-saver if you have only 8.5×11-inch paper. You also get four full-page sheets, two microperforated sheets each with enough room for 2 5×7-inch photos, six wallet-size photos, or ten business cards.

Shopping for printer media

So many varieties of papers and specialized inkjet materials are produced that you might have to look around to find the ones that you want. A good place to begin the hunt is at Office Depot, OfficeMax, Best Buy, or CompUSA, because they usually offer the widest selection. If you can't find a particular paper in a store, you can order directly from the manufacturer by visiting its Web site.

Printer and media tips

After you have a photo-quality inkjet printer and some good paper, you are almost ready to print. First, though, you need to check your print resolution. Has your digital image been created at the optimal resolution for your printer? If you are printing on a 300 dpi printer, then your image ought to be 300 dpi as well.

Before you print, you should also know what setting to use for the specific type of paper that you are about to print on. This information usually comes from the paper manufacturer. They generally list specific settings to use to get optimal print results when using some of the more common printers. Read the optimal print settings for each product you use. These settings might vary between printers and often the settings might not be what you think they should be. For example, the best print that you can achieve with most printers on some of the watercolor papers is normal quality, not photographic quality, as you might expect. Normal quality gives a softer, more watercolor-like image.

To find your printer settings, you can select the Print menu item on most applications. This will launch a dialog box. Then, click the Properties button, and a printer settings dialog box specific to your printer will be launched.

If you start with a good image—created at the right image resolution to match your printer—use a good-quality paper, and configure your printer settings where they should be, you'll have a good printed image. That is, unless you put your oily fingers on the paper. Most papers can be ruined if you don't handle them by the edges only and store them in a cool, dry place, sealed in their own packages. If you got all that right, then you'll be happy with your print.

That concludes this chapter. In the next, and final chapter, "Using AOL and 'You've Got Pictures,' " you will find out how you can use AOL to learn more about photography and digital imaging and learn how to share your images with AOL features.

14

Using AOL and "You've Got Pictures"

America Online's (AOL) subscriber base is greater than 20 million members worldwide, many times larger than its nearest rivals. The reason for this incredible success is well-known—AOL is exceptionally easy to use and offers an excellent set of content, merchants, and services on just about any topic you can name. This especially applies to digital imaging and photography, for which AOL offers many excellent choices. For this reason, I've included this chapter to help those of you who are already AOL members to get the most from the available AOL digital imaging and photography resources and services. For readers who are not yet members, this chapter will help you to learn how AOL can help you more fully enjoy digital imaging and share your images with others.

In this chapter, you will learn how you can use AOL to more fully enjoy your digital images and photography—professionally or just for fun. More specifically, you will learn how to do the following:

▶ Find your way around AOL's digital imaging and photography pages

▶ Learn about digital imaging and photography on AOL

▶ Use AOL's message boards dedicated to digital imaging and photography

▶ Use AOL Chat to talk about digital imaging and photography

▶ Use AOL's You've Got Pictures service

▶ Share your digital images with AOL e-mail

▶ Use a personal Web page at AOL Home Town to share digital images

▶ Shop on AOL for digital cameras, scanners, and other equipment and supplies

Finding your way around AOL

One of the more frustrating aspects of surfing the Internet is finding your way around. AOL has worked hard to make it easy to get where you want to go quickly. AOL's Welcome screen and AOL Keywords are the two most important tools to make your surfing productive and fun.

Channels

AOL categorizes the thousands of AOL pages in one of nineteen categories, which are listed on the left side of the Welcome screen, as shown in Figure 14.1. These categories are known as *AOL Channels*. With a single mouse click, you can open a page that provides links to most of the AOL content that fits into that specific channel. You should also notice the Mail Center and You've Got Pictures icons on the Welcome screen—more on those features later.

Figure 14.1
AOL's Welcome screen and Keywords make it easy to find your way around.

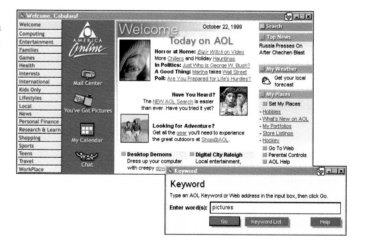

To get to a topic of choice, simply click the Interests channel to open the page shown partially covered in the bottom-left side of Figure 14.2, and then click the hot-link for Digital Imaging and Photography to get to the page shown in the foreground of Figure 14.2. From there, we can get to some of the more useful pages that cover aspects of digital imaging and photography such as building a personal Web page or learning how to edit images.

Part IV Sharing & Enjoying Images

Figure 14.2
AOL's digital imaging
and photography page.

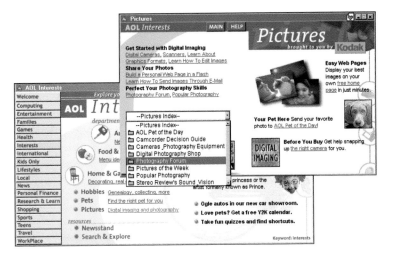

Keywords

The second feature AOL offers to help you get where you want to go fast is AOL Keywords. *Keywords* are shortcuts to online places—but I don't mean shortcuts with that "http://www….com" stuff! An AOL Keyword is a keyword such as "shopping" for when you want to go shopping online or "pictures" when you want to view your pictures online. By now, you probably get the idea. Yes, "photography" will take you directly to the main Photography Interests page, where you can then select a subcategory to visit. "Pop Photo" is one Keyword that you might not be familiar with until you use it; it takes you to an online version of *Popular Photography* magazine. Entering Keywords is as easy as clicking the Keyword button in the top-right part of the AOL window. You then type the Keyword in the dialog box that was previously shown in Figure 14.1.

If you have ever used one of the major search engines on the Internet and have had a page returned listing the first twenty pages matching your search criteria out of 17,452 sites, you'll appreciate the small, select number of choices that AOL provides you. As you might have assumed, AOL can provide this wonderful way of getting around on the Internet because the pages (or sites) that are accessed from AOL are actually pages selected, managed, and controlled to some extent by AOL. Some of these sites are even proprietary to AOL and have exclusive offers for AOL members, although an increasing number of them are also available directly on the Internet.

If you were on the Internet (not behind the AOL community wall) and wanted to find sites on photography and digital imaging, you would have to use one of the search engines. Using Excite, Yahoo!, or any other search engine, you will get an enormous list of sites, usually numbering in the thousands. Searching using the phrase "photography" on Yahoo!, for example, yields approximately 8,900 products for photography on Yahoo! Shopping, fifteen Yahoo! Category Matches, and 6,225 Yahoo! Site Matches, which are viewed twenty pages at a time. How helpful is this? Even worse, when visiting sites that are listed after searching for "digital images," you might suddenly find yourself looking at images that you wish you had never seen!

In sharp contrast to the Internet, you can use the AOL Interest channel on digital imaging and photography and get a very balanced selection of content on both photography and digital images, as previously shown in Figure 14.2. From this single page, you can select various topics that you would like to learn more about, visit galleries, shop at online stores, read an online version of *Popular Photography,* visit forums, and access photography-related Chat sites. If you want more than what is offered on AOL, AOL members can simply launch an Internet browser to venture outside the AOL community.

By the way, if you want to search outside of AOL pages, AOL 5.0's Search facility, NetFind, gives you the option of searching both AOL and the Web or either one individually, as shown in the window on the left side of Figure 14.3. The window on the right side shows an organized view of the sites it found—in fact, these sites are some of the 675,000 hand-selected sites that have already been judged by AOL as being quality sites that represent AOL values.

Figure 14.3
Using AOL's Internet
Search facility.

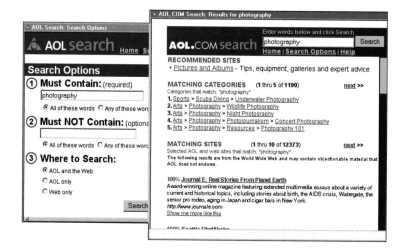

Learning about digital imaging and photography on AOL

Okay, let's see how we can learn more about digital imaging and photography on AOL. Where do we go and what can we learn? If you answered, "Type the Keyword 'photography' in the Keyword box," you've been reading carefully. Let's do that now. After clicking the Go button, you will see the page shown earlier in Figure 14.2. From there, you have many choices. You can choose from categories titled Get Started with Digital Imaging, Share Your Photos, and Perfect Your Photography Skills or follow links to pages for creating a home page, sharing pictures of your pet, and picking the right camera.

Under the Perfect Your Photography Skills heading is a link that gives you another full page of resources to help you learn to take better pictures. If you click a link under Top 10 Techniques, you will get the page shown in Figure 14.4—"Guide to Better Pictures," offered by Kodak. These are simple, to-the-point techniques that will help everyone. One of my favorite pages is the *Popular Photography* page shown in Figure 14.5. This online magazine offers everything—photo galleries, how-to articles, camera/lens test reports, articles on digital imaging, and much more.

Figure 14.4
Learning how to take better pictures on AOL.

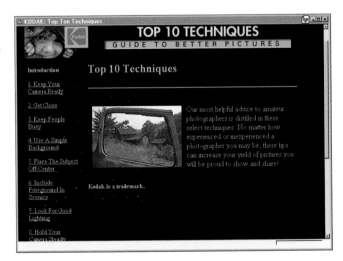

Figure 14.5
AOL's online version
of Popular Photography.

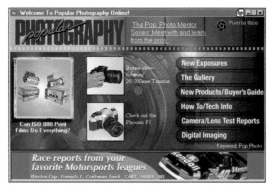

These are just two of the many useful pages you'll find on AOL to help
you learn more about digital imaging and photography. While you are
online, don't just read about how to take better pictures—also look at
pictures taken by others. You'll learn a lot by viewing other
photographers' work at online photo galleries or even by visiting some of
the AOL member-created galleries. Figure 14.6 shows the home page of
the California Museum of Photography.

Figure 14.6
Viewing photos at the
California Museum of
Photography.

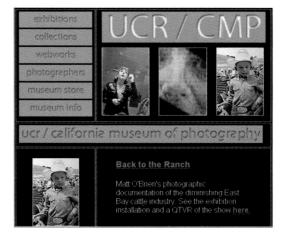

Another great way to learn about digital imaging and photography is to
use AOL's message boards—the topic covered in the next section.

Using AOL's photography message boards

Online message boards are the digital equivalent of the cork bulletin boards that are commonly found in schools, lunchrooms, and offices. Instead of writing or typing a message on paper and tacking it to the board with a few thumbtacks, you just type a message and post it to an electronic bulletin board. Sometimes bulletin boards are also referred to as *discussion boards* or *discussion groups*.

Message boards that have a lot of postings and are focused on a specific topic can be an invaluable tool to learn more about digital imaging and photography. AOL bulletin boards are conveniently located in places where visitors are most likely to want to post messages. For example, when you visit AOL's *Popular Photography* page, you will find the list of bulletin boards shown in Figure 14.7.

Figure 14.7
Bulletin boards found on AOL's Popular Photography page.

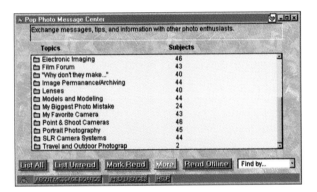

You can find many other active message boards on the front page of the AOL Interests page on photography. The Digital Imaging Message board is one that you might want to look at. It offers more than fourteen different subjects, including Digital Cameras, Digital Imaging Questions, Image Output, Inkjet Printing, and Scanning. After you click a subject, another window opens that lists the messages by subjects. Figure 14.8 shows the sequence of windows that you open to find a topic category appropriate for the messages that you want to read or post.

Figure 14.8
Using AOL's
Photography Message
Center to ask a question
about digital printing.

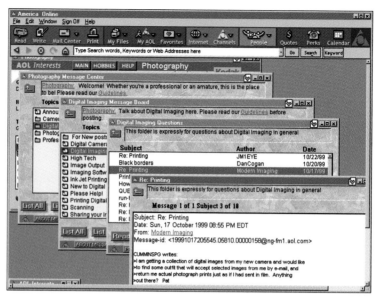

After you find a bulletin board that interests you, you can read the posted messages or you can add to the content yourself by replying to an existing message or creating a new subject and posting a new message. When you find a bulletin board that is especially useful to you, click the Favorite Places heart icon in the upper-right corner, and the bulletin board will be added to your Favorite Places list. This makes it easy to revisit and read responses to your questions or to read new messages.

Using AOL Chat to talk about digital imaging and photography

If you like a more interactive method of communicating than message boards provide, maybe you'll find AOL Chat more to your liking. AOL Chat is like real-time e-mail. You type a line and then send it by clicking the Send button. Whoever is in the chat room will instantly see your message, as shown in Figure 14.9. If you read the chat text in Figure 14.9, you can see that this particular discussion was about the different kinds of film that each photographer preferred. It included a bit of lamenting over a few types of film that were no longer being made. If you happen to be someone who used VPS film for years, as I did, you might have really enjoyed the chat. If not, you might have left or waited until a subject was started that was more to your liking.

Figure 14.9
Using AOL Chat to discuss photography issues.

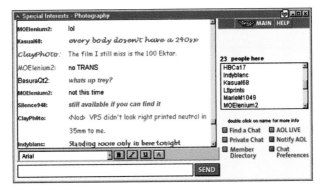

When you want fast answers, you can't beat a chat room, provided that you have a few knowledgeable people in the room. There will be times when all the people in a chat room are professionals and you can get excellent answers. Other times, you might think that no one in the room even owns a camera!

If you visit the same chat room frequently, you will soon recognize the "regulars." When they are there, you can participate in some good discussions. There are also times when the discussions are good but too many people are trying to participate, and the text flies by too fast to read.

Another great reason to use AOL Chat is to get feedback on your digital images. You can post your images to a Web site or send them to several people with AOL e-mail and then have an open discussion about the images. You can also post a message on a bulletin board, asking for some feedback on one of your images.

NOTE

After spending several hours digitally editing a photograph of a bird, the photographer posted it on a free AOL Home Town home page. Beneath the picture, the photographer requested that visitors page her on AOL Instant Messenger to discuss the image. Within a week, the photographer was paged six times and had several useful chats with visitors. With this feedback, the photographer was able to digitally edit the image again with much better results. The interactive feedback not only was useful, but she also received several good tips on how to further improve her image.

Using AOL's You've Got Pictures service

AOL and Kodak have teamed up to create the You've Got Pictures service, which is likely to change photography as much as e-mail has changed personal communications. That might seem like a bold statement. However, consider that Americans take about 20 billion pictures each year. A large percentage of these 20 billion pictures are taken so that they can be shared with others.

Unfortunately, sharing printed photographs can be both costly and rather inconvenient. After you have selected the pictures that you want to share, you have to find the negative and make two trips back to a photo-processing retailer to drop off and then pick up the images. These prints then must be carefully packaged and mailed. There is also the cost of printing, packaging materials, and postage. Just imagine if you could send your pictures to one or even one hundred people for next to nothing as easily as you send e-mail. Well, that is what You've Got Pictures enables you to do.

Do you take pictures with a film camera? Do you regularly use e-mail or plan to use e-mail in the future? If your answer to these two questions is "Yes," you're going to love AOL's You've Got Pictures. It is a fantastic service that enables you to share your pictures digitally with others. Using your same camera and film, you drop the film off to get processed at the same place you always have—maybe a one-hour lab, drug store, or camera retailer.

If the photo-processing retailer is a Kodak processor (odds are good that they will be, because there are more than 40,000 of them), you just check off a box on the film-processing envelope indicating that you'd like to have digital images uploaded to the Internet. You will also need to include your AOL e-mail address.

To find the closest location to you, you need a list of participating photo-processing retailers in your area. To get such a list, use the AOL Keyword "pictures" and click the text, "Click here to receive a list of participating photo developers." After entering your ZIP code, you will receive an e-mail listing all the retailers in your area.

Alternatively, you can mail your film in photo-mailer envelopes. Two mail-order photo-processors who develop for AOL are Mystic Color Lab (**www.mystic.photonet.com**) and York Photo (**www.york.photonet.com**).

Within a few days, you will hear that familiar voice that says "You've got mail!" say "You've got pictures!" With a mouse-click, you can view the uploaded rolls of film, as shown in Figure 14.10.

Figure 14.10
Viewing rolls of film that have been uploaded to an AOL account.

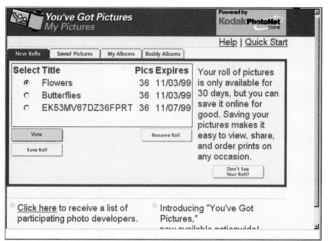

The window in Figure 14.10 shows four tabs:

▶ **New Rolls**—Review a list of recently uploaded rolls, which are available for 30 days. If you want to keep all or some of those images, you need to save them by clicking the Save Roll button. The saved pictures are then saved to the Saved Pictures section.

▶ **My Albums**—Create albums and save them.

▶ **Buddy Albums**—Save images that others have sent to you.

▶ **Saved Pictures**—View thumbnails of your images after they have been saved, as shown in Figure 14.11. From this same window, you can individually select images to be used in a new album, downloaded, or deleted, or you can order prints and photo gifts.

Figure 14.11
Viewing saved images on AOL's You've Got Pictures service.

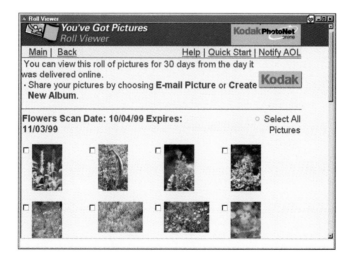

You can select a roll and have one or more photos downloaded to a file directory, free of charge, in e-mail or Web-page quality (384×256) or print quality (768×512). You can also choose to have them downloaded in a premium-quality format (1536×1024) at $1 each with a minimum of three images.

Now, you have digital copies of each of your pictures available online. What else can you do with them? The list of answers to this question is endless—but the most useful answer is that you can share them with others. The two common ways of sharing digital images are sending them as an e-mail attachment and sending e-mail with a link to where they are stored on the Kodak PhotoNet network or on a Web page, such as one in AOL Home Town. After your images have been uploaded, you can also download them, order prints, or have them put on photo gifts, such as a photo mug, photo mouse pad, photo jigsaw puzzle, or photo T-shirts or sweatshirts. You can also organize them into albums and safely store them.

Here is the cool part of this service. Now that the images are on the Kodak PhotoNet site, anyone to whom you provide a roll number and password can view them, download digital files, or use them in the same ways that you can. They can order prints or have them put on photo gift items.

Sharing images with AOL e-mail

It is very easy to share images with AOL e-mail, and numerous ways are provided to do so. You can go to the AOL Mail Center, click the Write icon, fill in the boxes, and then send one or more images as an attachment.

Attaching digital images to AOL e-mail is as easy as clicking the Attachments button on the bottom of the e-mail window and then selecting the file or files that you want to attach. It will even automatically zip your files, if you include more than one, to conserve file space and increase the speed of uploading and downloading files. If multiple images have been sent, it is just as easy for recipients to unzip the files for viewing.

You also can send a single image by inserting a picture, as shown in Figure 14.12, by clicking the camera icon on the style toolbar and selecting Insert a Picture. If your image is too large to display in the e-mail window, you are asked whether you would like the image to be resized; if you choose to have your image resized, it automatically will be resized for you.

Figure 14.12
Sending AOL e-mail
with an inserted image.

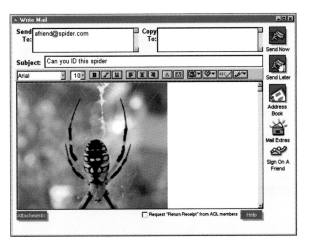

It is also possible to post your digital images on a Web site and to send
e-mail with a pointer to the images.

A completely different approach is to share your images from the You've
Got Pictures screen, as shown in Figure 14.13. A significant advantage to
this approach is that it enables the recipients of your e-mail to not only
download the image but also order prints and photo gifts directly from
Kodak. Another advantage is that your e-mail does not actually contain
the images; rather, they merely have a pointer to the image files that
remain on the AOL PhotoNet site. This decreases the upload time
required for you to send a message and the download time required for
your recipients to receive e-mail. Because they can view thumbnails on
the PhotoNet site, recipients can also elect not to actually download the
full-size images, which saves hard-disk space as well as the time that it
takes to download larger images.

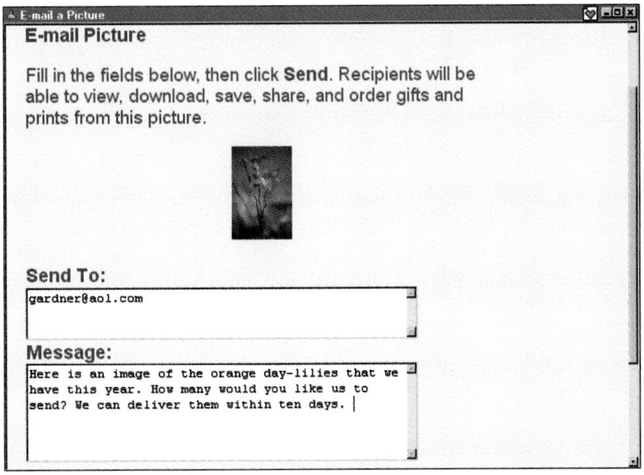

Figure 14.13
Sharing images with
AOL's You've Got
Pictures service.

You also can share entire photo albums from the You've Got Pictures page, as shown in Figure 14.14. Once again, your recipients can download images and order prints or photo gifts directly from Kodak.

Figure 14.14
Using AOL's You've Got Pictures to share photo albums.

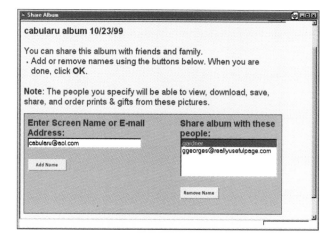

When someone shares an album with you, you can save it in the Buddy Album section, previously shown in Figure 14.10. After the album is saved, you can order prints or photo gifts directly from Kodak.

Besides using your AOL service to access your regular AOL e-mail service, AOL also offers AOL NetMail 2.0, which you can access directly from the Web with any browser from anywhere, as shown in Figure 14.15. You can learn more about the advantages and disadvantages of these entirely different approaches in Chapter 11, "Sharing Images Electronically."

Figure 14.15
Accessing AOL e-mail from the Web with NetMail 2.0.

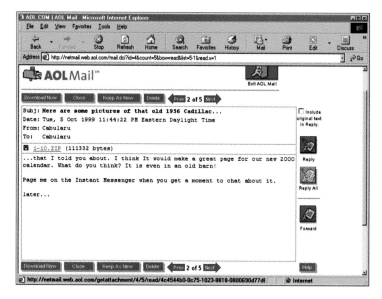

TIP

After hosting a large family gathering of more than seventy-five relatives one summer, the hosts wanted to give each family that had attended an opportunity to have copies of about ten photographs of the event. To save money, the ten photographs were put into an album on AOL's PhotoNet service. They then sent e-mail with a roll number and password to each family so that they could download and view the images or even get their own prints made directly by Kodak. The cost to make these images available to everyone was about $12, which was the cost of having the images scanned and uploaded to the host's AOL account through AOL's You've Got Pictures service.

Using a personal Web page on AOL Hometown to share images

AOL offers each member up to 12MB of free space for a home page on the AOL Hometown Web site. Web pages can be created and posted to the site in several ways. The easiest way is to use the AOL 1-2-3 Publish wizard, shown in Figure 14.16, which consists of seven simple steps that take about three minutes to complete.

Figure 14.16
Using AOL's 1-2-3 Publish wizard to create a home page on the AOL Hometown site.

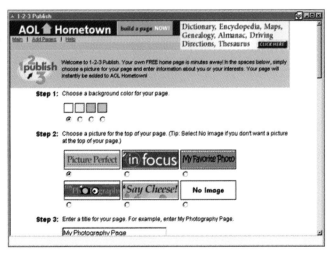

Figure 14.17 shows an AOL Hometown site that was created with 1-2-3 Publish. The page is shown in an ordinary Internet browser. It features a large digital image of a frog.

Figure 14.17
AOL Hometown Web page featuring a frog image.

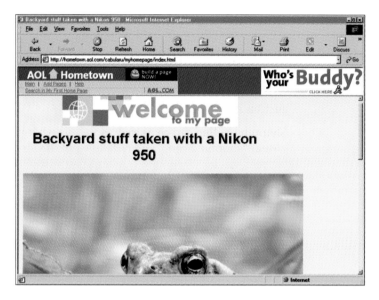

Besides enabling others to search for your page by using topics that you choose, AOL also enables you to use free special services, such as a personal chat room on your site. Web page addresses are all created as part of the Hometown page, such as **hometown.aol.com/cabularu/myhomepage/index.html**.

After you create a Hometown Web page, any AOL member or anyone else who has access to the Internet can access the Web page. If you want to do something more sophisticated than is possible with 1-2-3 Publish, you can use many of the standard Web page creation tools, including many of the portfolio tools that can create image portfolios for a Web site. Chapter 4, "Managing and Storing Images," discusses several software products that will help you create image portfolios or even Web-based slide shows.

Shopping on AOL

Have you bought anything online yet? If not, save some shoe leather and grab your mouse—let's go shopping online on AOL. First, make sure that you are ready. Just as you would prepare for a shopping trip at your local mall, you also ought to prepare for online shopping. If you know what you want to buy, you can start shopping now. If you don't know what to buy, then I suggest that you complete the necessary research to figure out what you want. On the other hand, maybe you just like window shopping—that's okay too.

If you need to do some research first, I suggest doing it online in the forums, in the chat rooms, or by using some of the online references discussed earlier in the chapter. After you have an idea of what you want, you can begin the online hunt for the best price. The more research you do, the more likely you are to get what you want and not something that won't meet your needs.

If you would like to buy a new digital camera, a scanner, or maybe just a new storage media card for your images, AOL offers many good places for you to shop. Maybe you don't want to shop but would rather bid at an auction site. Well, you can do that too.

Shopping online can be as easy as finding what you want, filling your virtual "shopping cart," and checking out! If you type the AOL Keyword "shopping" and click the Go button, you will be taken to the main shopping page on AOL. Depending on what you are looking for, you can then select from the many options that are presented.

One of my favorite places to shop is CNET, because it not only provides tremendous "how-to-buy" articles for a wide variety of products but also enables you to compare various products by manufacturer, by price range, and by key features, as shown in Figure 14.18.

Figure 14.18
Shopping online on
AOL at CNET.

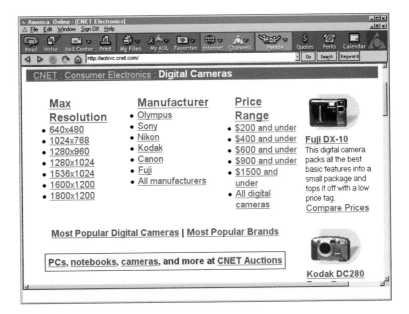

The AOL Shop Direct Digital Shop groups its offerings into eight different categories to make your shopping easier (see Figure 14.19). You'll notice that each time you visit, a special offer appears on this front screen. These special offers are often quite good deals that have been specially arranged between AOL and the vendor. If you need a product like the one displayed, you're not likely to find a better deal elsewhere. It's kind of like the special sale display at the front of most retail stores in a mall. If by chance you are looking for what they are offering, you're likely to get a good bargain.

Figure 14.19
The front window of AOL's Shop Direct Digital Shop.

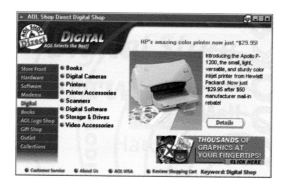

With online resources like those provided on AOL, and the wide range of online merchants who frequently offer special deals to AOL members, how can you not get a deal that will please you? You should have successful shopping trips on AOL every time!

NOTE

After browsing at a few online stores and reading online reviews of inkjet printers, an AOL member decided to purchase a specific brand and model of inkjet printer. To confirm his selection, he posted a message about his decision on an AOL message board. Within a week, he received several reply messages telling him that the printer he had selected was an excellent printer but needed to be used regularly, because the inkjets were known to dry out when not used frequently. The recommendation was to choose another printer if he wasn't going to use it at least once a week. Because he was not likely to use the printer once a week, he wisely chose another printer to avoid the problems associated with clogged inkjets.

Oh, I almost forgot to mention, if you are a bargain hunter and you like auctions, several auctions sites are available to you on AOL, including the famous eBay site, which is shown in Figure 14.20. Auction sites are lots of fun, and you really can get some good deals. Be careful, though.

If you win a bid on a large-ticket item, consider using one of the escrow services. An escrow service is a third party that holds payment for the goods until delivery is confirmed. Using an escrow service costs a little more, but it will prevent you from a big loss if you run into a disreputable vendor, which can and does happen at auction sites.

Figure 14.20
Getting a bargain at an online auction site, eBay.

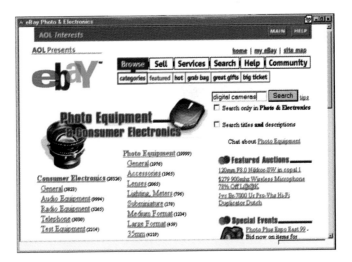

If you are reluctant to spend your hard-earned money over the Internet because of concerns about the merchants and the safety of transmitting your credit card number, using AOL should make you feel much better. AOL's Certified Merchant Guarantee is shown here—read it, because it truly makes AOL stand far apart from other online services:

> *For your protection, all AOL Certified Merchants offer return policies that are backed up by AOL's money-back guarantee. If, for any reason, you are not satisfied with your purchase, please contact the merchant through the store's Customer Service area. To view each Certified Merchant's satisfaction guarantee and customer service policies, go to Shopping Customer Service. If, after contacting the merchant, you do not get a satisfactory resolution that is consistent with the store's posted customer service polices, outline your complaint and notify our Customer Service Help Desk at screenname ShopHelp. We will intervene on your behalf to assist you in obtaining full satisfaction from the merchant. Should any AOL Certified Merchant not comply with its return policy as stated in the merchant's Customer Service area, then AOL will provide you a refund for the full purchase price.*

You can't beat that policy anywhere else that I know of. Furthermore, AOL makes the claim that it has never received a report of a credit card that was compromised during a shopping transaction with a Certified Merchant on AOL since it opened online shopping in 1996. If you have been concerned about credit card fraud and paying for products and services online, AOL makes it as safe as it can be—which is often safer than paying with a credit card at many retail stores.

In this chapter, you learned how AOL can be used to easily post images to a Web site, share digital images with others via e-mail, receive digital images via the You've Got Pictures service, use forums and chats rooms to learn more about photography and imaging, and go shopping for the products and services that you need. What more could you want to do? You can see why AOL has so many subscribers and enjoys the incredible success that it does. If you want to feel like you are part of a small community and prefer viewing just a few well-selected sites, then AOL is for you. If you are a big-city person and want lots of variety, then you might want to choose another service.

A few last words...

That's about it folks—for this chapter and the book! I truly hope you enjoyed reading it as much as I enjoyed writing the chapters and creating the images and projects that have been included. Even more, I hope that this book inspires and motivates you to do creative, fun, and useful things with your digital images and that you will enjoy sharing them with friends, family, and business colleagues.

Combining the Internet, PCs, and digital images gives you so many options than have ever been available to share and more fully enjoy the benefits of digital imaging. Keep your eyes open for new products and services and help become a pioneer in the new world of PC photography.

My challenge to you is to buy a digital camera, if you haven't already done so. They are better than you might think. They make it easier to create and use digital images, and they are useful and fun.

Index

Part V Index

Part V Index

Part V Index

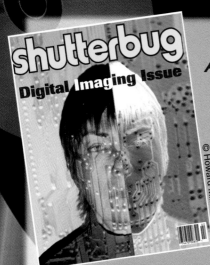

CREATING PAINT SHOP PRO WEB GRAPHICS

Price: $44.99
ISBN: 0-9662889-0-4
Pages: 384
Author: Andy Shafran

- Full Color
- Foreword by Chris Anderson, VP of Marketing, Jasc Software

Highlights

- Sixteen focused chapters teach you how to understand layers, special effects, plug-ins, and other important Paint Shop Pro features
- Integrates with a comprehensive Web site that contains updated information, complete examples, and frequently asked questions
- Detailed Web-specific topics such as transparency, animation, Web art, digital photography, scanners, and more

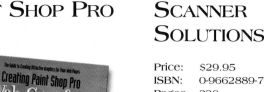

SCANNER SOLUTIONS

Price: $29.95
ISBN: 0-9662889-7-1
Pages: 320
Author: Winston Steward

- Full Color
- Tabbed Sections
- Index for easy use

Highlights

- Shows readers how to use their scanners for personal entertainment, in their home office, and in conjunction with the Internet
- Describes how to purchase and install scanners, specific hardware and software performance tips, and how to use the scanner as an important piece of office equipment.
- Discusses photo editing, graphic design, desktop publishing, OCR, saving and archiving, and retrieving files

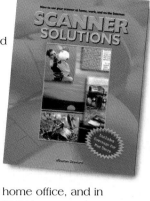

PAINT SHOP PRO 6 POWER!

Price: $39.99
ISBN: 0-9662889-2-0
Pages: 416
Author: Lori Davis

- Full Color
- Tabbed Sections
- Technically edited by Jasc

Highlights

- Completely updated for Paint Shop Pro 6, this book is geared for PSP users who want to get the most out of their new software
- Written by a well-known expert in the Paint Shop Pro field
- The focused chapters explain how to use layers, masks, animations, and filters

eBAY ONLINE AUCTIONS

Price: $14.95
ISBN: 0-9662889-4-7
Pages: 240
Author: Neil J. Salkind

- Glossary
- Question and Answer format

Highlights

- Explains the concepts behind how eBay works
- Fully explains the bidding, buying, and selling process for items, handling payment, and obtaining the auctioned items
- Describes the different types of auctions, options available for bidders and sellers, and limitations of each format

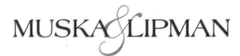

Order Form

Postal Orders:
Muska & Lipman Publishing
2645 Erie Avenue, Suite 41
Cincinnati, Ohio 45208

On-Line Orders or more information:
http://www.muskalipman.com
Fax Orders:
(513) 924-9333

Title/ISBN	Price/Cost

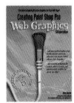

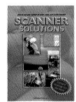

eBay Online Auctions
0-9662889-4-7

Quantity _____

× $14.95

Total Cost _____

Creating Paint Shop Pro Web Graphics
0-9662889-0-4

Quantity _____

× $44.99

Total Cost _____

Paint Shop Pro 6 Power!
0-9662889-2-0

Quantity _____

× $39.99

Total Cost _____

Digital Camera Solutions
0-9662889-6-3

Quantity _____

× $29.95

Total Cost _____

Scanner Solutions
0-9662889-7-1

Quantity _____

× $29.95

Total Cost _____

Subtotal _____

Sales Tax _____
(please add 6% for books
shipped to Ohio addresses)

Shipping _____
($4.00 for the first book,
$2.00 each additional book)

TOTAL PAYMENT ENCLOSED _____

Ship to:

Company _____

Name _____

Address _____

City _____ State _____ Zip _____ Country _____

Educational facilities, companies, and organizations interested in multiple copies of these books should contact the publisher for quantity discount information. Training manuals, CD-ROMs, electronic versions, and portions of these books are also available individually or can be tailored for specific needs.

Thank you for your order.